ISBN 978-88-8398-046-6
Copyright © 2007 by European Press Academic Publishing
Florence, Italy
www.e-p-a-p.com
www.europeanpress.it
Proprietà letteraria riservata—Printed in Italy

Proceedings of the

V Legislative XML Workshop

European Press Academic Publishing

Contents

6

SOFTWARE FOR LEGISLATION

Introduction

The adoption of shared or interoperable standards for legal information represents an important precondition for enabling access, communication, processing, and integration of legal sources through IT technologies, in an open and cooperative framework. Standards need to address different aspects of legal information:

— abstract (logical) ways of identifying legal documents, so that official texts can be retrieved and made available over the Internet, regardless of their physical location and legal information pertaining to different sources and States, and can be queried from single access-points;

— ways of structuring legal documents and data, so that their elements can be automatically identified and processed;

— ways of dealing with changes in the law, so that textual modifications can be clearly identified, the current content of legal texts can be automatically constructed, the applicable law can be more easily determined;

— ways of distinguishing and representing the different stages of the life cycle of legislative texts (from first drafts, to parliamentary discussions, to amendments, to subsequent modifications);

— ways of defining and applying conceptual classifications to legislative texts so that, possibly according to appropriate mappings and translations, legal conceptualisations can be applied in understanding and retrieving laws of different countries and different languages;

— ways of building rich executable representations of legal knowledge, which can capture the essential components of legal knowledge, can be transferred from one computer platform to another, can provide a basis for knowledge-based systems supporting the application of laws of different countries.

Today is exactly the time when studies and proposals on legal standardisation at the European level can be most useful: knowledge of the issues involved in standardisation, awareness of best technological solutions and practices, proposals for improvements, suggestions for convergence and interoperability can be very useful for European policy-makers, National authorities and all private and public providers of legal information. Only a few years ago it would have been too early, since the technologies for the informational unification of the laws of Europe would not have been available or would not yet have been in use. A few years from now it would be too late since different countries would possibly have gone in different directions, organising their legal information according to incompatible (or sub-optimal) standards.

Providing shared or interoperable standards for legal knowledge can bring various advantages:

- An increased accessibility of European legal materials (of the different countries) over the Internet is an important factor for developing the European market and favouring transnational business. In this regard, further problems are to be addressed, like linguistic barriers, but access to texts (in a structured forms), navigation over their links, availability of the law in force and ease of retrieval are the preconditions of any further use of law texts;

- An increased accessibility of laws, decisions, and legal data over the Internet, through shared or interoperable standards, promotes cooperation between different legal authorities of different Member States (e.g. accessibility of case law, of all judicatures, can contribute to the harmonisation of European case law, and to the trans-jurisdictional dialogue; accessibility under appropriate legal warranties of data concerning individual cases can facilitate judicial cooperation on cases involving different jurisdictions; accessibility of all legislative and regulatory acts, and of the corresponding preliminary documents, can contribute to the harmonisation of legislation and to spreading the best solutions);

- An increased accessibility of legal materials contributes to providing the necessary input for studies and policies aimed at the harmonisation-unification of European laws;

- The availability of legal materials of different countries, structured or enriched according to shared or interoperable standards, increases competition in the provision of legal services (assuming that the information is provided on non-discriminatory bases), since the same software systems can then be used for processing laws of different countries;

- The availability of legal materials according to shared or interoperable standards reduces the costs of developing certain legal services (for instance, legal documentation) and thus paves the way for new actors to provide for legal information to the public, both in commercial and non-commercial ways.

— The adoption of appropriate standards for texts of law and associated documents is the precondition for efficient information management of all legislation-related documents, and thus can favour openness and transparency of the legislative process, and access to information relevant to legal interpretation (legislative history).

— Legislative standards also have an impact on legislative quality, since compliance with appropriate legislative standards can contribute to obtaining a clearer, better structured and more consistent legislation.

A number of projects on Internet-based standards for legal information have already been developed in different Member States (like Italy, Austria, Denmark, the Netherlands, Switzerland and Britain). There is at present a need need not only to stimulate similar initiatives being developed in other countries (particularly in new Member States, who are just starting to develop up-to-date approaches to legal information), but also to give a specifically European direction to legal standardisation: besides facilitating the communication of information about national experiences, we need to promote shared or interoperable standards at the European level.

These initiatives show that, just as protocols for the Internet have achieved a global dimensions, so can and should standards for legal information. They also show that it is necessary that such standards, rather than being unilaterally imposed by commercial or political interests (or reflecting the idiosyncrasies of particular legal traditions), result from a discussion as broad and inclusive as possible, involving experts, lawyers, computer scientists, public authorities and private companies.

The ideas just sketched out provide the backdrop of the V Legislative XML workshop, which took place on in Florence on 14-16 June 2006, hosted by EUI (the European University Institute) and organised by EUI in cooperation with ITTIG-CNR (the Institute of Legal Theory and Techniques of the Italian National Research Council) and CIFSFID (the Legal Informatics Centre of the University of Bologna). The title of the workshop refers to XML (eXtended Markup Language), the tag-based language which is nowadays increasingly used for expressing in machine-readable format the structure of any kind of information made accessible on the web, and in particular for organising legal materials and for enriching them with further data.

The workshop was characterised by a large and diverse participation: more than 100 people from more than 20 countries (in 4 continents: Europe, North America, South America, and Africa) were present, coming from public administrations (national and regional parliaments and governmental bodies), academic institutions and IT companies.

As in the previous editions of the XML workshop, the focus was on the presentation, comparison and discussion of concrete experiences and projects on legislative standards, especially those carried out by public administrations, with the purpose of sharing knowledge and best practices. This was indeed the subject of the first day of the workshop, which was devoted to ongoing projects. Initiatives from European countries like Switzerland, Austria, Italy, Denmark, the Netherlands, France, Germany, Ireland, Hungary, UK, Spain were presented, together with activities promoted within the EU institutions (especially by the Office for Official Publications), and experiences or non-European countries, like Nigeria, Kenia, South Africa, Brazil and the USA. The first day of the workshop also included a session devoted to the comparison of the results obtained by marking up a single legislative text according to different national standards.

The second day of the conference was concerned with new ideas and developments in the domain of legislative markup, like the emerging country-independent standards, techniques for automatic consolidation, the semantic markup of texts and rules, the use of ontologies (conceptual dictionaries and networks) for supporting multilingual information retrieval.

On the third day the first session was devoted to the presentation of various standards-based software programs for supporting the publication, the drafting and the consolidation of legislation. This session included the presentation of prototypes but also of software systems already in use within national and regional parliaments, publication offices and private companies.

The conference ended with a roundtable aimed at identifying the prospects for the development of legislative markup standards. In particular, ideas were discussed for a roadmap towards common and interoperable standards in Europe, and a commitment was made toward defining a project proposal on European standards for legislation, to be submitted to the next call of the program framework for EU projects.

It is difficult to synthesise the outcomes of such a rich program in a few conclusive remarks. We think that two indications had particular saliency and significance for future activities.

The first indication is that not only the technologies, but also national and European institutions are now mature for realising significant standards-based IT systems in the legal domain. Important applications

have already been developed both at the national level and at the
European level. However, it is not always the case that the standards
adopted at the national and subnational level reflect the best technological knowledge, and not always do they take into account other
experiences, either on learning or on convergence grounds. Thus it is
urgent to compare existing standards and improve upon them, so that
an agreement can be reached at least on a shared common denominator
having the most advanced features.

The second indication is the emergence of country-independent standards, and the possibility of far-reaching international cooperation. As
announced at the workshop, proceedings have been started at the European Committee for Standardization (CEN), for the definition of an
Open XML interchange format for legal documents. At the same time,
an African standard for legislation has been defined which is based on
and improves upon the results of some European experiences (in the
framework of the Africa i-Parliaments Action Plan, an initiative supported by United Nations Department of Economic and Social Affairs,
the Global Centre for ICT in Parliaments, and the Panafrican Parliament). This African project is particularly significant, since it shows
how shared or interoperable machine-readable standards for legal information can contribute to technological development, but also how they
can support communication, democracy and participation, and how the
adoption of such standards could be based upon a wide discussion,
bridging different legal traditions, and merging technical considerations
with social and political requirements. A joint African-European working group is now emerging where such issues are addressed in an open
and cooperative way, within a shared framework.

These proceedings collect revised and extended versions of the contributions presented at the workshop. The first section of the proceedings
(entitled Legislative standards) includes the papers addressing the basic
level of the standardisation of legal documents, namely, the structure
of such documents and their identification through univocal names.
This is the aspect that has already been addressed in various national
experiences, though as these contributions show there is space for development toward adopting best practices and enabling interoperability.
The second section includes papers devoted to legal dynamics, an aspect of standardisation that is now at the center of scientific debate
and of implementation efforts. It regards defining ways of specifying
textual modifications within the concerned documents, in such a way
that the law in force can be automatically constructed. The adoption
of such standards (supported by adequate software programs and or-
ganisational structure) would provide a much needed relief to citizens,
professionals and administrators, greatly facilitating knowledge of the

law. The third section is devoted to another much-needed development in access to, and use of, legislative information. This is the availability of conceptual architectures, or ontologies, which indicate the connections between legal concepts and specify aspects of their meaning. Shared and reliable legal ontologies would enable users to access documents, in different languages, on the basis of their conceptual contents (rather than only on the basis of their wording) and appropriately use legal terms (for instance, in preparing new legislation). The fourth and final section collects contributions presenting some significant innovative software-development projects in the domain of legislative information. They show how standards for legal texts can provide (and have indeed provided) a stimulus for starting software projects: standardisation enables software to match the needs of a larger basis of users and facilitates cooperation in joint initiatives.

The contributions collected here do not exhaust the many issues that are involved in current standardisation projects, but they do provide, we believe, a broad-enough account of the achievements so far obtained, the developments now underway, and the debates accompanying them. We hope that presenting them to a larger public than the attendants at the Florence conference can contribute to promote awareness of, and participation in, the debate on standards for legal documents.

Florence, October 2006

Carlo Biagioli
Enrico Francesconi
Giovanni Sartor

CNIPA and legislative XML: an update on projects and new initiatives

Caterina Lupo, Luca De Santis
Centro Nazionale per l'Informatica nella Pubblica Amministrazione (CNIPA)
Via Isonzo 21/b, 00198 Roma, Italy
`{lupo,luca.desantis}@cnipa.it`

Abstract. In the last two years CNIPA has been involved in several projects related to Legislative XML. Some of them directly adopt NormeinRete standards, while others are influenced by NormeinRete results. Currently, CNIPA's projects mainly focus on back office issues, in order to make information systems effective in supporting the whole laws management process. In this paper we illustrate current and forecast CNIPA's initiatives in the field of Legislative XML.

Keywords: Italian national projects, e-Leges, CNIPA, NormeinRete, Legislative XML

1. Introduction

The Italian National Centre for Information Technologies in the Public Administration (CNIPA) was established in 2003, from the merger of the Italian National Authority for IT in the Public Administration (AIPA), which had been operating since 1993, and the Italian National Technical Centre. Its tasks are the promotion, the coordination, the planning and the control of the development of information systems within Government central organizations and agencies, through standardization, interconnection and integration.

Some CNIPA's projects on legislative XML achieved notable results over the last years. They concern both standardization and system architectures in order to manage legal document processes at different stages in their life cycle.

The first important CNIPA's project on legislative XML was NormeinRete. Starting from this experience, CNIPA took part to several other projects, enlarging its interests from front office (e.g., services to citizens) to back office (e.g., enactment process). Currently, an important initiative in which CNIPA is involved is the Italian National "ex 107" program.

In this paper some CNIPA projects are briefly described. The paper is structured as follows: Section 2 is dedicated to a description of NormeinRete project; in Section 3 the "107" program is illustrated. Section 4 describes the new proposal for NormeinRete project, a short summary of other CNIPA relevant projects is provided in Section 5. Finally, in Section 6 there are some final considerations.

2. NormeinRete initiative

The project NormeinRete (Lupo and Batini, 2003) (i.e. Norms in the net) has been promoted since 1999[1] by Italian Authority for information technology in Public administration (AIPA - now CNIPA) and Ministry of Justice. Its main objective was to improve the access to legislative and regulatory acts (laws, decrees, rules) by citizens and professionals through the Internet, adopting a federative approach. Moreover, it allows to fulfil the citizens' right to acquire knowledge of norms and to support Public Administration in managing legislative documentation life-cycle efficiently.

During the last years, the project has achieved lasting and shared results:

— a standard for XML representation of norms (AIPA, 2002). It has been defined a specific format for Italian legislation, with particular regard to the peculiarity of legislative documents structure, metadata representation and other significant information useful to provide advanced automatic functions. Moreover, the availability of documents marked-up according to shared formats allows the creation of advanced search and retrieval functions operating on distributed data bases effectively.

— A standard for norms persistent identification (AIPA, 2001; Spinosa, 2001), based on IETF Uniform Resource Name specification (Masinter and Sollins, 1994) that allows to identify each document regardless of its physical address (e.g, URL) and to automatically hyperlink resources through a resolution system.

— A portal as a unique point of access to the Italian legislative corpus. www.normeinrete.it provides search and retrieval functions operating on all the Italian laws from 1904, published on more than 50 different web sites. It also provides utilities to automatically transform references contained in the laws into navigable links. The portal contains the entire project documentation (in Italian) and other information related to the project. It includes e-learning tools on technical matters, a software download section and a best-practices section to encourage experiences sharing, in

---

[1] At the beginning as experimental project

order to create a virtual space for knowledge sharing within the public administrations community.

— An infrastructure for identifier resolution and management. Currently, the mechanism to resolve identifier is provided within the portal itself, by means of a CGI component.

Both XML standard and URN derived standard are adopted by a growing number of private operators in addition to the majority of Italian public administration. European institutions and other countries have also shown interest in them.

3. Italian National "ex 107" program

One of the most important recent initiative concerning the use of information and communication technologies in the legal field is the Italian National program for free access to in force laws. The program was set up by the Italian law n. 388/2000 (i.e., financial act 2001) in the article number 107 and therefore it is commonly named "ex 107" program. The main objectives are:

— to produce the in force version of the whole Italian legislative corpus;

— to allow free access to in force legislation through the Internet;

— to support mark-up, legislative process, classification and consolidation.

The "ex 107" program is managed by a Steering Committee composed by general Secretaries of the Italian Senate, the Chamber of deputies and the Prime Minister office. Moreover it involves the Italian Ministry of Justice, Supreme Court of Cassation and CNIPA.

The "ex 107" program and NormeinRete project, *despite of deep differences in architectural and organizational philosophy*, have some relevant points in common. In fact the program adopts both NormeinRete standards and the NormeinRete cooperation registries will be linked to the infrastructure that will be implemented to fulfil the program objectives. Moreover, the document repository of the program will use the navigation facilities provided by NormeinRete resolution service.

3.1. CNIPA PROJECTS FOR THE "EX 107" PROGRAM

Within the above mentioned program, CNIPA proposed a project named *e-Leges* (where "e" stands for electronic), composed by several sub-projects, which aims to increase the effectiveness of normative processes. The sub-projects are s-Leges, x-Leges, p-Leges, c-Leges and r-Leges. Each sub-project concerns a very specific aspect; nevertheless all together concur to improve the way laws are enacted and managed in their life cycle. s-Leges, x-Leges and p-Leges projects are briefly described in the following:

s-Leges The s-Leges project ("s" stands for standards) regards standardization of formats and the providing of tools for supporting legislative processes. The project directly supports the enrichment and the extension of CNIPA's XML and URN standards. In 2006 the project activities mainly focused on formats able to manage bills and also to identify documents not enacted yet.

x-Leges The objective of x-Leges project (De Santis et al., 2006) ("x" stands for eXchange) is to implement a system that will support legislative production processes through i. the exchange of documents (e.g., draft of the laws to be discussed, accompanying documents, etc.) by means of Certified email, ii. the management and the exchange of added-value information related to the overall process and its phases and iii. the possibility to receive notifications when relevant events happen.

p-Leges The p-Leges project ("p" stands for portal) concerns the implementation of a web site providing access to in force version of laws. The site will inherit some infrastructure elements from NormeinRete in order to support consolidation activities.

The e-Leges project achieved notable results, especially concerning standardization. New standard versions have been released both for XML document format (version 2.2 of DTD and XML Schema) and URN law identification (version 1.3). Moreover, the web site of the program is in the implementation phase and it is going to be on line within 2007.

As a result of x-Leges project, a call for tender for the implementation of a system enabling electronic documents exchange within normative process has been published, arousing much interest (16 proposals). The end of implementation phase is foreseen by the end of 2007.

4. NormeinRete evolution

Normeinrete project is facing up a deep reorganization, both for its long term objectives and for the services it will provide. As illustrated in the previous section, some architectural elements have been taken up by p-Leges project while part of standardization effort has been delegated to s-Leges project.

However, besides these elements, NormeinRete and "ex 107" program are clearly complementary, because of their different architectural approach and main aims. As a matter of fact, the first adopts a completely decentralized architecture that is clearly more coupled with local administrations and can easily deal with sectorial and specialized legislation. On the other hand, the former adopts a centralized architecture and limits its field of action to National laws.

In the last months, CNIPA has been involved in the definition of NormeinRete new outlook and in the re-engineering of online services. Effort has been mainly focused on the implementation of a new version of:

— Norms repository, in order to support laws consolidation and re-order;

— mechanisms for URN resolution and services for URNs registration;

— NormeinRete portal, with specific regard to accessibility, in accordance with the Italian law.

Concerning URN standard, a new distributed resolution architecture, abstractly depicted in Figure 1, is currently under design. In this architecture each official normative web site should have its own resolution table and should be responsible of registering the norm URNs of its competence. The architecture potentially allows integration with information sources different from those of Public Administration, for example the ones of private publishers.

The evolution of XML and URN standards will continue in being taken into consideration, for example to represent and manage local laws.

Finally, the possibility of integration with the Italian Public System of Cooperation (named SPCoop[2]) has been examined. SPCoop aims to provide the technological infrastructure (based on XML and Web Services) for applicative cooperation, with the formal definition of rules and SLA, in order to make high quality services available to citizens.

---

[2] Project documentations (in Italian) can be found on the web site http://www.cnipa.gov.it/

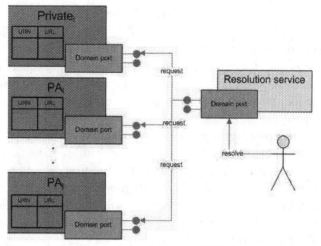

Figure 1. The new architecture of NormeinRete URN resolution mechanism

CNIPA is studying the possibility to integrate NormeinRete cooperation registries into the SPCoop system, in order to exploit both technological and organizational infrastructure.

5. Other relevant projects

CNIPA is involved in, and in some case directly conducts and funds, many other initiatives concerning legal documents management and access. Some of these projects are briefly described below, pointing out the opportunities of cooperation with NormeinRete and "ex 107" program.

ESTRELLA The ESTRELLA (European project for Standardized Transparent Representations in order to Extend Legal Accessibility) project[3] aims at developing an open platform enabling citizens and businesses to easily access, understand and apply complex legislation and regulation. In this project CNIPA is leader of Standardization activities, which regard the definition of an XML format for legal documents and the proposal of an open source content management system to enable interoperability among different legal document formats. One of the main milestone expected is the publication of a proposal for an open XML standard for legal documents. The standard should take into account the standardization experiences made in several European countries, such as Dutch

---

[3] Website: http://www.estrellaproject.org/index.php/Main_Page

METAlex and Italian NormeinRete. In particular, the project can effectively exploit NormeinRete standard in order to enrich metadata representation of the new format.

African i-Parliaments The African i-Parliaments is an initiative funded by the UN/DESA (United Nation Department of Economic and Social Affairs) with the objective to provide African Parliaments with the opportunity to modernise their information management capabilities. It consists of standardization activities, addressed by AKOMA NTOSO project[4], and a project (named BUNGENI[5]) which objective is to design and implement information systems for managing the whole legal documents life cycle in African countries. CNIPA has given a contribution at the first step of the project as consultant, providing know how in document formats standardization and best practice for cooperative architecture design, derived by both NormeinRete and "ex 107" program experiences.

AUGUSTO . The objective of AUGUSTO (Acronym for AUtomazione Gazzetta Ufficiale STOrica) project[6] is to digitalize all the Italian Official Journal as images with basic indexing service. In the future it will be possible to link the XML text of a law produced by x-Leges system or available on p-Leges site with the image of the page of the Official Journal where the law has been published. In such a way, it is possible to provide a "certification" with respect to printed text. This is a very important issue, because in Italy the printed text on Official Journal is the only source with legal validity.

6. Conclusion

CNIPA's effort is currently focused on several initiatives, both national and international, each regarding a specific aspect of the normative life cycle. Notwithstanding, CNIPA is trying to maintain a coherent and global vision over the projects, in order to simplify the scenario and to enable cooperation and results sharing.

Starting from a situation where several initiatives tend to overlap (see Figure 2), it is possible to identify three well defined areas that

---

[4] http://www.akomantoso.org/

[5] http://www.bungeni.org/

[6] http://www.cnipa.gov.it/site/it-IT/In_primo_piano/Progetto_AU.G.U. STO/

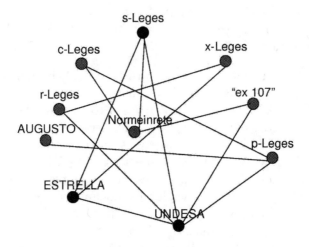

Figure 2. A naïf vision of CNIPA involved projects interaction

can be used to categorize the projects that see CNIPA involved with
respect to their main objectives:

— standardization;

— access;

— back office.

Figure 3 illustrates how projects place in the above-mentioned categories with respect to their main objectives.

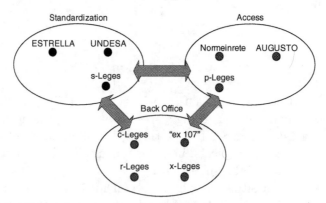

Figure 3. CNIPA's global vision on projects cooperation

Currently the main italian project in Computer science and Law
is really the "ex 107" program. Several CNIPA initiatives are in their
final stage. Moreover, in a short time other CNIPA projects should

start, specifically the analysis of automatic classification software tools for legal documents and the study of mechanism and tools to support normative reorder.

References

AIPA (2001). Definizione delle Regole per l'Assegnazione dei Nomi Uniformi ai Documenti Giuridici. Circolare n. AIPA/CR/35 (in Italian), `http://www.cnipa.gov.it/site/_contentfiles/00127800/127896_CR_35_2001.zip`.

AIPA (2002). Formato per la Rappresentazione Elettronica dei Provvedimenti Normativi tramite il Linguaggio di Marcatura XML. Circolare n. AIPA/CR/40 (in Italian), `http://www.cnipa.gov.it/site/_contentfiles/00127500/127544_CR_40_2002.pdf`.

De Santis, L., Lupo, C., Marchetti, C., and Mecella, M. (2006). The x-leges system: Peer-to-peer for legislative document exchange. In *Proceedings of the fifth international EGOV conference,Krakow, Poland.*

Lupo, C. and Batini, C. (2003). A Federative Approach to Laws Access by Citizens: The "Normeinrete" System. In *EGOV 2003 Conference, Prague, Czech Republic.*

Masinter, L. and Sollins, K. (1994). Functional Requirements for Uniform Resource Names (RFC 1737). `http://www.faqs.org/rfcs/rfc1737.html`.

Spinosa, P. (2001). Identification of Legal Documents Through URNs (Uniform Resource Names). In *EUROWEB 2001 Conference "The Web in Public Administration".*

Spain on Going Legislative XML Projects[†]

Dámaso Javier Vicente Blanco*, M. Mercedes Martínez González°

* Grupo de investigación sobre Derecho de las nuevas tecnologías y delincuencia informática. Universidad de Valladolid (Spain)
° Grupo de Recuperación de Información y Bibliotecas Digitales. Universidad de Valladolid (Spain)

Abstract. The current state of the use of XML in legislative projects is presented. The experiences presented are classified in four groups: commercial databases, official databases, other projects and experiences, and finally, current research in this area. The analysis considers four aspects for each legislative XML project examined: a) *what* it is; b) starting *date*; c) *who* is doing it; and d) *how* it is being developed.

Keywords: legislative XML, Spain, legal databases

1. Introduction. The Spanish experience with legislative XML: scope.

This paper presents a synthetic overview of the state of the art of current legislative XML projects in Spain. That is, the projects we consider are restricted to the geographical area of Spain, and which are related with the use of XML in the legislative environment. Therefore, other applications of XML to Law-related aspects, but not to legislative projects, are not included in this survey[1].

By the term "legislative XML" we refer to the application of the XML technology to legislative texts, to permit their organisation, their manipulation and/or to manipulate relationships between them. The goal is to permit their use, either by Law professionals, or by non-expert users (users with little or no knowledge of Law), e.g. citizens who are interested in accessing the content of normative documents.

[†] This work was presented in the V Legislative XML Workshop, Fiesole (Florencia), 14 -16 June 2006. This participation was supported by the Legal Framework for the Information Society, LEFIS network, which is co-ordinated by professor Fernando Galindo Ayuda, Universidad de Zaragoza (Spain).

[1] There are some general studies into the current state of the application of computer technologies to Law and legal documentation, within which those by ALVITE DÍEZ, M.L. («Evolución de las bases de datos jurídicas en España», *Anales de Documentación, 2004, vol. 7, p. 7-27*) and GARCÍA PALOMEQUE, REBECA & PÉREZ CAMPOS, RAFAEL («Las nuevas tecnologías : un paso adelante en la documentación jurídica», *Biblioteconomia i Documentació: textos universitaris de biblioteconomia i documentació, junio 2003, 10,* http://www2.ub. es/bid/consulta_articulos.php?fichero=10garcia2.htm, retrieved: 01-06-2006) are particularly interesting.

We use the generic term "projects" to refer to a collection of efforts in the application of XML technology, which offer an overview of the current situation in Spain. We classify them in four groups: A) commercial databases; B) official databases; C) other projects that have been developed in this area; and finally D) current research in this matter.

It is worth noting that this survey revises experiences that have been disseminated, in either scientific publications, or by other means, such as, for example, web pages. We use a set of representative examples and analyse them to offer an overview of the current state of the art in Spain. This is the option taken, given the difficulty of attempting an exhaustive revision of all the experiences available in the Spanish public administration, legislative courts, and judicial administration. The plural reality of Spain, where the central government and the Spanish Parliament coexists with the regional governments and Parliaments of the 17 "autonomous communities" and with the city councils, makes it really difficult, unless time extensive research is carried out, to be sure that all existing cases of XML use are considered.

With each project, we analyse four aspects: a) *what* it is; b) starting *date*; c) *who* is doing it; d) *how* it is done.

2. Commercial databases

Commercial, legal databases that include legislative texts have been present in Spain since the mid-eighties[2].

Now there are several CD-ROM legislative and jurisprudence databases from commercial firms, *Aranzadi-Thomson*[3], *El Derecho*[4], some databases of the *Kluwer Group* (*La Ley*[5] and *Colex Data*[6]), *Lex Nova*[7] and others, such as *Bosch*[8] or the *Revista General de Derecho*[9].

In addition, there are two commercial XML databases available on the web: *Derecho.com*[10] and *Tirant On Line*[11].

Derecho.com (see Figure 1) is a legal portal dated from 1999, which uses XML with legislative texts since 2003.

---

[2] ALVITE DÍEZ, M.L., *op. cit.*

[3] http://www.aranzadi.es/

[4] http://www.elderecho.com/

[5] http://www.laley.es/

[6] http://www.colex-data.com/

[7] http://www.lexnova.es/

[8] http://www.bosch.es/

[9] http://www.rgid.com/

[10] http://www.derecho.com/. In particular, see http://www.derecho.com/xml/quiensomos.xml.

[11] http://www.tirantonline.com/index.do

Figure 1. Derecho.com

The developer of this server is a Catalonian enterprise, *Cometa Technologies*, and content management tools have been developed for this aim. Content management is XML-based; their application servers are *Linux*; and the framework used is *Cocoon*[12].

3. Official databases

There are multiple official databases in Spain[13]. Official administrations have chosen the Web as the preferred instrument for the e-administration, and the best way to offer services to citizens. It is important to remember that Spain has a broad and heterogeneous sector of "public power", including central government (Government, national Parliament and Judicial Power), the governments corresponding to the 17 regional autonomies in which Spain is divided (each with its own government and regional parliament), and city councils. In some cases, the XML technology is used to provide public access to legislative databases, but in some other cases, it is used to organise information and documentation, with the aim of facilitating its use by the administration, simplifying its manipulation for their own employees. We study some examples that show different possibilities in different administrations.

---

[12] http://www.content0.com/cms-spain/cases/view.asp?cid=536

[13] About electronic government in Spain, see the study *eGovernment in Spain*, from November 1995, by *The IDABC eGovernment Observatory*, in http://ec.europa.eu/idabc/servlets/Doc?id=21024. Additional information about Spain can be found in http://ec.europa.eu/idabc/en/chapter/343.

3.1. Portal "Administraciones Públicas", www.060.es

The first example is the Official portal of the Spanish Public Administration (Figure 2), *Red 060 (060 Network)*, whose URL is http://www.060.es.

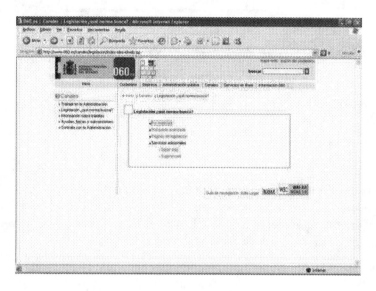

Figure 2. Spanish Public Administration, *Red 060.*

This portal has been created recently. It was presented at the end of May / start of June 2006, in the technologies and public administration "fair" (*Tecnimap*), celebrated in Sevilla between May 31, and June 2, 2006[14].

This portal has been developed by *XimetriX Network troughts*[15]. Its aims are to establish a closer relation between the administration and citizenship and to progressively unify the access of different departments of the General Administration (Administración General del Estado) to electronic services. In addition, it offers citizens the information they need in their relation with the public administration. This web portal is the successor of http://www.administración.es. It offers a document management system and the content management uses XML.

It contains a legislative database where it is possible to search for legislative documents[16], either by using a subject index (Figure 3) or a search engine. However, there are no links between these documents

---

[14] http://www.map.es/gobierno/muface/map.htm, Muf@ce nr. 203, June-July-August, 2006.

[15] http://www.ximetrix.com/

[16] http://www.060.es/canales/legislacion/index-ides-idweb.jsp

Figure 3. Topic index used with legislative documents in the Spanish Public Administration Web Server http://www.060.es/canales/legislacion/servicios/index-ides-idweb.jsp.

or any other type of relationship; that is, it does not exploit all the possibilities of XML. However, there are links to several web pages corresponding to the different Spanish Ministries in which the special legislation about a topic can be found.

Additional features of this server are an area "of citizens' participation" that citizens can use to express their opinion about rules and projects. This portal is also accessible through mobile devices, such as PDAs.

3.2. The *SIDRA* Proyect, (Asturias Government)

The second Project we study corresponds to an "autonomous community", the Principality of Asturias. It is a document management and 'knowledge management' system called *SIDRA* (*Sistema de Información Documental en Red de Asturias*)[17], whose web presentation can be seen in Figures 4 and 5.

This Project is a collaboration between the government of the Principality of Asturias and *Software AG España*, filial of the German parent

---

[17] A description of this project can be found in the developer's web page http://www.softwareag.com/es/customers/references/SIDRAProject_page.asp

Figure 4. The SIDRA Project.

company *Software AG*[18]. [19]. It has recently received the Adolfo Posada 2005 prize that recognises its value in using the new technologies to improve the functioning of the Public Administration. This document management system has been developed with XML, using the XML platform *Tamino XML Server.*

SIDRA is a system built on a single tool, which is responsible for the treatment, retrieval, distribution, and loan of all documents and information, public or private, necessary for the functioning of this organisation. SIDRA is presented as a dynamic information network that exploits the resources, information exchange, and cooperation between the different entities of the Public Administration of the Principality of Asturias, which has 32,000 employees. This system permits the sharing of information that, until now, each organism had managed in an isolated manner. The main idea of this project can be summarized in the term "Networked Administration" so that sharing information would permit "it to be transformed into knowledge" (*sic*). However, the connections and relationships between documents are not completely exploited.

There are other examples that use XML for the treatment of legislative texts, in other regional communities, for example, the Basque Country, Catalonia, or Valencia[20]. In most cases, it has proved impossible to

---

[18] http://www.softwareag.com/es/News/latestnews/20051201_ProyectoSIDRA_page.asp

[19] The Adolfo Posada award 2005 recognises relevant efforts in the research, study, teaching, and "broadcasting" of topics related with the Public Administration.

[20] See the web page of the Basque Government, and its services, at http://www.juslan.ejgv.euskadi.net/r45764/es/contenidos/informacion/fichero_xml/es_fich_xml/informacion_fichero_xml.html. For Catalonia, see http://www.gencat.net/nougencat/cas/web20.htm. The experience in Valencia is presented in http://www.tramita.gva.es/difusion/cs_/rss.jsp. Note that these projects, despite their undoubted value, do not exploit all the possibilities

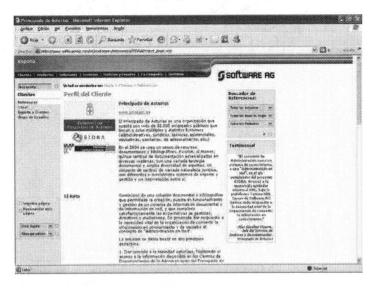

Figure 5. Web page of the SIDRA Project.

get any scientific publication that describes their implementation. This is a serious difficulty to evaluating their technological contribution[21].

3.3. ACTIVITY IN THE SPAIN SENATE: THE USE OF *EUROVOC*

The Spanish Senate (see Figure 6) uses the *Eurovoc Thesaurus* to index its document databases. With this thesaurus as starting point, the Senate makes its own development[22].

Eurovoc is a multidisciplinary, multilingual thesaurus, developed jointly by the European Parliament and the *Office for Official Publications of the European Communities (Publications Office)*, and it is used by at least fifteen European Parliaments to index their documentation and, particularly, legislative texts[23].

---

that XML offers for the multiple connections between legal texts. In some cases, they transfer the normative text to the end user in PDF or Word format, which implies that relationships between texts are not accessible to the end user.

[21] The Basque Country case is somehow different, as the research group DELi from the University of Deusto, has a research line in Information Technologies, within which it has developed (as we shall see later) the bilingual corpus used in the Basque Official Bulletin. See http://www.deli.deusto.es/Resources/BOPV for more information.

[22] http://www.senado.es/tesauro/intro.html

[23] The information about Eurovoc, and its multilingual versions in the eleven official communitary languages is available at http://europa.eu.int/celex/eurovoc/index.htm

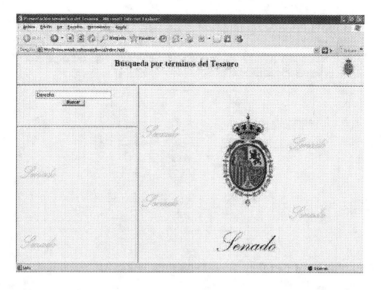

Figure 6. The Spanish Senate

The Senate maintains the structure of EUROVOC, making adapta-
tions and additions necessary for the correct management of documentation in this court, which manages several types of documentation,
laws and other rules, jurisprudence, bibliography and other archive
documents.

EUROVOC is mainly used in the Spanish Senate with juristic and
political micro-thesauri, focusing on those related with this parliament[24].

4. Projects and experiences

4.1. THE *LEXML.ES* COMMUNITY

The international community *LEXML* presents itself as a "European
network searching for the automatic exchange of legal information". It
uses XML as the tool to facilitate this exchange, as it is understood
that XML facilitates the standardazition of legal documents, in a co-
ordinated manner, thus allowing different schemas (e.g., DTDs) that
facilitate interoperability to be obtained[25].

This network is composed of national communities, which use a web
site and a distribution list as a meeting point. In Spain, it is coordinated

---

[24] See the presentation by CUETO, M., "EUROVOC Thesaurus use at the Senate
of Spain", in the *Cape Town – XML Workshop* del "*Africa i-Parliaments*", 27-30
june 2006, at http://www.parliaments.info/Capetown/09%20Marina%20Cueto%20-
%20The%20use%20of%20EUROVOC%20in%20the %20Spain%20Sentate.pdf. Nev-

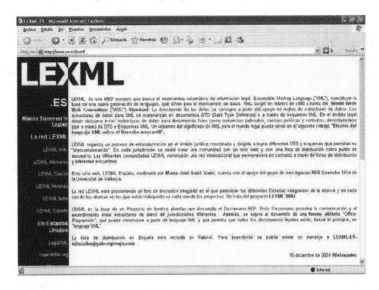

Figure 7. LEXM.ES

by María José Vañó Vañó with the research group RED Derecho TICs from the Valencia University[26]. Its presentation web page appears in Figure 7.

4.2. THE EXPERIENCE IN THE CARLOS III UNIVERSITY (MADRID) WITH THE OFFICIAL BULLETIN OF THE MADRID COMMUNITY.

A collaboration Project started in the year 2000 between the Department of "Librarianship and Documentation" of the Carlos III University of Madrid, and the Official Bulletin of the Madrid Community.

Its main aspects are described in an article published in the workshop on digital libraries "Primeras Jornadas de Bibliotecas Digitales", that took place in Valladolid in the year 2000[27].

---

ertheless, no information about how the Spanish Senate is using XML with EUROVOC could be obtained for this presentation.

[25] See the LEXML.ES web page at http://www.uv.es/lexml/

[26] See the work by Mª José Vañó Vañó, «Efectos del lenguaje XML sobre el Derecho mercantil», in its presentation version at http://www.uv.es/lexml/MjVanyoXML.pdf; and the corresponding paper, «XML, una herramienta al servicio del buen gobierno corporativo», *Revista Aranzadi de Derecho y Nuevas Tecnologías*, nr. 8, 2005, pp. 101-116.

[27] NOGALES FLORES, J. T., RODRÍGUEZ, D., ARELLANO PARDO, M. C. MARTÍN GALÁN, B. y HERNÁNDEZ, T., «Un repertorio legislativo hipertextual mediante marcado de texto: las Disposiciones Generales del Boletín Oficial de la Comunidad de Madrid», *Jornadas de Bibliotecas Digitales* (1ª. Valladolid 2000). Valladolid: Departamento de Informática, Universidad de Valladolid, 2000, pp. 89-

This proposal has an precursor in a hypertextual version of the "Código del MERCOSUR", the set of legislation for the Common Market of South America (*Mercado Común de América del Sur*) –Argentina, Brasil, Paraguay, Uruguay, and the associations of Bolivia, Chile, and Venezuela). In this work, the texts used were the legislative texts of this commercial area dated from 1993 to 1998, which were provided by the Publisher "Editorial Ciudad Argentina" in order to create a hypertextual product available in Internet, or in CD-ROM.

The aim of the new project was to transfer this experience to the legislation of the Community of Madrid, adapting it to the peculiarities of this legislation.

5. Research

The last part of this paper synthesizes the current research in Spain related with the use of XML for legislative texts. There is other research related with the use of XML for other legal domains, such as intellectual rights management, but it is outside the scope of this study.

Most of this research is done in public universities, but some is also done in private universities.

5.1. CARLOS III UNIVERSITY OF MADRID

The Librarianship and Documentation Department of the Carlos III University in Madrid, already mentioned as collaborating with the Community of Madrid, has a long tradition of research into the application of XML to legal texts, with the perspective of documentalists.

This research team is made up of M.C. ARELLANO PARDO, T. HERNÁNDEZ, B. MARTÍN GALÁN, J. T. NOGALES FLORES and D. RODRÍGUEZ. Since the year 2000, it has brought out several publications related to the analysis of legal documents so as to transform them into electronic documents in XML format in order to permit their

---

104 (available at `http://gaia.dcs.fi.uva.es/~jbidi2000/comunicaciones/09_Reper.pdf`).

manipulation and use[28]. The PhDs of B. MARTÍN GALÁN[29] and M.C. ARELLANO PARDO[30], dealing with the treatment of jurisprudence texts, and legislative texts respectively, were written in this context.

5.2. DEUSTO UNIVERSITY

The research team DELi, in the University of Deusto, started its work in 1998 with the collaboration of some lecturers of the Faculty of Arts and ESIDE, who had common interests in areas such as information manipulation and transmission (memetics, intertextuality, edition and hypertexts, etc.) and the Semantic Web (ontologies, metadata harvesting, *Web* services, etc.).

---

[28] In chronological order, starting with the already mentioned work in collaboration with the Community of Madrid: a) NOGALES FLORES, J. T., RODRÍGUEZ, D., ARELLANO PARDO, M. C. MARTÍN GALÁN, B. and HERNÁNDEZ, T., «Un repertorio legislativo hipertextual mediante marcado de texto: las Disposiciones Generales del Boletín Oficial de la Comunidad de Madrid», *I Jornadas de Bibliotecas Digitales*, Valladolid, Departamento de Informática, Universidad de Valladolid, 2000, pp. 89-104; b) MARTÍN GALÁN, B., NOGALES FLORES, J. T. and ARELLANO PARDO, M. C., «Modelos formales para la definición estructural y semántica en documentos XML: comparación de posibilidades en un corpus textual de documentación jurisprudencial», *III Jornadas de Bibliotecas Digitales (JBIDI'02), El Escorial (Madrid) 18-19 de Noviembre de 2002*, José Hilario Canós Cerdá, Purificación García Delgado (ed.), Facultad de Informática, Universidad Politécnica de Madrid, Madrid, 2002, pp. 97-106; c) NOGALES FLORES, J. T., MARTÍN GALÁN, B., ARELLANO PARDO, M. C., «Informática, Derecho y documentación. Experiencias y posibilidades de aplicación de los lenguajes de marcado de texto (SGML, HTML Y XML) a los documentos jurídicos», DAVARA RODRÍGUEZ, M.A. (ed.), *Actas del XVII Encuentro sobre Informática y Derecho*, Madrid, Instituto de Informática Jurídica, Universidad Pontificia de Comillas, 2003, pp. 355-374; d) ARELLANO PARDO, M. C., NOGALES FLORES, and J. T., MARTÍN GALÁN, B., «La organización hipertextual del ordenamiento jurídico. Posibilidades de XML y estándares relacionados», *Revista General de Información y Documentación*, 2003, vol. 13, nr. 2, pp. 181-191; e) NOGALES FLORES, J. T. , ARELLANO PARDO, M. C. and MARTÍN GALÁN, B., «Propuesta de aplicación de los criterios de técnica legislativa a un sistema de información de legislación usando tecnologías XML», en DAVARA RODRÍGUEZ, M.A. (coord.), *Actas del XVIII Encuentro sobre Informática y Derecho*, Madrid, Instituto de Informática Jurídica, Universidad Pontificia de Comillas, 2004, pp. 273-288; and, f) ARELLANO PARDO, M. C., *Aportaciones de la Técnica Legislativa y XML a la Informática Jurídica Documental*, Universidad Carlos III de Madrid/Boletín Oficial del Estado, Madrid, 2005.

[29] *Tratamiento y difusión en Internet de información jurisprudencial mediante tecnologías XML: aplicación al caso de Tribunal Constitucional*, Universidad Carlos III de Madrid, February 2002.

[30] *La organización hipertextual del ordenamiento jurídico por medio de tecnologías XML: aplicación a la normativa del IRPF*, Universidad Carlos III de Madrid, abril de 2003.

Currently, this team brings together full-time lecturers of the University of Deusto. Unai Aguilera, David Buján, Josuka Díaz Labrador, Inés Jacob and Txus Sánchez are computer engineers belonging to ESIDE; Joseba Abaitua, Patricia Fernández Carrelo and Koldo Garai Bilbao are linguists in the Faculty of Arts.

The research of this team has focused, as far as legal texts are concerned, on the elaboration of a bilingual corpus in which they compiled, in an exhaustive manner, the official bulletins published in the Official Basque Bulletin (Boletín Oficial del País Vasco) (BOPV) between 1994 and 2004, obtained from the institutional web http://www.euskadi.net[31]. The publications of this team are related to linguistic aspects[32].

5.3. MURCIA UNIVERSITY

In the Faculty of Computer Science of the University of Murcia, within the research team "Intelligent Systems" (*Sistemas inteligentes*) of the department "*Departamento de Ingeniería de la Información y las Comunicaciones*"[33], Antonio F. Gómez Skarmeta, and Javier de Andrés Rivero, are working on the creation of a system that permits the automatic retrieval of legislation in force. The results of this work are explained in more detail in the publication entitled *Cronolex: One System for the Dynamic Respresentation of Laws*[34].

5.4. UNIVERSITY OF THE BASQUE COUNTRY

The team made up of Sara Sanz , Silvia Sanz , Mikel Villamañe, Julián Gutiérrez, José A. Vadillo and Tomás A. Pérez, all members of the department of "*Lenguajes y Sistemas Informáticos*" of the University of the Basque Country (UPV/EHU), is responsible for a project consisting in the development of a Digital Library of Historical Basque Law (Derecho Histórico Vasco). The particularity of this project is that the documents considered are bibliographis and other documents related

---

[31] See http://www.deli.deusto.es/Resources/LEGE-Bi/; http://www.deli. deusto.es/Resources/BOPV; and http://www.deli.deusto.es/News/1128469312/ index_html.

[32] See http://www.deli.deusto.es/AboutUs/Publications.

[33] See   https://habidis.cpd.um.es:8001/servlet/um.curie.ginvest. ControlGrinvest?accion=verficha&grin_codigo=02&dept_codigo=E096.

[34] See also GÓMEZ SKÁRMETA, A.F., MARTÍNEZ GRACIÁ, E., and GALIANO ROMERO, A.M., «Una arquitectura de metadatos para la gestión de información en el web », *Novática*, nr. 146, may-august 2000, pp. 9-11. See also the work by GÓMEZ SKÁRMETA, A.F. and ANDRÉS RIVERO, J., «XML for the Recovery of the Law in Force», presented in *IAAIL Workshop Series - The Role of Legal Knowledge in E-Government*, Bologna (Italia), 2005.

to "Historical Basque Law", instead of modern, legal texts currently in force[35].

5.5. VALLADOLID UNIVERSITY

The University of Valladolid also has some researchers investigating the application of XML to legislative documents, using information extraction and paying special attention to structure manipulation. Mercedes Martínez González and Pablo de la Fuente — members of the research team *Grupo de Recuperación de Información y Bibliotecas Digitales* of the Computer Science Department — are collaborating in this research with Dámaso Javier Vicente Blanco — *Grupo de investigación sobre Derecho de las nuevas tecnologías y delicuencia informática*, of the Faculty of Law —.

This research began in 1996, with two research projects on the topic of Internet-accessible public servers of legislative information[36]. This research continued after these projects, in collaboration with the French research institute *Institut Nacional de Recherche en Informatique et ses Applications (INRIA)*[37]. Additional results of this research are published in several international and national publications[38].

---

[35] See SANZ, S., SANZ, S., VILLAMAÑE, M., GUTIÉRREZ, J., VADILLO, J. and PÉREZ, TOMÁS A., «BD-IDHV. Una Biblioteca Digital de Derecho Histórico Vasco», *IV Jornadas de Bibliotecas Digitales (JBIDI'03), Alicante, 10-12 de Noviembre de 2003*, Eduardo Mena and Jesús Tramullas (ed.), Alicante, 2003, pp. 125-134.

[36] Project *Estudio, diseño y puesta en marcha de un servidor público de información legislativa sobre red INTERNET. CICYT (TEL96-1296)*; and *Estudio y realización de un servidor público de información Legislativa de Castilla y León sobre red INTERNET (VA10196)*.

[37] This PhD was supervised by Dr. Pablo de la Fuente Redondo, University of Valladolid, and Dr. Jean-Claude Derniame, *INRIA*. It was presented in Spain and France in April 2001 and September 2001 respectively. The respective titles were « *Principios para la explotación dinámica de relaciones entre documentos en las bibliotecas digitales: aplicación al entorno jurídico*» and «*Principes d'explotation dynamique des relations inter-documents dans les bibliothèques électroniques: application au domaine juridique*».

[38] In chronological order: a) MARTÍNEZ-GONZÁLEZ, M., DE LA FUENTE, P., DERNIAME, J.-C., PEDRERO, A., «Explotación dinámica de relaciones en las bibliotecas digitales: aplicación a una biblioteca jurídica», *II Jornadas de Bibliotecas Digitales (JBIDI 2001)*, Almagro, 2001, pp. 169-180; b) MARTÍNEZ-GONZÁLEZ, M., DE LA FUENTE, P., DERNIAME, J.-C., PEDRERO, A., «Relationship-Based Dynamic Versioning of Evolving Legal Documents», *INAP (LNCS)* vol. 2543, 2001, pp. 290-305; c) MARTÍNEZ-GONZÁLEZ, M., DERNIAME, J.-C. and DE LA FUENTE, P., «A method for the dynamic generation of virtual versions of evolving documents», *ACM Symposium on Applied Computing (SAC)*, 2002, pp. 476-482; d) MARTÍNEZ-GONZÁLEZ, M., DE LA FUENTE and P., DERNIAME,

Currently, Mercedes Martínez González and Dámaso Javier Vicente Blanco are collaborating in a regional research Project (Junta de Castilla y León) with the Association of Attorneys of Valladolid (Colegio de Procuradores de Valladolid)[39]. The goal of this project is to provide these professionals with automatic tools that facilitate the treatment of legal texts related to the topic "judicial cooperation on civil matters in the European Union".

6. Conclusions

This study of on-going legislative XML projects in Spain shows that there is a varied and interesting activity on this topic in this country, even if it is not always possible to know the technological contributions of commercial and official activities, due to the lack of scientific publications describing them.

References

Alvite Díez, M.L., «Evolución de las bases de datos jurídicas en España», *Anales de Documentación*, 2004, vol. 7, pp. 7-27.

Arellano Pardo, M. C., Nogales Flores, and J. T., Martín GALÁN, B., « La organización hipertextual del ordenamiento jurídico. Posibilidades de XML y estándares relacionados», *Revista General de Información y Documentación*, 2003, vol. 13 (2), pp. 181-191.

J.-C., «XML as a means to support information extraction from legal documents», *International Journal of Computer Systems, Science and Engineering*, vol. 18, n° 5, 2003, pp. 263-277; e) MARTÍNEZ-GONZÁLEZ, M., DE LA FUENTE and P., DERNIAME, J.-C., «Una propuesta integrada de extracción de información para gobierno electrónico: estructura, referencias y evolución de los documentos jurídicos», *IV Jornadas de Bibliotecas Digitales : (JBIDI'03), Alicante, 10-12 de Noviembre de 2003*, Eduardo Mena and Jesús Tramullas (ed.), Alicante, 2003, pp. 201-210; f) MARTÍNEZ-GONZÁLEZ, M., DE LA FUENTE, P. and VICENTE BLANCO, D.J., «Dealing with the automatic extraction of references from legislative digital libraries», VSST 2004 (Veille Strategique, Scientifique et Technologique), 2004, pp. 281-288; g) MARTÍNEZ-GONZÁLEZ, M., «Document Versioning in Digital Libraries», *Encyclopedia of Database Technologies and Applications*, 2005, pp. 201-205; h) MARTÍNEZ-GONZÁLEZ, M., DE LA FUENTE, P. and VICENTE BLANCO, D.J., «Reference Extraction and Resolution for Legal Texts», *Lecture Notes in Computer Sciences (LNCS), vol. 3776, Springer-Verlag, 2005, pp. 218-221.*

[39] *Creación de una Aplicación de Web Semántica para el Tratamiento y Manipulación Electrónicos de los Textos Jurídicos de la Unión Europea y el Espacio Económico Europeo en materia de Conflictos Internacionales deJurisdicción (VA010B06).*

Arellano Pardo, M. C., *Aportaciones de la Técnica Legislativa y XML a la Informática Jurídica Documental*, Universidad Carlos III de Madrid/Boletín Oficial del Estado, Madrid, 2005.

Cueto, M., «EUROVOC Thesaurus use at the Senate of Spain», in the *Cape Town – XML Workshop* del *"Africa i-Parliaments"*, 27-30 june 2006, at http://www.parliaments.info/Capetown/09%20Marina%20Cueto%20-%20The %20use%20of%20EUROVOC%20in%20the%20Spain%20Sentate.pdf.

García Palomeque, Rebeca & Pérez Campos, Rafael, «Las nuevas tecnologías: un paso adelante en la documentación jurídica», *Biblioteconomia i Documentació: textos universitaris de biblioteconomia i documentació*, june 2003,10, http://www2.ub.es/bid/consulta_articulos.php? fichero=10garcia2.htm, Retrieved: 01-06-2006.

Gómez Skármeta, A.F., Martínez Graciá, E., and GALIANO ROMERO, A.M., «Una arquitectura de metadatos para la gestión de información en el web», *Novática*, nr. 146, may-august 2000, pp. 9-11.

Gómez Skármeta, A.F. and Andrés Rivero, J., «XML for the Recovery of the Law in Force», presented in *IAAIL Workshop Series - The Role of Legal Knowledge in E-Government*, Bologna (Italia), 2005.

Martín Galán, B., Nogales Flores, J. T. and Arellano Pardo, M. C., «Modelos formales para la definición estructural y semántica en documentos XML: comparación de posibilidades en un corpus textual de documentación jurisprudencial», *III Jornadas de Bibliotecas Digitales (JBIDI'02), El Escorial (Madrid) 18-19 de Noviembre de 2002*, ed. José Hilario Canós Cerdá, Purificación García Delgado, Grupo de Ingeniería del Software, Facultad de Informática, Universidad Politécnica de Madrid, Madrid, 2002, pp. 97-106.

Martínez-González, M., De La Fuente, P., Derniame, J.-C., Pedrero, A., «Relationship-Based Dynamic Versioning of Evolving Legal Documents», *INAP (LNCS)* vol. 2543, 2001, pp. 290-305.

Martínez-González, M., De La Fuente and P., Derniame, J.-C., «XML as a means to support information extraction from legal documents», *International Journal of Computer Systems, Science and Engineering*, vol. 18 (5), 2003, pp. 263-277.

Martínez-González, M., De La Fuente, P. and Vicente Blanco, D.J., «Dealing with the automatic extraction of references from legislative digital libraries», VSST 2004 (Veille Strategique, Scientifique et Technologique), 2004, pp. 281-288.

Martínez-González, M., De La Fuente, P. and Vicente Blanco, D.J., «Reference Extraction and Resolution for Legal Texts», *Lecture Notes in Computer Sciences LNCS*), vol. 3776, Springer-Verlag, 2005, pp. 218-221.

Nogales Flores, J. T., Rodríguez, D., Arellano Pardo, M. C. Martín Galán, B. and Hernández, T., «Un repertorio legislativo hipertextual mediante marcado de texto: las Disposiciones Generales del Boletín Oficial de la Comunidad de Madrid», *I Jornadas de Bibliotecas Digitales*, Valladolid, Departamento de Informática, Universidad de Valladolid, 2000, pp. 89-104.

Nogales Flores, J. T., Martín Galán, B. and Arellano Pardo, M. C., «Informática, Derecho y documentación. Experiencias y posibilidades de aplicación de los lenguajes de marcado de texto (SGML, HTML Y XML) a los documentos jurídicos», en DAVARA RODRÍGUEZ, M.A. (ed.), *Actas del XVII Encuentro sobre Informática y Derecho*, Madrid, Instituto de Informática Jurídica, Universidad Pontificia de Comillas, 2003, pp. 355-374.

Nogales Flores, J. T. , Arellano Pardo, M. C. and Martín Galán, B., «Propuesta de aplicación de los criterios de técnica legislativa a un sistema de información de legislación usando tecnologías XML», en DAVARA RODRÍGUEZ, M.A. (ed.),

Actas del XVIII Encuentro sobre Informática y Derecho, Madrid, Instituto de Informática Jurídica, Universidad Pontificia de Comillas, 2004, pp. 273-288.

Sanz, S., Sanz, S., Villamañe, M., Gutiérrez, J., Vadillo, J. and Pérez, Tomás A., «BD-IDHV. Una Biblioteca Digital de Derecho Histórico Vasco», *IV Jornadas de Bibliotecas Digitales (JBIDI'03), Alicante, 10-12 de Noviembre de 2003*, ed. Eduardo Mena and Jesús Tramullas, Alicante, 2003, pp. 125-134.

The IDABC E-Government Observatory, *eGovernment in Spain*, November 2005, http://ec.europa.eu/idabc/servlets/Doc?id=21024.

Vañó Vañó, M.J., «XML, una herramienta al servicio del buen gobierno corporativo», *Revista Aranzadi de Derecho y Nuevas Tecnologías*, 8, 2005, pp. 101-116.

A Schema Development for Brazilian Legislative Acts

Andrea Marchetti*, Isabella Martins Garcia Leite, Maurizio Tesconi*,
Salvatore Minutoli*, Marco Rosella*
* *CNR Institute for Informatics and Telematics*

Abstract. This is a brief of the research activities involved in the development of
a XML Schema for Brazilian Legislative acts.

Keywords: XML, legislative, Brazilian acts

1. Introduction

To start the development of a Schema for Brazilian legislative acts we
needed some basic information:

— The rules related to the Brazilian legislative drafting.

— The tools and criterions used to search for acts in the Official Web
site of the Brazilian Government.

— The electronic format used for legislative acts.

The first point is fundamental for the drafting of the Schema. The
other two are useful to understand the current technological state of
the Brazilian juridical documentation. Our first concern was to find out
if a Schema of the Brazilian laws already existed or if it were a matter
of some ongoing project.

In this project we tried to exploit our recent work "Norme In Rete"
where we participated in the definition of an XML Schema for Italian
Laws. Therefore we will occasionally refer to the structure of Italian
Laws so as to detect which elements could be reused for the new Schema.

2. Brazilian acts related to the rules of legislative drafting

The first research has been done with the goal of finding the rules related
the Brazilian legislative drafting.

For this purpose we visited all the websites of the bodies allowed by
the Constitution to legislate, as described in its article 61. These bodies
are:

1. Chamber of Deputies

2. Federal Senate

3. Presidency of the Federal Republic of Brazil

4. Supreme Federal Tribunal (STF)

5. Superior Tribunal of Justice (STJ)

6. General (Procure) of the Republic

7. Superior Electoral Tribunal

8. Superior Tribunal of the Work

9. Superior Military Tribunal.

Afterwards we found the email addresses of five deputies and five senators of the Republic[1] published in their related websites and we asked them about the existence of legislative technical instruments. It was the eve of the most important election of the nation, the one in which Brazilian people choose the President of the Republic, all the federal deputies, the 2/3 of members of the Senate and the leaders of all the 26 member states of Brazilian federation, as well as the members of the legislative houses of all the 26 federal states. Although a big number of the parliamentarians were in electoral campaign for the renewal of their legislative mandate, we received replies and documents in electronic and paper format by most of them.[2]

After the researches in the websites cited above and the review of the information received from parliamentarians, we finally characterized the Brazilian legislative acts (on a federal level) that contain rules for legislative drafting. These are:

1. Complementary Law 95 of 26th February 1998

2. Decree 4176 of March 2002

3. Manual of writing of the Presidency of the Republic.

---

[1] The criterions used for the choice of the nominative of parliamentarians were: national projection, certified juridical knowledge to be the President of a legislative house: Chamber of Deputies or Federal Senate.

[2] Thanks in particular to Federal Deputy Doctor Michel Temer, President of the Chamber of Deputies, Doctor Leany Barreiro de Sousa Lemos, Chief of the Gabinet of Senator Roberto Freire and Doctor Gileno, alderman of the Federal Deputy Augusto Franco Neto.

2.1. THE COMPLEMENTARY LAW 95 OF 26th FEBRUARY 1998

The most important Brazilian legislative drafting rule, is about the elaborating, editing, amending and consolidating laws, in compliance with the unique paragraph of art. 59 of the Federal Constitution, and establishes rules for the consolidation of the normatives cited in it.

The first remarkable aspect to analyze is that of the normative specie that regulates the subject: it's about the *Lei Complementar* (Complementary Law).

The *Complementary Law* is one of the seven normative species established in article 59 of the Constitution, and since it is founded directly on the Constitution, is considered a primary norm.

The Complementary Law is a normative specie, to which the Constitution expressly reserves a specific subject, and needs the absolute majority for its approval.

Despite the actual doctrinaire agreement about the fact that Complementary Law is not to be considered hierarchically superior with respect to the ordinary laws, for a long time this argument has generated controversies.

The thesis of the superiority of the Complementary Law was founded on the fact that it is a law aimed to complement the Constitution needing an absolute majority for its approval, whereas the ordinary law is approved with simple majority.

Nowadays the prevailing doctrine is clear about the horizontality and equality of the normative species contained in article 59 of the Brazilian constitution, because the Complementary Law differs form the other only on its subject and qualified quorum for its approval.

Obviously amendments to the Constitution are an exception, because after its approval, the Constitution amendment integrates the Constitution itself.

Analyzing the constitutional text we can understand that the constitutional lawmaker chose some subjects needing a careful consideration and wider political agreement.

The setting of a qualified quorum for the approval of the Complementary Law project shows the need for a qualified agreement for the approval of the chosen topics.

This is the case of the unique paragraph of art. 59 when it established that the Complementary Law will discipline the elaboration, editing, amending and the consolidation of the laws.

The resort to the Complementary Law as a juridical mean of regulation of the activities for legislative drafting, points out, without doubts, the big importance given to the subject and the political will for the effective improvement of the quality of the legislation.

2.1.1. *Object of the Complementary Law 95 of the February, 26 1995*
The topic of this law is cited in its first article*: the elaboration, editing, amending and the consolidation of laws.*
Its application sphere is the set of normative species listed in article 59 of the Constitution:

— Amendments to the Constitution,

— Complementary Laws,

— Ordinary Laws,

— Legislative Decrees,

— Delegation Laws

— Temporary Measures

— Decrees

— Regulation Acts sent to the organs of the federal Executive.

It contains nineteen articles organized in four chapters named respectively: preliminary dispositions; techniques for elaboration, editing and amending of the laws; consolidation of laws and other normative acts; final dispositions.

From the contents of this law we can understand that the structure of the Brazilian Law differs from the Italian one both on the formal structure and the functional point of views.
Most of the information used for the definition of the Schema originates from this law.

2.2. The Decree 4176 of March 2002

The Decree 4176 of March 2002, establishes norms and directives for elaboration, editing, consolidation and presentation to the President of the Republic of normative acts projects competing to the organs of the Federal Executive. It is a decree and, as such, it is a secondary normative specie, that specifies what is stated in the Complementary Law 95 of the February 1998, on the subject of the drafting rules about the law plans competing to the Federal Executive.
Since it is specific, besides repeating the rules of the above-cited Complementary Law, it is more detailed, containing sixty-four articles and two annexes with a lot of suggestions for the drafting, in check list form.
A particularity of this decree is that it contains very detailed indications about the form and the style to use for the law text visualization.

Among other things, this decree takes into account the use of the Internet to send law plans to the Presidency for their evaluation

2.3. MANUAL OF WRITING UP OF THE PRESIDENCY OF THE REPUBLIC

The Complementary Law 95/98 and the Decree 4.176 of March 2002 above analyzed are, without doubts, the consecration of the rules and recommendations contained in the Manual of Editing of the Presidency of the Republic.

Edited in the 1991, in the sphere of the Presidency of the Republic, the Manual constitutes the first attempt by the government to start the setup and standardization of the editing rules for acts and official communications, simplifying the administrative language and repressing archaic aspects.

Promptly followed by all the organs that compose the Brazilian public administration, the Manual uniformed the language and the structure of the official communications and the normative acts enacted in the federal executive, providing both a style code and a legislative drafting manual.

It is subdivided into two parts, the first under the authority of diplomatic Nestor Jose Foster Junior and the second under the authority of the Manual. The first part deals with the official communications, beginning from their essential aspects, giving the definition of the official editing and the principles that must be followed in the elaboration: impersonality, the use of the cultured form of the language, clearness, briefness, formality and uniformity.

The first part also presents the typology of the official communication, defining every species and their goals; uniforms the structure, displays models, introducing, at the end of this part, grammar elements to use in the official editing.

The second part is about the elaboration and editing of the normative acts competing to the executive, their definition and exemplification and the legislative procedure.

According to Pedro Parente, Chief of the Civil House of the Presidency of the Republic of the government Fernando Henrique Cardoso[3] the edition of the Manual gave rise to a monitoring system for the edition of the normative acts, allowing a more careful thinking over proposed normative acts, clearly characterizing the problem or situation that generated them, their expenses, their practical effects, the probability of juridical disputes, their legality and constitutionality and their consequences on legal order. After eleven years from the publication of

---

[3] President of the Federal Republic of Brazil from 1994 to 2002.

the first edition, the need for a revision and update of the Manual raised to conform to changes in the handled topics. The second edition of the Manual of Editing of the Presidency of the Republic, available in the site http://www.planalto.gov.br has been recently published in the Portaria N 91, in December 04, 2002 by Chief of the Civil House of the Presidency of the Republic.

The second edition maintains its original structure. In the first part the principal alteration has been the adjustment of the editing forms and communication with the public administration by means of innovative informatics technologies.

The second part, concerning the normative acts and the legislative procedure, has been largely modified, to comply to the constitutional alterations and to the rules dictated from the Complementary Law 95/1998 and the Decree 4.176/2002.

3. The formal structure of a Brazilian law

The Brazilian law is structured in three principal parts: preliminary part, normative part and final part.

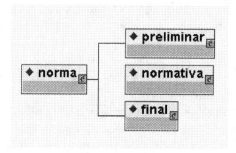

Figure 1. The Principal Components of a Brazilian Law

3.1. PRELIMINARY PART

The preliminary part includes the *epigraph*, the *ementa*, the *preamble*, the *enunciation of the object* and the *indication of the application scope* of the normative dispositions. The *epigraph* corresponds to the heading of the Italian law (except the Title), indicating the denomination of the normative species, sorting order and promulgation date. The *ementa* is a summary of the content of the normative act. The definition of *preamble* of Brazilian law is different from the Italian one, since it is only used to indicate the competing institution for the act procedure and its legal base. The Brazilian preamble matches the system of Italian promulgation, while Italian preamble, only used for non-legislative acts, matches the exposition of Brazilian theme.

The *enunciation of the object* and *indication of the application scope* of the normative disposition are showed in the first article of every law text.

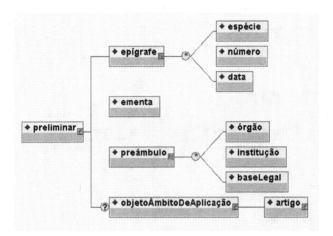

Figure 2. Preliminary Part Schema

LEI Nº 10.558, DE 13 DE NOVEMBRO DE 2002.

Cria o Programa Diversidade na
Universidade, e dá outras providências.

Faço saber que o Presidente da República adotou a Medida Provisória nº 63, de 2002, que o Congresso Nacional aprovou, e eu, Ramez Tebet, Presidente da Mesa do Congresso Nacional, para os efeitos do disposto no art. 62 da Constituição Federal, com a redação dada pela Emenda constitucional nº 32, de 2001, promulgo a seguinte Lei:

Art. 1º Fica criado o Programa Diversidade na Universidade, no âmbito do Ministério da Educação, com a finalidade de implementar e avaliar estratégias para a promoção do acesso ao ensino superior de pessoas pertencentes a grupos socialmente desfavorecidos, especialmente dos afrodescendentes e dos indígenas brasileiros.

Figure 3. Example of a Preliminary Part

```
- <preliminar>
  - <epígrafe>
      <especie>LEI</especie>
      N°
      <numero>10.558</numero>
      , DE
      <data ano="2002" mes="11" dia="13">13 DE NOVEMBRO DE 2002</data>
    </epígrafe>
  - <ementa>
      Cria o Programa Diversidade na Universidade, e dá outras providências.
    </ementa>
  - <preambulo>
      Faço saber que o Presidente da República adotou a Medida Provisória n° 63, de 2002, que o Congresso Nacional
      aprovou, e eu. Ramez Tebet,
      <institucao>Presidente da Mesa do Congresso Nacional</institucao>
      , para os efeitos do disposto
    - <baseLegal>
        no art. 62 da Constituição Federal, com a redação dada pela Emenda Constitucional n° 32, de 2001
      </baseLegal>
      , promulgo a seguinte Lei:
    </preambulo>
  - <objetoAmbitoDeAplicacao>
    - <artigo>
        <numero>Art. 1°</numero>
      - <caput>
          Fica criado o Programa Diversidade na Universidade, no âmbito do Ministério da Educação, com a finalidade de
          implementar e avaliar estratégias para a promoção do acesso ao ensino superior de pessoas pertencentes a grupos
          socialmente desfavorecidos, especialmente dos afrodescendentes e dos indígenas brasileiros.
        </caput>
      </artigo>
    </objetoAmbitoDeAplicacao>
  </preliminar>
```

Figure 4. Example of a Preliminary Part in XML Format

3.2. NORMATIVE PART

The normative part includes the text of the norms with substantial content related with the regulated topic.

The articulation of the Brazilian law includes the last element of the preliminary[4] part and the normative and final part.

Therefore, the first article of the law text will always indicate the object of the law and the related application scope (article 7 of the Complementary Law 95/1998).

3.2.1. *Article*

The basic unit of articulation is the article, container of the norm text and indicated by the abbreviation "Art." [5]

The content of every article of the law must deal only with a unique subject and principle.

---

[4] The one related to the statement of the object and the indication of the application sphere of the normative disposition, indicated in the first text of every normative act (see art. 7 of the Complementary Law 95/1998)

[5] In the Italian law, the article is not the container of the norm text, but of a rubric text (despite it is optional the rubric in an article is often used in Italian law). The norm is described in the paragraph The rubric of the article in the Brazilian legal system is not mandatory, but it's often used in unique texts and codifications.

The article can be divided into paragraphs or into parentheses; the paragraphs in turn can be divided into parentheses, the parentheses into *alinea* and the *alinea* into *itens*.

The paragraphs express the complementary aspects of the enunciated norm in the *caput* of the article and the exceptions to the rules established by them.

The parentheses, *alinea* and *itens* contain enumerations and distinctions.

Since the article and the elements that constitute it are different from the Italian model, we introduce, as an example, a fragment of the article 5th of the Brazilian Constitution of 1988:

Art. 5° Todos são iguais perante a lei, sem distinção de qualquer natureza, garantindo-se aos brasileiros e aos estrangeiros residentes no pais a inviolabilidade do direito à vida, à liberdade, à igualdade, à segurança e à propriedade, nos termos seguintes:

I - homens e mulheres são iguais em direitos e obrigações, nos termos desta Constituição;

(. . .)

LXXVI - são gratuitos para os reconhecidamente pobres, na forma da lei:

a) o registro civil de nascimento;

b) a certidão deóbito;

LXXVII - são gratuitas as ações de "habeas-corpus" e "habeas-data", e, na forma da lei, os atos necessários ao exercício da cidadania.

§ 1° - As normas definidoras dos direitos e garantias fundamentais têm aplicação imediata.

§ 2° - Os direitos e garantias expressos nesta Constituição não excluem outros decorrentes do regime e dos princípios por ela adotados, ou dos tratados internacionais em que a República Federativa do Brasil seja parte.

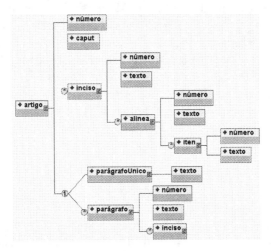

Figure 5. Article Schema

3.2.2. *Aggregation of Articles*

The aggregation categories, specified in the parenthesis V of art. 10 of the Complementary Law, are subsection, section, chapter, title, book and part.

A group of articles forms a subsection; a group of sections forms a chapter;

Figure 6. Normativa Schema

chapters form a title; titles form a book and books possibly a part (because the latter can be split into general part and special part).

The article, as described by Gilmar Mendes[6], is "*a unidade básica para a representação, divisão ou agrupamento de assuntos num texto normativo*", and, as such, is the unique element essential to a normative text, so the existence of the other groups are not mandatory, being part, as said by Gilmar Mendes, of the "*sistematizaçao das leis mais complexas*", as, for example, the codifications.

Making an example, we see below a part of the structure of the Federale Brazilian Constitution of 1988, without the Book and Part groups:

---

[6] Gilmar Mensdes in "Questões Fundamentais de Tecnica Legislativa", published in the Revista Dialogo Juridico, Ano I – Vol 1 – N 5 – August 2001 – Salvador – Bahia - Brasile

TÍTULO III

Da Organização do estrado
    CAPÍTULO I
    Da Organização
    Político-Administrativa (Arts. 18 e 19)
    CAPÍTULO II
    Da União (Arts. 20 a 24)
    CAPÍTULO III
    Dos Estados Federados (Arts. 25 a 28)
    CAPÍTULO IV
    Dos Municípios (Arts. 29 a 31)
    CAPÍTULO V
    Do Distrito Federal e dos Territórios
        Seçao I
        Do Distrito Federal (Art. 32)
        Seçao II

As we can see, despite the Complementary Law doesn't contemplate the rubric element, it is a part of the Brazilian legislative routine, often used to identify every law group, except for the article. The Brazilian article, in fact, unlike the Italian one, does not usually include a rubric, being it only present, sometimes, in the codification.

3.2.3. *Typographical Elements*

A very interesting aspect that is not present in the Italian Law is the identification, in the Complementary Law 95/1998, of a series of indications about the typographic styles to use for all the types of elements used in the normative part. These characterizations, that allow for a simple location of the single elements, are synthesized in Tab. I.

Table I.

Part, Book, Title, Chapter	Written in lower case letters identified by roman numbers. In conformity with the Complementary Law 95/1998 parts could be divided in parts expressed in ordinal numbering in full.
Subsection and Section	Written in lower case letters, in boldface or style that emphasize them, identified by roman numbers.
Article	Indicated by the abbreviation "Art.", followed by an ordinal numbering up to the ninth and cardinal numbering for the following numbers.
Paragraph	Represented by the graphical sign "§", followed by an ordinal numbering up to the ninth and cardinal numbering for the following numbers. When only a paragraph exists, the expression "unique paragraph" must be used.
Parenthesis	indicated by roman numbers.
Aliena	indicated by lower case letters.
Iten	indicated by arabic numbers

3.3. FINAL PART

The final part includes:

1. Dispositions pertinent to the necessary measures to the implementation of the substantial content norm;

2. Temporary dispositions;

3. The effective clauses;

4. The revocation clauses;

5. The *fecho* conclusions.

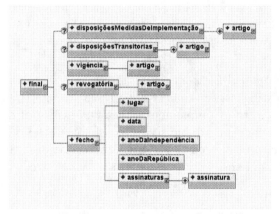

Figure 7. Final Part Schema.

4. The Formal Aspects

The Complementary Law 95/1998, besides the formal and systematic structure of the dispositions, enunciates also some rules about the morphological, syntactic and semantic aspects, when, in its article 11, enunciates norms that must be observed to achieve **clearness**, **precision** and **logical order** in normative dispositions. The term **normative disposition** cited in the Complementary Law is used as a reference to those contained in articles, paragraphs, parentheses, *alinea* or *itens*.

4.1. CLEARNESS

In order to obtain clearness, words and expressions of common use and meaning must be used (except when the norm is about a technical topic), using short and concise sentences, uniformly using the verbal tenses, giving the preference to present and past tenses and wisely employing the punctuation, avoiding stylistic excesses.

4.2. PRECISION

In order to obtain precision the above-said law suggests to correctly use the language with the goal of allowing the perfect understanding of the objective of the law; to always use the same word to express the same idea all over the text, avoiding the use of synonyms and words that cause ambiguity; to not use regional expressions; to use only common acronyms, accurately defining their meaning when used for the first time; to write in letters the references to numbers and percentages (except data and laws numbers or in cases the understanding of law text could result difficult).

It is important to emphasize that to achieve precision the object of the remission must be explicitly indicated, in place of the expressions "anterior", "following" or "equivalent".

4.3. LOGICAL ORDER

The logical order is obtained combining, under the aggregation categories, only the dispositions related to the object of the law, reducing the content of every article of the law to only one topic or principle.

4.4. NUMBERING AND OTHER

Some particular numbering criterions for articles are dictated in article 12 in the case of alteration, where a new article is inserted. In this case the same number of the article must be used, followed by lower case letters, in alphabetical order, as many times as sufficient to identify the additions.

For example we can see the following articles from the Code of Civil Procedure:

TITULO IV
DA EXECUCAO POR QUANTIA CERTA CONTRA DEVEDOR INSOLVENTE
(...)
CAPITULO IX
DAS DISPOSICOES GERAIS
(...)

Art. 786. As disposiçoes deste Titulo aplicam-se às sociedades civis, qualquer que seja a sua forma.

Art. 786-A. Os Editais referidos neste Título também serão publicados , quando for o caso, nos órgãos oficiais dos Estados em que o devedor tenha filiais ou representantes.

Artigo acrescentado pela Lei 9.462/97

(...)

The units that compose the article can be reorganized,: the article will then identified with the "NR" letters.

The Section III of the Chapter II states rules about the alteration of the laws.

References

A.Marchetti, F.Megale, E.Seta, F.Vitali. *Marcatura XML degli atti normativi italiani. I DTD di Norme in Rete.* In Informatica e diritto Progetto NIR – Fase 2 "Accesso alle Norme In Rete", November 2001.

F.Vitali, A.Marchetti *Using XML as a means to access law documents: Italian and foreign experiences* – EuroWeb2001, December 2001.

A.Marchetti, E.Seta, G.Gabriele, L.Abba *Documenti Parlamentari in XML.* In atti XML Italia 2000 pp. 109-135, May 2000.

An Adaptation of the FRBR Model to Legal Norms

João Alberto de Oliveira Lima
Senado Federal/PRODASEN - Brazil

Abstract. FRBR (*Functional Requirements for Bibliographic Records*) is an entity-relationship model developed in 1998 by IFLA (International Federation of Library Associations and Institutions) as a new way to model bibliographic records. Its main feature is the recognition of four entities (*Work, Expression, Manifestation, and Item*) representing different levels of abstraction of a certain work. This paper proposes an adaptation of the FRBR model to the modelling of the several levels of abstraction of a legal norm.

Keywords: Abstraction, Legal Norms, FRBR, Entity Relationship Model.

1. Introduction

According to Edsger W. Dijkstra (1972, p. 864) "the purpose of abstraction is not to be vague, but to create a new semantic level in which one can be absolutely precise".

Whenever we mention a certain legal norm, which entity do we mean? The original text promulgated after the legislative process? Or the compiled version of such norm for the present date, which somebody has edited? Or are we speaking about a version of such norm translated into another language? Or are we speaking about the content of a certain PDF file presenting the original text with an URL (Uniform Resource Locator) address available in a government site? A system that tries to model all these examples of entities as one singular entity will not allow for an adequate representation of the various relationship types between these entities.

Abstraction seen as a process is one of the most valuable modelling tools, and its use allows for the identification of entities at different abstraction levels in the universe of discourse. Abstraction seen as a product is the resulting model, which is used as a reference to systems development, since it expresses precisely the main existing entities and relationships.

The purpose of this paper is to adapt FRBR (Functional Requirements for Bibliographic Records), an example of judicious and adequate use of the abstraction process in the world of bibliographic records, to the world of legal records and norms.

The next session presents a brief history of cataloguing; thereafter, a short presentation of the FRBR model; and finally, considerations on adapting FRBR to legal norms.

2. Cataloguing and FRBR

Information Science and, more specifically, Library Science have been trying to establish standards of information organization and classification long before the first computers made their entrance in modern world. For instance, Anthony Panizzi's work, *"Rules for the Compilation of the Catalogue"* published in 1841, introduces 91 rules for book cataloguing. With the introduction of computers, the creation of a standard format was sought out in order to record cataloguing information on available books in a library. At present, the more used format for bibliographic description in the world is MARC (Machine Readable Cataloguing) format, created in the seventies by the American Library of Congress. Recently, the MARCXML format was published by Library of Congress. However, it was only a translation from MARC fields and subfields to XML elements and attributes, i.e., it was an evolution at the syntactic level only, leaving the semantics unchanged.

A MARC record represents several entities at different abstraction levels, from the work authorship (higher, conceptual level) to an exemplar of the work stored in a library shelf (lower, physical level). This raises a problem in case you intend to establish relationships between those entities.

2.1. FRBR

In 1998, IFLA (*International Federation of Library Associations and Institutions*) published the document *Functional Requirements for Bibliographic Records*. Although the work that originated the model was started in 1990, its origins goes back to 1961, with the publication of *"Statement of Cataloguing Principles"*, also known as *Paris Principles*. The FRBR document presents the conceptual model using Chen's Entity Relationship Model (1976), and divides entities into three groups:

- Group 1: consists of the products of intellectual or artistic endeavour;

- Group 2: comprises those entities responsible for intellectual or artistic content, safeguard or dissemination of Group 1 entities; and

- Group 3: includes the entities that serve as subject of Works.

Below, a brief description of each group. See (IFLA, 1998) for more details.

2.1.1. *FRBR - Group 1: Work, Expression Manifestation, and Item*

Entities called *Work, Expression, Manifestation, and Item*, as shown in Fig. 1, represent the different abstraction levels of an intellectual or artistic work. A **Work** is a distinct intellectual or artistic creation at the conceptual level. Since it is an abstract entity, it may be difficult to determine its boundaries precisely. For instance, text reviews or updates are seen as different "expressions" of the same "work". But to which extent do changes generate a new work? Furthermore, an **Expression** is the specific intellectual or artistic form that a work takes each time it is 'realized.' It is an abstract entity as well (at the conceptual level), which can be identified, for instance, in a translation work from the original text of a work to another language, thus generating a new "expression" of the same work. It has already been stated that any change in the original content by means of revision and/or updates originates a new expression. Fig. 2 shows other existing relationships: work-to-work, expression-to-expression, and expression-to-work relationships.

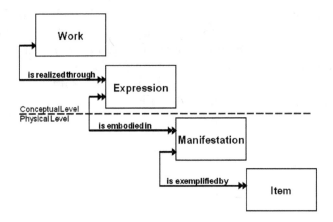

Figure 1. Group 1 FRBR Entities. (IFLA, 1998, p.13, adapted)

A **Manifestation** is the physical embodiment of an "expression" of a "work". The relationship between "expression" and "manifestation" is a "many-to-many" cardinality relationship.

Finally, an **Item** is a single exemplar of a "manifestation" of an "expression" of a "work". Such level of detail allows for the description of features of a specific example, like information on a book reserve or

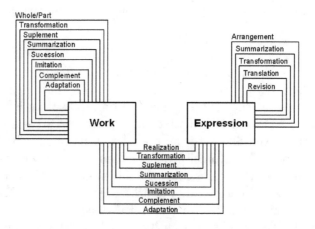

Figure 2. Work and Expression Relationships. (Aalberg, 1998, p.13, adapted)

loan request or even identification of an exemplar of the work with the author's autograph.

2.1.2. *FRBR - Group 2: Person, Corporate Body*

A **Person** is an individual consistently identified and independent from the way his name appears in a determined expression or manifestation of a work. **Corporate Body** is an organization, a group of individuals and/or organizations acting as a unit.

The relationships between the *Person* and *Corporate Body* Entities and Group 1 Entities are depicted in Fig. 3.

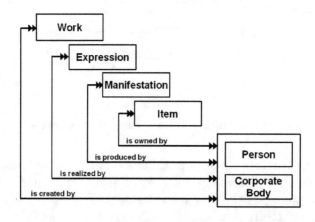

Figure 3. Group 2 FRBR Entities. (IFLA, 1998, p.14, adapted)

2.1.3. *FRBR - Group 3: Concept, Object, Event, Place*

Group 3 Entities serve as subject descriptors of Group 1 entity *Work*. The entity **Concept** is defined as an abstract notion or idea. Thus, a concept may be something of a general nature or something specific and precise. An **Object** is defined as a material thing. The entity **Event** is used to represent an action or occurrence, as for example, historic events, epochs or time periods. A **Place** represents locations, as a town, state or country; a historic or present location; geographical features, as a river or a mountain. Fig. 4 shows the relationships between entities that serve as Work subject descriptors. The diagram shows that not only Group 3 Entities serve as subject descriptors, but also Groups 1 and 2 Entities may be used to index the subject matter of a work.

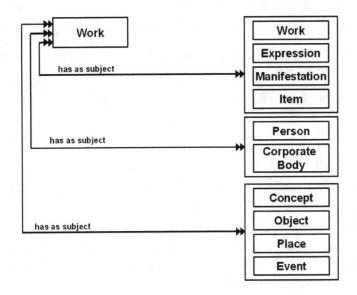

Figure 4. Subject Relationships. (IFLA, 1998, p.15, adapted).

One of the FRBR main innovations is the perception of the existing relationships between these entities which before were merged within the MARC record.

3. Adaptation of the FRBR Model to Legal Norms

The application of the FRBR Model to the world of legal norms does not require any structural changes. Each entity of the model can be mapped to the representation of entities and relationships of the universe of legal norms.

To present the considerations on adapting this model to legal norms we shall adopt the same organization of groups of entities.

3.1. FRBR Adaptation (Group 1)

A legal norm has two dimensions: content and form. The former is the semantic content that it carries, and the latter is the articulated text that composes it.

In our proposal, the entity Work (FRBR) refers to the "content of the legal norm", and the entity Expression refers to the "form" as defined by its original text. We have listed below some types of expression for a legal norm:

- Original Text – legally valid text;

- Republished Text – legally valid text (optional);

- Rectifying Text – legally valid text rectifying a text that has already been published;

- Updated Text – non official version updated to a certain date by a publisher;

- Translated Text – non official version translated into another language by a translator;

- Metadata – abridged version basically comprising metadata compiled by an information analyst;

"Metadata" is a "Work" and an "Expression" related to the Expression "Original Text" by a relationship (expression-to-expression relationship). Example of this configuration is depicted in Fig. 2 by the "Summarization" relationship of the entity "Expression". We present below an example of Work and Manifestation according to adaptation:

- W_1 – "Act n° 9 691, July 22, 1998 [creator = National Congress]"

  - $E_{1.1}$ – "Original Text"
  - $E_{1.2}$ – "Rectifying Text"

- W_2 – "Metadata to Act n° 9 691, 07/22/1998 [creator = Federal Senate]"

  - $E_{2.1}$ – "Metadata"

The entity "Manifestation" (FRBR) refers to the realization of the publishing work, which, in our proposal, is officially and mandatorily represented by the government press, and by the government bodies that publish or consolidate legislation texts, either on paper or in the Internet. With the inclusion of manifestations, the configuration of the above example is as follows:

- **W**$_1$ – "Act n° 9 691, 07/22/1998 [creator = National Congress]"

    - **E**$_{1.1}$ – "Original Text"
        - **M**$_{1.1.1}$ – "Official Publication in the Federal Journal, 07/23/1998"
        - **M**$_{1.1.2}$ – "Publication in the Federal Senate web site, 07/24/1998"
    - **E**$_{1.2}$ – "Rectifying Text"
        - **M**$_{1.2.1}$ – "Official Publication in the Federal Journal, 07/24/1998"

- **W**$_2$ – "Metadata to Act n° 9 691, 07/22/1998 [creator = Federal Senate]"

    - **E**$_{2.1}$ – "Metadata"
        - **M**$_{2.1.1}$ – "Publication in the Federal Senate web site, 07/24/1998"

Finally, Item (FRBR) refers to a univocally identified exemplar of a certain manifestation, which may be unique or not, on paper or in digital format. While the Item is identified by an URL, the Work or Expression instances can be identified by an URN (*Uniform Resource Name*) like the *Italian Norme in Rete Project*. Our example will now have the following structure:

- **W**$_1$ – "Act n° 9 691, 07/22/1998 [creator = National Congress]"

    - **E**$_{1.1}$ – "Original Text"
        - **M**$_{1.1.1}$ – "Official Publication in the Federal Journal, 07/23/1998"
            - **I**$_{1.1.1.1}$ – Exemplar on Paper in the National Library
            - **I**$_{1.1.1.2}$ – Exemplar on Paper in the Library of the Federal Senate
        - **M**$_{1.1.2}$ – Publication in the Federal Senate web site, 07/24/1998"
            - **I**$_{1.1.2.1}$ – `<http://www6.senado.gov.br/legislacao/ListaTexto.action?id=127883>`
    - **E**$_{1.2}$ – "Rectifying Text"
        - **M**$_{1.2.1}$ – "Official Publication in the Federal Journal, 07/24/1998"
            - **I**$_{1.2.1.1}$ – Exemplar on Paper in the National Library

- **W**$_2$ – "Metadata of Act n° 9 691, 07/22/1998 [creator = Senate]"

    - **E**$_{2.1}$ – "Metadata"
        - **M**$_{2.1.1}$ – "Publication in the Federal Senate web site, 07/24/1998"
            - **I**$_{2.1.1.1}$ – `<http://www6.senado.gov.br/legislacao/DetDoc.action?id= 149629>`

3.2. FRBR ADAPTATION (GROUP 2)

Group 2 entities are identified according to the legislative process of the norm in question. For example, the Federal Constitution, the country's main body of rules, is normally created and realized by a Constituent National Assembly, and produced by the National Press. In Brazil's case, the 1988 Constitution, art. 59, lists 7 types of norms prepared by the legislative process.

Table I identifies the roles of "Creator of the Work" and "Editor of the Expression" played by Official Agents according to the type of act. In the cases listed in Table I, the role of the "Manifestation Producer" is played by the "National Press" by means of the publication in the Federal Journal, and the role of "Item Custodian" is officially played by the National Library, and non-officially by any other agent that owns the Item.

Table I. Roles of the Agents according to the type of legal norm

Type	Creator of the Work	Editor of the Expression
Federal Constitution	Constituent National Assembly	Constituent National Assembly
Constitutional Amendment	National Congress	National Congress
Supplementary Law	National Congress	President of the Republic
Ordinary Law	National Congress	President of the Republic
Delegated Law	President of the Republic	President of the Republic
Provisional Measure	President of the Republic	President of the Republic
Legislative Decree	National Congress	National Congress
Resolution	National Congress	National Congress
	Federal Senate	Federal Senate
	House of Representatives	House of Representatives

Although "Supplementary Laws" and "Ordinary Laws" are created by the National Congress and passed on both Houses, they are actually realized with the sanction of the President of the Republic, who has the authority to put a veto to the whole or to part of the bill received from Congress.

Art. 61 of the Brazilian Federal Constitution deals with the initiative of supplementary and ordinary laws, and establishes that "laws can originate in any member or committee of the House of Representatives, the Federal Senate or the National Congress, the President of the Republic, the Supreme Federal Court, the Higher Courts, the Federal Prosecutor General and the citizens, in the manner and in the cases as specified...". Although the initiative may belong to agents outside the

National Congress, the debate and deliberation procedures legitimate the National Congress as the intellectual author, even when the bill has not been officially altered during its procedures in Congress.

The legislative process of the different types of legal norms is not simple and must conform to the Standing Rules on both legislative Houses. The purpose of this paper is not to exhaust details of the legislative process, but to show that the entities of the FRBR model may be naturally adapted to the world of legal norms.

3.3. FRBR ADAPTATION (GROUP 3)

Subject indexing is closely linked to the stage of information retrieval, i.e., a good indexing task will have a direct positive impact upon the quality of information retrieval. Indexing tasks must be viewed as existing relationships between indexer (descriptor) and indexed (target) entities, and not as simple listing of keywords in a subject field.

The FRBR model helps define various access ways to the works and, in this particular case, to the legal norms. Besides allowing indexing by Concept and Place, a common procedure in systems of legal information retrieval, it is possible to use the entities Event, Object, Person and Corporate Body as subject of a legal norm or even use another Work, Expression, Manifestation or Item as indexing descriptors, as shown in Fig. 4.

3.4. FRBR (RELATIONSHIPS)

Relationships between Group 1 entities, as shown in Fig. 1, do not need any adaptation or extension, when applied to legal norms, sufficing to follow the suggestions listed in section "FRBR Adaptation (Group 1)". Table II shows some Work-to-Work relationships, which are part of the FRBR model, and suggests new relationships applied to the world of legal norms.

Table II. Work-to-Work Relationships

Relationship	Roles	Uses
Successor (FRBR)	has a successor → ← is a successor to	Inform on the next and previous norms on dealing with the same content (e.g.: new/previous civil code).
Supplement (FRBR)	has a supplement → ← supplements	Relationship between legal norms and respective annexes.
Summarization (FRBR)	has a summarization → ← is a summarization of	Relationship between legal norms and metadata.
Whole-Part (FRBR)	has part → ← is part of	Allows for the division of a legal norm into smaller parts (Part, Book, Title, Chapter, etc.)
Alteration	alters → ← is altered by	Relationship of alteration or revocation of provisions between the altering and the altered norm;
Revocation	Revokes → ← is revoked by	Revocation relationship between legal norms.
Regulation	Regulates → ← is regulated by	Regulation relationship between norms

The "Alteration" relationship between norms occurs at the level Work-to-Work as shown on the Table above. The consolidation of this alteration in the original text, if achieved, will generate a new expression ("consolidated text") to the altered norm.

Table III shows some "Expression-to-Expression" relationships of the same work, which are part of the FRBR model.

Table III. Expression-to-Expression Relationships of the same work.

Relationship	Roles	Uses
Revision (FRBR)	has a revision → ← is a revision of	Relationship between the revised and the original norm.
Translation (FRBR)	has a translation → ← is a translation of	Relationship between the original text and the translated version.

Table IV shows some "Expression-to-Expression" relationships of different works that are part of the FRBR model, and suggests new relationships applied to the world of legal norms. According to IFLA (1998, p. 73), when Expression-to-Expression relationships involve expressions of *different* works, they include the same type of relationship acting at the "Work-to-Work" level.

Table IV. Expression-to-Expression Relationships of different works.

Relationship	Roles	Uses
Successor (FRBR)	has a successor → ← is a successor to	specifies the previous and next norm in dealing with the same matter (i.e., new civil code / previous civil code).
Supplement (FRBR)	has a supplement → ← supplements	Relationship between legal norms and respective annexes.
Abridgement (FRBR)	has an abridgement → ← is an abridgement of	Relationship between legal norms and Metadata.
Whole-Part (FRBR)	has part → ← is part of	Allows the division of a legal norm into smaller parts (Part, Book, Title, Chapter, etc.)
Alteration	alters → ← is altered by	Relationship of alteration or revocation of provisions between the altering and the altered norm;
Revocation	revokes → ← is revoked by	Total revocation relationship between legal norms.
Regulation	regulates → ← is regulated by	Regulation relationship between norms

According to IFLA (1998, p.74), relationships between "Expression of one Work" and a "Work" (different) are more frequently made when it is not easy to identify the expression of the second work to which reference is made. In this case, the same relationships as in Table IV occur, except in the case of the relationship "Whole/Part". One example of this relationship in the world of legal norms is the occurrence of a second alteration in the same provision without a republishing of the "Updated Text" containing the first alteration. Since it is impossible to identify the expression of the intermediate text, reference is made to the Work.

Table V shows the "Manifestation-to-Manifestation" Relationship present in the FRBR model.

Table V. Manifestation-to-Manifestation Relationships

Relationship	Roles	Uses
Reproduction (FRBR)	has reproduction → ← is reproduced	Inform the existence of copy in microfilm or in a mirror site
Alternate (FRBR)	has alternate → ← is alternate to	Informs an alternate manifestation
Whole/Part (FRBR)	has part → ← is a part of	Allows for the division of a legal norm into smaller parts.

4. Conclusion

Similarly to Dijkstra's quote in the beginning of this paper, Maria Helena Diniz (2006, p. 354), author of works on Law, makes the following considerations on the abstraction process:

"It must not be thought, as *Miguel Reale* so adequately states, that with the abstraction effort, inherent to the philosophic knowledge, we will gradually lose contact with reality, suspended in a world of pure fantasy since what differentiates and particularizes the "philosophic abstraction" is that the more we overcome the contingent and accessory, the more we capture reality in its true essence".

As we have tried to show in this paper the FRBR model resulting from a thorough work of analysis and abstraction achieved by IFLA, offers a rather simple reference model that can be applied to the organization of legal norms. The proposed adaptation did not involve structural changes but the information on how to map FRBR entities and relationships to the universe of legal norms.

Acknowledgements

My thanks to the Brazilian Federal Senate, Subsecretaria Especial de Informática do Senado Federal (PRODASEN) and Secretaria de Informação e Documentação (SIDOC). I am grateful for comments and suggestions by João Batista de Holanda Neto, Fernanda Passini Moreno and Flavio Roberto de A. Heringer.

References

Chen, P. P. The Entity-Relationship Model - Toward a Unified View of Data. *Transaction on Database Systems*, v.1, n.1, p.9-36. 1976.

Dijkstra, E. W. The Humble Programmer. *Communications of ACM*, v.15, n.10, p.859-866. 1972.

Diniz, M. H. *Compêndio de Introdução à Ciência do Direito*: Saraiva. 18ed, 589p, 2006.

IFLA (International Federation of Library Associations and Institutions) - Study Group on. *Functional Requirements for Bibliographic Records*, 144p. 1998. Available in: <http://www.ifla.org/VII/s13/frbr/frbr.pdf>

Towards a country-independent data format: the Akoma Ntoso experience

Fabio Vitali*, Flavio Zeni°

* *Department of Computer Science, University of Bologna, fabio@cs.unibo.it*
° *UN Department of Economic and Social Affairs, Nairobi, Kenya, zeni@un.org*

Abstract. AKOMA NTOSO (*Architecture for Knowledge-Oriented Management of African Normative Texts using Open Standards and Ontologies*) is an operating framework and a set of guidelines for driving e-Parliament services in a Pan-African context by formalizing and harmonizing the storage, publication and exchange of Parliamentary documents using a precise, common and easy to understand data format based on XML. The AKOMA NTOSO XML document schema provides sophisticated description possibilities for Parliamentary document types (including legislative documents and parliamentary records), and supports document structures by systematically relying on international standards, best practices, guidelines and widely recognizable design patterns.

Keywords: AKOMA NTOSO, Open Access, Pan-African Interoperability, Parliamentary records, XML

1. Introduction

In 2004 and 2005, the UNITED NATIONS Department for Economics and Social Affairs (UN/DESA) project, "Strengthening Parliaments' Information Systems in Africa", has aimed at empowering legislatures to better fulfil their democratic functions, using ICTs to increase the quality of parliamentary services, facilitate the work of parliamentarians and create new ways to promote the access of civil society to parliamentary processes.

A strategic role in this project is played by the AKOMA NTOSO (Architecture for Knowledge-Oriented Management of African Normative Texts using Open Standards and Ontologies) framework, a set of guidelines for e-Parliament services in a Pan-African context. The framework addresses information content and recommends technical policies and specifications for building and connecting Parliament information systems across Africa.

In particular, the AKOMA NTOSO framework proposes an XML document schema providing sophisticated description possibilities for several Parliamentary document types (including bills, acts and parliamentary records, etc.), therefore fostering easier implementation of Parliamentary Information systems and interoperability across African Parliaments, ultimately allowing open access to Parliamentary information.

The AKOMA NTOSO Framework reaches three main objectives which are instrumental for the success of the overall project:

— to define a common standard for data interchange between parliaments;

— to define the specifications for a base document model on which parliamentary systems can be built;

— to define an easy mechanism for citation and cross referencing of data between parliaments.

The AKOMA NTOSO framework aims at providing two basic types of interoperability: *semantic interoperability* is concerned with ensuring that the precise meaning of exchanged information is understandable by any person or application receiving the data; *technical interoperability* is aimed at ensuring that all AKOMA NTOSO-related applications, systems, interfaces are based on a shared core of technologies, languages and technical assumptions easing data interchange, data access and reuse of acquired competencies and tools. AKOMA NTOSO ensures technical interoperability by enforcing the use of open standards and open document formats, based on the XML (eXtensible Markup Language) language whose specifications are a world-wide standard and for which numerous tools and applications have been developed and are widely available.

In this paper we plan to describe the genesis and the fundamental aspects of the AKOMA NTOSO documents.

2. The need for a country-independent data format

Parliaments are currently exploiting ICT to improve the quality of their services and to improve access to all Parliamentary information: In Africa, this is particularly considered a strategic resource for its young and active democracies. In a Pan African context, Parliaments are also promoting collaboration among Parliaments and co-operation among countries in order to tackle the enormous problems that Africa is facing. At present, most interactions within and among Parliaments require numerous disparate transactions across multiple departments and Parliaments and there is very limited consolidation and aggregation across national Parliaments' boundaries.

Yet, Parliaments in Africa are continually confronted with demands for ever-greater dialogue between the electors and the elected, and have to examine how the management of information and official documents can improves transparency and citizens' access to political decisions, thereby permitting greater understanding of the democratic process. Needless to say, improved access to documents regarding activities of the Parliaments enable citizens to hold Parliaments accountable, stimulate greater efficiency and enhance democracy.

Connecting Parliaments has many benefits: in addition to its value as a knowledge transfer mechanism – whereby one Parliament can learn from the other – it also can be a tremendous boost to Parliamentary positive imitation. By seeing what others are doing, members of Parliaments can discover the possibility of doing the same in their own Parliaments. The explosion of Internet-based systems has increased the possibilities and range of such dialogue but this can be achieved and exploited only if common standards to produce, classify and share Parliamentary and legislative electronic documents are agreed and used by African Parliaments.

Providing access to primary legal materials and parliamentary documents is not just a matter of providing physical or on-line access to them, what we could be termed *formal access*. What we call *open access*, on the other hand, requires that the information content and the tools for search and retrieval of data are organized so as to allow users (MPs, the Executive, public administration, enterprises and citizens) to access and use the information in the form that is most convenient to them.

In order to build an information system that provides open access, there is the need to establish both common specifications for document models on which parliamentary systems can be built and a mechanism for citation and cross referencing of legal documents. To embark on the development of an information system without defining and agreeing on a standardised way for Parliaments to classify and structure their documents, e.g. bills, debate records, etc., would be to ignore the lessons learnt and the best practices of ICT development.

AKOMA NTOSO[1] (*Architecture for Knowledge-Oriented Management of African Normative Texts using Open Standards and Ontologies*) is an enabling framework for the effective access to and exchange of machine-readable Parliamentary Documents such as legislation, debate record etc. It aims to standardize simple, technology-neutral representations of Parliamentary Documents in order to improve inter-Parliamentary cooperation, and reduce the costs of Parliamentary IT support systems

---

[1] "Akoma Ntoso" (linked hearts) is the symbol used by the Akan people of West Africa to represent understanding and agreement. Likewise, AKOMA NTOSO represents common standards that provide open access to parliamentary documentation and allow Parliaments to exchange information more efficiently, like "linked hearts" [Akoma Ntoso, in "West African Wisdom: Adinkra Symbols & Meanings", http://www.welltempered.net/adinkra/htmls/adinkra/akon.htm].

To obtain interoperability between Parliamentary information systems for the purpose of providing open access, it was necessary to develop and adopt a framework for interoperability between IT systems at all levels that could foster co-operation between different institutions, administrations and Parliaments.

The framework takes the form of a collection of specifications aimed at facilitating the data interchange of Parliaments' systems and services using common open standards that avoid vendor lock-in and allow for greater public access to information.

By bringing together the relevant specifications under an overall framework, IT management and developers can have a single point of reference for the interoperability specifications that should be followed. By adopting these specifications, Parliamentary system designers can ensure interoperability between systems while at the same time enjoying the flexibility of selecting different hardware, operating systems and application software to implement solutions.

In 2004 and 2005 the UNITED NATIONS Department for Economics and Social Affairs (UN/DESA[2]) "Strengthening Parliaments' Information Systems in Africa" project started to address the need that Parliaments have to exchange information amongst themselves. With the establishment of the Pan African Parliament, this need has become an institutional requirement for the Parliaments that are represented there. It is clear that it would have been inappropriate to proceed with the development and implementation of the Parliamentary Information systems without establishing common guidelines on the structure and classification of digital parliamentary documentation, and it would not be following international best practices in such matters. In practice, it could jeopardize the long-term sustainability of such complex systems. To address this issue, the Project developed the AKOMA NTOSO framework proposal[3], based on the best practices and drawing from the experience of other continents. It was apparent that it would have been imprudent to deploy information systems in the National Parliaments without a Pan-African framework, and relying on no set of recommendations and guidelines for e-Parliament services in a pan-African context. By adopting AKOMA NTOSO, Parliamentary System designers can ensure interoperability between systems while at the same time enjoy the flexibility of selecting different hardware, systems, and application software to implement specific solutions.

---

[2] UNDESA, the United Nation Department of Economic and Social Affairs, http: //www.un.org/esa/desa/

[3] Pan African Parliamentary Interoperability (AKOMA NTOSO) Report and Documentation, published in http://www.parliaments.info/AKOMANTOSO/docs/ AKOMANTOSO\%20Draft\%20Proposal\%20V\%202.2.pdf

In order to enlist the support of the African Parliaments, UN/DESA organised, on 10 and 11 February 2005, an International Conference, "Parliaments' Information Management in Africa: Challenges and Opportunities of ICTs to Strengthen Democracy and Parliamentary Governance". The participating Parliaments were introduced to the AKOMA NTOSO framework proposal as well as to "Eurovoc-Africa" - a multilingual parliamentary thesaurus; and the proposal for the development of a common, but customisable Parliamentary Information System that included cooperative information services and repositories.

The Conference was attended by speakers and high-level delegations from the Parliaments of Algeria, Angola, Cameroon, Ghana, Kenya, Madagascar, Malawi, Mauritius, Mozambique, Rwanda, Sao Tomé and Principe, Somalia, Sudan, Tanzania, Tunisia, Uganda, Zambia and Zimbabwe, the Pan African Parliament, East Africa Legislative Assembly, ECOWAS Parliament, SADC Parliamentary Forum and the Italian Chamber of Deputies. Parliamentary officials from the above countries as well as from South Africa, the European Parliament, some European Union countries, representatives from international organisations, development partners, the private sector, and civil society organisations also attended the Conference.

The Conference unanimously adopted the "Nairobi Declaration" which, among other issues, recommends to promote the exchange of information by supporting the AKOMA NTOSO framework and a common Parliamentary multilingual thesaurus thereby establishing "*a coordinating mechanism to adopt, promote and maintain the Pan-African Parliamentary Interoperability (PAPI[4]) proposal*" and through the development of Parliamentary Information Systems "*based on open and interoperable standards, innovative technologies and full access to information*".

AKOMA NTOSO was developed as a necessary foundation for the development of a comprehensive Parliamentary Information System (PIS). The goal of the Parliamentary Information System is to maximize the operational efficiency and effectiveness of National Legislatures by implementing a solution which provides secure, reliable, and timely collection, storage, access, and transmission of information. The system will equip Parliaments with a solution that fosters accessibility, transparency and accountability of Parliaments by exploiting open source multi-platform applications based on open standards and available in multiple human languages.

---

[4] PAPI was later renamed to "AKOMA NTOSO". This was done in order to give the framework, as requested in the Nairobi Conference, an African name to reflect its Pan African nature and ownership.

Individual country Parliaments should use the guidance provided
by the AKOMA NTOSO Framework to supplement their national e-
Government initiatives with a Pan-African dimension and thus enable Pan-African interoperability of Parliaments. Thus the AKOMA
NTOSO framework is meant to supplement, rather than replace, national interoperability guidance that may exist, and to add a pan-
African dimension to them.

3. Objectives

AKOMA NTOSO (Vitali and Zeni, 2006) is an enabling framework
for the effective exchange of machine readable Parliamentary Documents such as legislation, debate record etc. AKOMA NTOSO aims
to standardize simple, technology-neutral representations of Parliamentary Documents in order to improve inter-Parliamentary cooperation,
and reduce the costs of Parliamentary IT support systems.

Parliaments are major producers of data and information that are vital
for the democratic well-being of a country and the lifeblood of political participation. The lack of a standardized way for Parliaments to
classify and structure their data resources, information technology and
business processes stands in the way of increased integration of information exchange and this in turn limits the efficiency and effectiveness
of Parliamentary activities.

The goal of AKOMA NTOSO is to fulfil the citizens' right to access
Parliamentary proceedings and deliberations and to support Parliaments in managing legislative documentation life-cycles efficiently. This
is facilitated through the definition and adoption of technical rules to
improve data exchange, document life-cycle automation and standardized representations of data and metadata in the African Parliamentary
domain. This goal can be further specified in three major subgoals:

3.1. DATA INTERCHANGE BETWEEN PARLIAMENTS

Parliaments function through the medium of documents. Debate in
Parliamentary chambers is recorded as documents. Legislation is passed
through the voting process via a combination of documents – the proposed legislation itself, proposed amendments, committee working papers and so on.

Given that the process is document-centric, the key enabler of stream-
lined Information Technology in Parliaments is the use of open document formats for the principal types of documents. This allows easy
exchange and aggregation of Parliamentary information – in addition

to reducing the time required to make the information accessible via different electronic publishing media.

The Information Technology industry has coalesced around a standard technology for open document formats known as XML (eXtensible Markup Language)[5]. The AKOMA NTOSO framework uses of industry standard XML to define a comprehensive set of XML-based Parliamentary document formats. This comprehensive set open document formats includes:

— Primary Legislation – covering the lifecycle of a piece of legislation

— Parliamentary Debates

— Amendment lists

— Committee briefs

— Journals

3.2. A SCHEMA FOR AFRICAN PARLIAMENTARY METADATA

Metadata is structured information about a resource. Metadata enables a resource to be found by indicating what the resource is about and how it can be accessed with a series of structured descriptions. Metadata facilitates the discovery and use of online resources by providing information that aids and increases the ease with which information can be located by search engines that index metadata.

The AKOMA NTOSO metadata format is primarily concerned with resource discovery and records management. The aim of this metadata format is to ensure that people searching the Parliaments information space online have fast and efficient access to descriptions of many different resources. The access to XML documents thanks to such shared metadata allows the creation of advanced search and retrieval functions across heterogeneous databases.

Structured collections of shared metadata will generate a thesaurus of legislative terms even across disparate documents, and documents occurring in disparate locations. These in turns will allow faster and more precise searches and categorizations of available legislative documents. The AKOMA NTOSO metadata format is designed to be extensible, so that those Parliaments with different, or more specific, metadata needs may add those extra elements and qualifiers needed to meet their own requirements.

---

[5] XML, the extensible Markup Language, http://www.w3.org/XML

3.3. Easy citation and referencing

Official documents, bills, laws and acts contain numerous references to other official documents, bills, laws and acts. The adoption of a common naming convention to reference a distributed document corpus like the one of the African Parliaments greatly enhances the accessibility and richness of cross references.

The naming convention enables comprehensive cross referencing and hyper-linking, so vital to any Parliamentary corpus, for instance:

— From debate records into legislation;

— From sections of legislation to sections of legislation in the same act;

— From sections of legislation to sections of legislation in another act of the same Parliament;

— From sections of legislation to sections of legislation of a different institution, such as acts of lesser authorities, acts of different countries, international treaties, or acts of superior authorities such as the Pan African Parliament.

The AKOMA NTOSO Naming Convention is intended to enable a persistent, location-independent, resource identification mechanism. The adoption of a scheme based on this Naming Convention allows the full automation of distributed hypertext.

4. Key issues in the development of AKOMA NTOSO

Developing a full model for legislative documents requires full awareness of a particularly complex environment of uses and applications and an environment that widely extends in space, time, and availability.

In particular, thinking about long term storage and an open set of applications requires making format choices completely independent of the tools that will be used for them, and ensuring that new tools can be used now and in an unspecified future for tasks as yet unclear or completely unknown.

In many ways, the AKOMA NTOSO data model derives from an analogous initiative brought forth in Italy by the National Centre for Informatics in Public Administration (*Centro Nazionale per l'Informatica nella Pubblica Amministrazione* or CNIPA[6]), a project called *NormeIn-*

---

[6] CNIPA, Centro Nazionale per l'Informatica nella Pubblica Amministrazione, http://www.cnipa.gov.it/site/it-IT/

Rete (Norms on the Network [7]), aimed at providing a common data model for XML versions of national and regional norms. The NormeIn-Rete schemas (NIR DTD and NIR XSD) and naming standards (NIR URN) have been published as national standards and are adopted by a number of local and national authorities, including the Italian Parliament and the Italian Court of Cassation. A brief description in English of the NormeInRete principles can be found in (Marchetti et al., 2002).

4.1. SIMPLE DOCUMENT MODEL

Data models created to handle complex document types (as legislation) need to deal with two apparently opposed requirements: on the one hand, they need to be sufficiently sophisticated to handle all possible occurrences and situations that may occur in the actual documents. On the other, they need to be speedily understood and used by the people who would need to apply these models.

These opposed requirements can be jointly satisfied not by simplifying the vocabularies of available structures and elements, which would reduce the available descriptive sophistication of the language, but rather by simplifying the structure variability and types (in XML lingo, the *content models*), thereby reducing the learning time and the software complexity without compromising a full and detailed descriptive power of the language. The idea therefore is to identify a number of basic, fundamental classes of structures (containers, hierarchies, blocks, etc.) that can be immediately understood and used appropriately, regardless of their actual names.

One of the main users considered when developing the AKOMA NTOSO model has been what we call the *future toolmaker*: this is a computer programmer that, fifteen years from now, will be asked to create new tools to manage AKOMA NTOSO documents or to activate new and currently unforeseeable computations with them. Differently from *current toolmakers*, the future toolmaker will not have access to complete documentation of the system, but only to sparse remaining documents, outdated by a fairly stratified situation where the basic ideas (on which the current toolmaker has worked) have evolved, modified, expanded and changed emphasis, often slowly and without documentation. The only reliable source of information available to the future toolmaker will be more than 15 years of actual legislation available in AKOMA NTOSO format.

Since the XML format has been created to be as complete and as self-

---

[7] NormeInRete, a joint project by the CNIPA and the Italian Ministry of Justice, http://www.normeinrete.it/

explanatory as possible, we expect the future toolmaker, in principle, to deduce all undocumented facts about AKOMA NTOSO by simply examining a few relevant XML instances of the legislation and discovering there how it should work. In a sense, the future toolmaker is more a key user for our system than the current toolmakers, and the possibility for him/her to deduce fundamental properties of AKOMA NTOSO from the visual examination of XML documents is a guarantee of long-term existence and usefulness of the AKOMA NTOSO system itself.

Thus the AKOMA NTOSO model is by no means a one-time exercise. Given the quantity and diversity of Parliaments and Parliamentary documents under consideration, it is unavoidable that the AKOMA NTOSO model grows substantially over time. Besides being as much as possible self-explanatory, the AKOMA NTOSO model has been built to stand evolutions and changes regarding the number of actual functionalities provided: features such as the number of metadata, or the automatic generation of amended text, or the activation of special analysis tools on the text may require with time an evolution of the schema.

4.2. Presentation, Structure and Semantics

Modelling Parliamentary documents – particularly legislation – requires giving consideration to the interplay between **presentation** (how the information looks), **structure** (how the information is organized, e.g. in document parts) and **semantics** (what the information is/represents). The mainstream philosophy of descriptive markup languages (to whose family XML belongs) dictates that

— *semantic markup* is the richest and most complete, whereby fully semantically identified parts of the document (e.g., headings, names, references, etc.) imply both their structural role and the expected presentation,

— some *structural markup* may need to be added for those document parts (e.g., organization of parts, hierarchies, preambles, conclusions, etc.) that have no specific semantic role; on the other hand, the presentation related to this markup can also be implied by their structural role.

— Finally, *presentation markup* deals with purely typographical aspects of text: there might be some remaining text parts with no identifiable semantic or structural role, yet with a different presentation (e.g., a part of text that is in bold for no discernible reason). These situations may occur because the current semantic/structural model is incomplete, or because the structure or semantics the part represents is a sporadic occurrence that was not deemed worth of being described, or because simply there was no real reason for putting a specific presentation but aesthetics. In these cases a full presentational model need to be described and used. Fortunately there are well known presentation models (e.g., XHTML + CSS) that can be directly applied to easily obtain full and sophisticated presentation effects.

There exists a continuum between explicit and hierarchical vocabularies that are specifics to a given domain, and flat, presentational vocabularies such as XHTML, as long as they allow descriptive information to be specified (e.g., the class attribute of XHTML elements) and allows unambiguous deductions as to the hierarchy they express.

This equivalence lets documents be created well across the semantic/presentational continuum, and still can be correctly converted into the final (fully descriptive) AKOMA NTOSO format automatically. For instance, it is be fairly easy to customize MS Word, Open Office, or any of a number of standard HTML editor, to produce texts with styles that can be automatically converted into the full AKOMA NTOSO format by deducing the actual names and hierarchy that the classes express.

4.3. EXPLICIT AND IMPLICIT STRUCTURE IDENTIFIERS

An issue whose support in AKOMA NTOSO can been seen as problematic is explicit naming. By design, AKOMA NTOSO needs to serve and deal with documents coming from several different African countries, where the names used for document parts may vary considerably from country to country, and where the same names can be used in different levels of the hierarchy.

A common practice, in SGML- and XML-derived languages, is to use tags that either reveal the name, or the structural role, of the parts being tagged. For instance, the hierarchical *sections* called "Part" and "Title", would be rendered as <section> elements under an implicit naming approach, and as <part> and <title> under the explicit naming approach.

In AKOMA NTOSO we assume that the advantages of proper, explicit naming of objects are prevailing over the increased software complexity in managing multiple partially overlapping sets of element names. In fact, we believe that the added complexity is not very impractical to implement, and that the expected future advantages (especially for long-term understanding of structures) definitely overcomes the initial implementation disadvantages.

AKOMA NTOSO expects documents to use explicit names, yet at the same time allows different document types to use the same names in completely different contexts and order. This apparent difficulty is overcome by the adoption of two related families of schemas. Similarly to XHTML Transitional and Strict DTDs, in fact, AKOMA NTOSO defines one Generic Schema and as many related Detailed Schemas as needed.

The *Generic Schema* is designed as a very loose schema, containing the full elements' vocabulary, but very few constraints on them; it allows all elements in all positions, and it is used as a baseline check for all situations in which no constraint can be imposed. Thus the GS validates all documents regardless of their provenance. Conversely, each individual *Detailed Schema* contains the same vocabulary, but imposes a larger number of constraints, compatible with the drafting rules of that specific document type. Detailed Schemas are subsets of the Generic Schema, and thus any document that is valid according to one of the DSs will also be perfectly valid according to the GS.

The only objection to this approach is that the Generic Schema also validates very absurd structures, and cannot be used to verify the structural correctness of documents. This is done on purpose: AKOMA NTOSO must accepts documents that were formally approved by the relevant Parliaments regardless of how absurd they happen to be. On the contrary, if a Parliament wishes to prevent the generation of absurd documents, it only needs to generate a Detailed Schema preventing inappropriate structures. This approach is more clearly detailed in the next section.

4.4. VERIFICATION OF THE VALIDITY OF DATA

Validation is the act of checking the correctness of an XML document according to pre-defined structural rules expressed in one or more DTDs and XML Schemas. The validation verifies whether the XML document contains, in number and position, all the expected elements of the type this document is an instance of.

The problem with being too restrictive in the constraints of the AKOMA NTOSO schema is that the Parliaments may have approved, and may decide to approve in the future, documents that do not conform to these rules: although in most countries there are guidelines for the correct drafting of legislation, but this is just what they are: guidelines, that can be ignored and modified at will by a higher authority such as a Parliament.

This fact has a very important effect on the generation of XML versions of documents: everything that gets approved by Parliaments have to be accepted by the system, and everything that has already been approved even more so. Therefore, failing XML validation (i.e., violating one or more of the constraints and restrictions expressed in the schemas) cannot have the effect of rejecting documents, but, at most, of pointing out issues and differences from the guidelines that the authority itself, if it wants and has time to spend on this, can consider for editing and modifications.

In reality there are two different actors in the complex issue of validating a piece of legislation: the Parliament, who is writing the actual content of the document, and the markers, who convert it into XML by identifying all interesting bits of the text and marking them up using the AKOMA NTOSO vocabulary.

In fact, we have designed the validation schema as a contract that only binds the marker, leaving the Parliament free to decide as it wishes. Thus compliance to rules such as "An identifier will always be added to each substructure of the act" or "The enactment date will be specified" can be safely required, as they bind the behaviour of the marker only, while structural rules (such as "Every subpart will have a heading", or "A section will contain paragraphs which contain clauses") cannot be imposed, as they would interfere with the authority and independence of the Parliaments.

Forcing markers to fully describe in XML all document parts, and yet leaving to the Parliament the maximum freedom in writing, may seem incompatible and hard-to-reach goals, but they can be and are reached in the AKOMA NTOSO framework. AKOMA NTOSO clearly separates data and metadata, thereby clearly distinguishing the contribution of the Parliament (data) and the contribution of the marker (metadata); AKOMA NTOSO provides a richly evocative vocabulary of structures and elements, so that the marker can correctly and precisely describe what is actually contained in the documents. AKOMA NTOSO imposes little or no constraints on data, letting the legislator write and organize the text matter as he wishes, but imposes a number of constraints on the metadata, forcing the marker of texts to provide all bits of information that are necessary to manage and organize the documents.

Yet it might be appropriate to also give guidance and help in following the drafting guidelines enacted in each country. This is the reason to provide both a General Schema and several Detailed Schemas: the GS is fully descriptive, only binding the marker and not the legislator, but allowing the marker to describe as precisely as possible the actual structure of the document as approved and generated by the Parliament. The DSs are more prescriptive, and are used to check whether the document actually conforms to the existing legal drafting guidelines in each individual country. Successful validation of documents will only be required against the GS, as errors would signal incorrect markup from the marker, while the DSs can be used, at the discretion of the Parliament itself, to automatically check conformance of the proposed bill against the local drafting guidelines, and thus be able to modify it accordingly in case conformance is sought.

5. Design approaches in AKOMA NTOSO

The AKOMA NTOSO model deals with a rather complex situation of five document types and several African countries, by creating two classes of document types, the Generic Schema (GS) and several Detailed Schemas (DSs) that provide support for differences in document types. Interoperability across these schemas is granted by a generalized approach that maintains full descriptions of the element while unifying and limiting in scopes the structures.

This is obtained through the systematic use of patterns. Patterns are the abstraction and distillation of past experiences in designing and resolving design problems. They are general and widely applicable guidelines for approaching and justifying design issues that often occur in XML-based projects.

We distinguish between patterns in content models (a restriction of content models to the ones that are actually useful) and patterns in schema design (guidelines on how to make a schema more modular, flexible and understandable by users). Both types of patterns are well known and well established in the literature, although by different experts in different ways. For patterns in content models we rely on (Vitali et al., 2005), while the authoritative resource for patterns in schema design is (XML Patterns, 2006).

5.1. SUPPORT FOR MULTI-LINGUISM

Due to the multi-language nature of the AKOMA NTOSO project, spanning across at least three European languages (English, French and Portuguese) and a number of African languages, all AKOMA NTOSO documents are required to use UTF-8 as their character encoding format.

Furthermore, although the schema has been designed to use English as the main language, it is expected that many users might have problems in using elements expressed in this language, and that relying on English alone would void the principle of descriptiveness of the documents.

For this reason, a (currently incomplete) list of equivalent names is provided in French and Portuguese and can be provided for any other languages as well, that allow sophisticated tools to evaluate and use these documents as if they were written using the main English-based AKOMA NTOSO vocabulary.

5.2. DESIGN PATTERNS IN SCHEMA ORGANIZATION

Design patterns are distillation of common wisdom in organizing the parts and the constraints of a schema. AKOMA NTOSO refers systematically to patterns listed in (XML Patterns, 2006). Whenever there has been a design choice to be made that was not immediately obvious and naturally acceptable, a relevant pattern has been sought and properly used. In fact, a large number of patterns from (XML Patterns, 2006) have been used, but only a few of them need to be explicitly described and explained :

— *Universal Root:* One generic root element contains all elements describing the document types. The AKOMA NTOSO schema covers five different document types: acts, bills, parliamentary debate records, parliamentary order papers, and miscellaneous parliamentary documents. The naïve solution would be to create five different schemas, one for each document type. This would mean activating five different processes for editing, marking up, validating, converting and displaying these documents, all of which driven by information contained within the document itself, and unavailable in advance. By creating a single root element containing the actual document elements, on the other hand, we have a single schema describing correctly and completely all document types.

— *Consistent Element Set*: many elements share similar or identical internal structures (in XML lingo, they have the same content model). As mentioned in the previous section, all elements rely on five types of content models only, and all document elements share just two content models (a strictly hierarchical structure and a loosely hierarchical structure). The advantage of this approach is that the proliferation of element names does not detract from the overall clarity and simplicity of the overall schema.

— *Generic document & role attribute*: Besides named elements, the AKOMA NTOSO schema also provides for a generic element for each of the five main types of content model. These are elements called just like the corresponding pattern (thus they are called <hierarchy>, <block>, <inline>, <marker> and <container>), and are meant to be used for markup that fits the content model but for which no specific element was provided. A 'name' attribute is provided for explicitly naming the element. A similar approach is taken in XHTML with the `<div>` and `<span>` elements, which are generic elements qualified by the 'class' attribute. It is also a characteristic of the AKOMA NTOSO schema that all named elements are equivalent, and can be substituted to the corresponding generic element with their name as the value of the name attribute. Thus, by definition, `<p>` is in AKOMA NTOSO the same as `<block name="p">`, `<part>` is the same as `<hcontainer name="part">`, `<act>` is the same as `<container name="act">`, etc.

— *Reuse Document Types* (partial): many AKOMA NTOSO element types mean exactly the same as corresponding elements in XHTML. For this reason, rather than inventing new names that need to be learnt from scratch, correctly understood and actually used when marking documents, only to have them translated into the corresponding XHTML terms for display, we have decided to just use the XHTML name, saving time in explanation, documentation, learning and usage. Therefore, for instance, a table in AKOMA NTOSO uses the tags `<table>`, `<tr>`, `<td>` and `<th>` that were introduced in HTML, a paragraph is `<p>`, bold and italic are simply `<b>` and `<i>` respectively.

5.3. DESIGN PATTERNS IN CONTENT MODELS

The AKOMA NTOSO 1.0 Schema uses systematically five of the seven patterns described in (Vitali et al., 2005). This means that all content models and complex types used in the schema follow precisely the form of the relevant pattern, and all elements can be simply described and treated according to their pattern rather than individually.

These patterns are:

— The *hierarchy*: a hierarchy is a set of arbitrarily deep nested sections with title and numbering. Each level of the nesting can contain either more nested sections or blocks. No text is allowed directly inside the hierarchy, but only within the appropriate block element (or, of course, titles and numbering).

— The *blocks*: a block is a container of text or structures that is organized vertically on the display (i.e., has paragraph breaks) and can contain either substructures or text. Most blocks in AKOMA NTOSO are based on the HTML language.

— The *inlines*: an inline element is an element placed within a mixed model element that identifies some text fragments as relevant for some reason. There are both semantically relevant inlines and presentation oriented inlines. There is but one content model using inlines (and markers), which means that all mixed model elements (i.e., those that allow both text and elements) also allow the a repeatable selection of all inline elements.

— The *markers*: markers are content-less elements that are scattered here and there in the document and are meaningful for their names as well as their attributes. Markers are also known in literature as *empty elements* or *milestones*. There are two main families of markers in the AKOMA NTOSO schema: placeholders in the text content (e.g., note references) that can appear in any position that also has text, and metadata elements that only appear in some subsection of the <meta> section.

— The *containers*: containers are sequences of specific elements, some of which can be optional. Containers are all different from each other (as the actual list of contained elements vary), and so there is no single container content model, but rather a number of content models that share the record pattern.

The following is an example of a hierarchy of sections:

```
<clauses>
  <chapter id="chap2">
    <num>Chapter 2</num>
    <title>Traditional communities and...</title>
    <paragraph id="chap2-para2">
      <num>2</num>
      <title>Recognition of traditional...</title>
      <clause id="cla1">
        <num>1</num>
        <p>A community may be recognised as ...</p>
      </clause>
      ...
    </paragraph>
    ...
  </chapter>
  ...
</clauses>
```

5.4. METADATA ELEMENTS

The meta section contains all the meta-information that needs or can be added to the actual content of the document. As a rule, all editorial content (i.e. content added by the editorial process out of Parliament rooms) need to be placed in the meta section, except for markup and note references.

Meta elements are divided in four subsections:

— *Descriptors*: i.e., a set of metadata providing info about the document and its publication and edition details, including its official promulgation date, its official URI, and so on.

— *Lifecycle*: the lifecycle element provides information about the events that the document has undergone, and references to the documents that have caused these events.

— *Notes*: the notes element contains the text of the editorial notes that are produced to comment and expand the actual text of the document. Note references inside the text point to notes contained here.

— *Proprietary*: this subsection allows any additional metadata to be specified in any order and vocabulary (provided it uses a different namespace than AKOMA NTOSO). Proprietary metadata can be used within a specific document management system to provide additional information useful for internal search and document management that is not worth standardizing and imposing across all AKOMA NTOSO implementations.

The development of the meta section is not finished yet. For instance, support for Dublin Core metadata is currently imperfect (there are semantic equivalences between Dublin Core elements and AKOMA NTOSO elements, but they are not complete nor officially described as equivalent).

5.5. IDENTIFIERS

Identifiers are systematically used in AKOMA NTOSO. All AKOMA NTOSO elements allow an identifier. Many relevant elements and sections *require* it. Identifiers are the main way to identify fragments and parts of the document in an unambiguous form. They can be used in document references (e.g. links and amendment commands) as a precise pointer to the actual part of the document mentioned (as opposed to simply referring to a document as a whole). Also internal links need to use identifiers.

The AKOMA NTOSO schema also specifies a syntax for identifiers, composed by juxtaposing sub-identifiers of the path needed to access them. Legal documents provide explicit global numbering for sections and articles, and local numbering for hierarchical subparts of them. The following (Table I) is a table with some examples of identifiers:

Table I.

Example	Identifier of example
Section 2 of this act	#sec02
Part 1 of section 2 of this act	#sec02-prt01
Paragraph 3 of part 1 of section 2 of this act	#sec02-prt01-par03
Chapter 5 of paragraph 3 of part 1 of section 2 of this act	#sec02-prt01-par03-chp05
Article 12	#art12
Clause 3 of article 12	#art12-cla03
item "c" of clause 3 of article 12	#art12-cla03-itm03
Third paragraph of clause 3 of article 12	#art12-cla03-blk03

Identifiers *never change* even if and when the elements get officially renumbered.

5.6. DOCUMENT URIS

A naming convention provides a simple mechanism for ensuring that Parliamentary Documents can be named and referred to in a consistent way. Being able to refer to documents in an unambiguous way that is both human and machine readable is very useful. In particular, a naming convention is critical in order to ensure that intra- and inter-Parliament hypertext linking can be achieved cost effectively.

All AKOMA NTOSO documents (and documents not converted into AKOMA NTOSO format, but referred to within a AKOMA NTOSO document) is identified by a unique name expressed as a specific URI. The actual syntax for AKOMA NTOSO URIs is being defined and is as yet unavailable.

6. Conclusions

The initial results of the AKOMA NTOSO framework are encouraging. Version 1.0 of AKOMA NTOSO is now complete, and contains schema and stylesheets for five different document types adapted to the needs of several different African Parliaments. Through the activity of UNDESA,

these schemas will soon evolve into local National Specifications for ten
African Parliaments that signed the Nairobi Declaration.

Given the importance of long term life span of the ideas behind
AKOMA NTOSO ideas, data and systems, it is vital that focused
activities for maintaining the project alive and active are taken. An
AKOMA NTOSO Management Board is being set up to ensure continu-
ing usefulness and adoption of the AKOMA NTOSO specifications, and
to engage in capacity building and users training at all levels (technical,
clerical, managerial) wherever the AKOMA NTOSO specifications have
been adopted, and to foster further adoption of the same.

References

Marchetti A., Megale F., Seta E., Vitali F., "Using XML as a means to access
   legislative documents: Italian and foreign experiences", *ACM SIGAPP Applied
   Computing Review*, 10, n. 1, pp. 54-62 (2002)
Vitali F., Di Iorio A., Gubellini D., *Design patterns for document
   substructures*, Extreme Markup 2005 Conference, Montreal, 1-5 August
   2005, http://www.mulberrytech.com/Extreme/Proceedings/xslfo-pdf/2005/
   Vitali01/EML2005Vitali01.pdf
Vitali F., Zeni F., Working Towards Interoperability in African Parliamentary In-
   formation Systems, IST-Africa 2006 Conference Proceedings, Paul Cunningham
   and Miriam Cunningham (Eds). IIMC International Information Management
   Corporation, 2006, ISBN: 1-905824-01-7
XML Patterns, http://www.xmlpatterns.com/

Internationalization of the Legal URN Schema

Pierluigi Spinosa
Institute of Legal Information Theory and Techniques (ITTIG-CNR)
Italian National Research Council

Abstract. In order to facilitate trans-national references, a proposal for an international extension of the schema of uniform names which will make it possible to identify any legal measure, issued anywhere in the world, is presented. The requested changes in the international scheme put forward by the Federal Senate of Brazil are also discussed and, in detail, the motivations, the positive and critical aspects and finally the still open issues are analysed. In the final part a proposal of official registration to IANA organization of a specific 'lex' namespace is proposed. The requirements of the IANA submission and the assessment of their satisfaction are also presented. Finally the proposal to charge Italian CNIPA organization with IANA registration is put forward.

Keywords: Legal document identification, URN.

1. Introduction

In the *III Workshop on Legislative XML* held in Furore, Italy, in April 2005, the extensions added, in the course of the past year, to the schema of uniform names (URN) adopted in Italy, in order to identify unambiguously and univocally any legal document or measure, were described. This evolution enables to correctly represent: annexes of annexes, multiple versions of a document which were generated by a single act of amendment, and communications referring to legal norms. Also the extended namespace which needs to be adopted for references in order to communicate to the resolver both the desired partition and the properties of the referred document were presented. Finally, in order to facilitate trans-national references, a proposal for an international extension of the schema of uniform names, which will make it possible to identify any legal measure issued anywhere in the world, was proposed.

In this document the proposal, suggested by the Brazilian federal Senate for changes in the international scheme proposed in Furore will be discussed, focusing on positive considerations, critical aspects and still open issues. As the benefits to have a common international legal scheme are acknowledged, the need to register the related namespace is emerged. This registration will be the base to create a shared infrastructure to access legal documents directly by URN without conversion in HTTP schema. For this reason, in the final part, the proposal to charge

CNIPA (Italian National Centre for ICT in Public Administration) with IANA (Internet Assigned Number Authority) registration is advanced.

2. Proposal of internationalization of the legal URN schema

2.1. MOTIVATIONS

The idea of assigning a uniform name as an unambiguous and univocal identifier to a legal measure is spreading all over Europe and in the world. Thanks to various events (conferences, workshops, seminars, etc.) focused on the use of XMLs in the legal field, Italian schema has started to circulate and, as a result, direct contacts were established with Switzerland, Denmark and Brazil.

Different countries have expressed the intention to adopt a schema characterised by a structure similar to the one which is defined and used in Italy. In fact, the method of identification of a legal measure through its issuing authority, the nature of the measure and its details is practically adopted in every country. Obviously, the schema will need to be adapted to the different countries in order to better reflect each country's normative, administrative and legal specificities (for example, the form of the State, the decentralization of the functions, its juridical organisation, etc.).

The proposal to create a common international schema was conceived within this context. Such a schema will have to take into account the schemas adopted in each country. Every schema will share with the others an homogeneous structure with regard to:

- the number, the meaning and the position of the main elements;

- the punctuation used to separate the elements and the sub-elements;

- the conventions used (for example, the allowed characters, labels and abbreviations, etc.);

- the formats in which dates, ordinal and cardinal numbers, etc., are represented.

In a scenario which sees a remarkable increase in various kinds of relationships among countries (treaties, agreements, conventions, etc.) and which sees the growing need to be familiar with the foreign norms, the adoption of a common international schema, at least at European level, will indeed foster the navigation among trans-national references, the creation of multinational services as well as the inter-exchange of experiences and tools all of which will be important to manage uniform names (from the recognition to the resolution).

2.2. THE STRUCTURE

The proposed structure of a uniform name of the international schema is the following:

"urn:lex:" <country-code> ":" <national-name>

where:

- lex is the name of the common meta-space of uniform names of legal measures at international level. In other words, the names assigned in each country which adopts the common schema begin with the following prefix;

- <country-code> is the identification code of the country where the measure was issued. This code follows the standard ISO 3166 of 2 letters (it=Italy, fr=France, dk=Denmark, etc.);

- <national-name> is the uniform name of the measure in the country where it was issued. Its internal structure is the same as the Italian schema which indicates, in the following order: the issuing authority, the type of measure, the details, the annexes, the version, etc.

For example, the uniform name of an Italian law would be urn:lex:it:stato:legge:2003-09-21;456, a French law would be urn:lex:fr:etat:lois:2004-12-06;321 and a Spanish law would be urn:lex:es:estado:ley:2002-07-12;123.

This structure also fosters the creation of an effective system of distributed resolution. The routing towards the proper resolver takes place first and foremost on the basis of the country code; each nation will decide autonomously the chain of proxies to activate on the sub-groups (by region, by province, etc.).

3. Proposal of extension of the Brazilian Senate

3.1. MOTIVATIONS

On the basis of an experimentation with Brazilian types of documents, the suitability of specifications developed in the Italian NIR (Norme in Rete: Legislation on the Net) Project to their reality has been very satisfactory. For this reason Brazil has adopted the legal URN schema to identify any kind of measures and is a great supporter of the internationalization initiative.

The idea that induced Brazilian Senate to propose an extension of the schema is, however, slightly beyond the need of internationalization. Brazil has a political and governmental structure that can be summarized as follows: a federal state with 27 federation units and more than 5,000 city houses. The legislative production is distributed among the three levels (federal, state and city house) and each of them possesses at least two different "authorities" able to issue legal measures. The Brazilian experts have considered a solution to avoid an unordered explosion of the authorities table and to help the effectiveness and the delegation of the resolution process.

This situation is similar in many countries. In the most part of them the legislative production is split at least between two levels: federal and state ambit in the federal form of government; state and regional ambit in the state form. Moreover all the countries have a very large number of bodies having the power to issue local measures (from regulations to administrative acts).

3.2. THE PROPOSAL

To fully adopt the URNs in Brazilian scope, the experts consider it necessary the addition of a <locality> element over the original NIR specification, as it has been foreseen for the new "urn:lex" namespace proposal.

This would be achieved by creating a <locality> element composed by the country code and one or more specifications able to support degrees of hierarchical specialization (using the separator character ';' as in the other NIR elements).

In other words, considering the following schema:

"urn:lex:" <locality> ":" <national-name>

The element locality would be:

<locality> ::= <country-code> *[;<specification>]

According to this schema and to the philosophy of distributed name resolution, it would be up to each country the definition, in the locality element, of the sub-structure that fits their needs at its best.

As an illustration example, in Brazil there would probably be a definition of this kind:

<locality> ::= "br" [;federation-unit-acronym [;city-name]]

Some examples deriving from this definition would be:

1. federal Constitution

   "urn:lex:br:federal:constituicao.federal"

2. resolution of the Secretary of the São Paulo State

   "urn:lex:br;sp:secretaria.fazenda:resolucao:2005-01-15;322"

3. petition of Câmara Municipal of São Paulo city

   "urn:lex:br;sp;sao.paulo:camara.municipal:requerimento:..."

4. bill of Prefeitura of Campinas (state of São Paulo)

   "urn:lex:br;sp;campinas:prefeitura:projeto.lei:..."

The <locality> element for a given document would have the minimum necessary level of detail to indicate the geographic context (area of influence or effectiveness) of the measure. As all cities in Brazil have the same basic set of authorities (one "prefeitura" - the local executive branch, and one "camara.municipal" - the local legislative house), identifying the city in the <locality> element would avoid the creation of the authority's complete name ("camara.municipal.campinas" or "camara.municipal.sao.paulo" in the above 3-4 examples).

Table I.

Official name	Locality	Authority
Brasil	br	federal
Presidència da Repùblica	br	presidencia.republica
Governo da Repùblica	br	governo
Estado de Minas Gerais	br;mg	estado
Governo do Estado de Minas Gerais	br;mg	governo
Prefeitura de São Paulo	br;sp;sao.paulo	prefeitura
Prefeitura de Campinas	br;sp;campinas	prefeitura
Càmara Municipal de São Paulo	br;sp;sao.paulo	camara.municipal
Càmara Municipal de Campinas	br;sp;campinas	camara.municipal

The complete univocal name of the authority would be determined by the combination of the two information: the locality element and the authority element, as shown in the Table I.

As we can see, the extended authorities table has the same number of rows as it would have had without the adoption of the <locality> element. However this approach benefits from a more compact dimension of the authority field and the "normalization" of the information.

Furthermore in a scenario like that of Brazil, this separation would make easier the implementation of a distributed "resolvers" architecture.

3.3. POSITIVE CONSIDERATIONS, CRITICAL ASPECTS AND OPEN ISSUES

The Brazilian proposal contains positive aspects as:

-   the further specification of the <country> element can be useful most of all for the federal states, where two levels of legislative production exist (federal and state) and the same bodies are present in every single state. Then similar acts issued by similar authorities in two different areas differ only for the locality specification. An example can be the following: "br:governo:decreto" (decree of federal government) and "br;sp:governo:decreto" (decree of São Paulo government);

-   the country specification is also very useful, in a distributed resolution system, to foster the delegation of the competence zones and the routing forward the proper resolver, like the DNS (Domain Name System);

-   it resolves the problem of the homonyms among Public Administrations, for instance the municipalities: the local prefixes make the complete name unique.

There are also some critical aspects:

-   the proposal uses frequently abbreviations: such possibility has been rejected in the Italian schema where only full denominations are used. The reason is that it constrains editors to learn or search them and is a potential cause of errors;

-   the split of enacting authority in two elements, the <locality> field and the <authority> one, makes the <authority> element not self-explaining and it must be read always in conjunction with the locality element. It would be better to use in the <locality> element only the organization or geographic component (state, region, etc.) while the institutional denomination of the body should be reported integrally, also if it involves some duplication. For example, the Tuscany Region institution in Italy would be coded as "it;tuscany:tuscany.region" instead of "it;tuscany:region".

However some problems are still to be solved, in particular those concerning the attribution of the names to:

- institutions interesting several states-regions-municipalities. One criterion might be the indication of the minimum territorial area able to include all of them, even though it would be necessary to go back up the hierarchical tree more than one level. For example, in case of a public body pertaining to two municipalities belonging to two different regions the common area is the state. The alternative solution might be to list all the territorial areas interested;

- the creation of a new intermediate geographic level (i.e a region) with migration of a institution (e.g. a municipality) from an area to an other one. While the denomination of the body remains the same, the locality changes and, as a consequence, the relative acts have a different initial part of the URN depending on the time in which each measure has been enacted. In the references this is particularly hard as it requires to know the exact date of the shift. This difficulty can be overcome either by an *alias* for each act or by a translation software (normalization process) which must be present in both nodes of the resolution tree. This problem is similar to a change of body denomination;

- finally, the identification of the administrative / geographic level which an institution belongs to is easy for an editor of the same state. On the contrary this information is difficult to know from the foreign countries as it requires the knowledge of the internal organisation (e.g. which *Land* Köln belongs to?).

In conclusion, the Brazil proposal contains some positive aspects even though it is necessary a verification at international level before adopting it in a generalized manner. The most significant points are the specificity level definition of the <locality> element and a shared answer to the open questions.

4. Official registration of "lex" namespace

4.1. WHY ASKING FOR THE OFFICIAL REGISTRATION?

Currently URN schema for legal documents is stable and robust. In Italy it is widely used by many institutions and it has also been tested successfully to identify acts contained in the official collection, which starts in 1861. This is a demonstration of its ability to identify also ancient documents characterized by authorities and types of measures no more existing.

The schema is regularly maintained (the last version 1.3 has been issued on May 2006) and some countries are going to adopt it (as Switzerland and Denmark).

The official registration of the "lex" namespace identifier (NID) by IANA organisation provides several advantages and mainly:

- to have a standard mechanism to link norms for Internet community in a persistent way;

- to address the standard evolution according to IANA general principles;

- to share a common infrastructure for routing the resolution via DNS.

4.2. OFFICIAL IANA REGISTRATION REQUIREMENTS

The official IANA registration of a formal URN namespace identifier (NID) is regulated by RFC 3406; this document requires the submission of a specific RFC (Request for Comments) and the IETF (Internet Engineering Task Force) consensus. The RFC must contain the following aspects:

1. technical requirements concerning the URN namespace and schema:

    - benefits to some subset of users on the Internet: a formal NID proposal must be functional on and with the global Internet and the potential use of names within that NID must be open to any user on the Internet;

    - uniqueness of the uniform names belonging to the namespace: the rules of assignment of the URN must guarantee that two different resources cannot have the same name;

    - persistence in the time: the name of the resource must be stable so that references to it guarantee the access in the future;

    - the providing of a resolution system: this service must guarantee the real access to resources through the URN, transforming it in a well known protocol (as http, wais, etc.). Moreover this system must guarantee its availability and persistence in the time;

2. administrative requirements concerning the organisation promoting the URN:

- to provide elements demonstrating that this body is consolidated and stable and it has a well defined structure;

- the body must be able to maintain for a long time the namespace and the registration service; this involves also the updating of the first level information to delegate the responsibility of sub-domains in a distributed architecture.

4.3. ANALYSIS OF THE ITALIAN SCHEMA

International legal URN based on the Italian schema satisfies all the technical requirements needed for the official registration. In facts it is:

- useful for a large Internet community: the related benefits are spreading over the PAs sites and involve any type of documents that refer to legal measure;

- IETF compliant: it respects all the rules defined in the RFCs about URN, as the use of the namespace ID and the related name specific string (NSS), the set of accepted, reserved and prohibited characters, etc., and, as a consequence, it has a compliant syntactic structure;

- well-defined with respect to all the technical requirements: uniqueness of uniform name, persistence in the time, rules for the assignment to a resource of its proper URN and a operative resolution mechanism.

Moreover, with respect to the organizational and administrative structure for the maintenance in Italy:

- legal URN standard was proposed within the Normeinrete project, a national project funded by CNIPA and Ministry of Justice;

- it has been issued by CNIPA as national technical norm, a recommendation for all the PA bodies;

- a specific Working Group, funded by CNIPA and coordinated by ITTIG/CNR, continues to maintain it; in this WG, in addition to CNIPA itself and national experts, are present the most important institutions as Senate, Chamber of Deputies, Ministries, etc.;

- the Italian branch of the international schema could be made soon operative: in fact it would be sufficient to translate the Italian namespace "nir" in the international "lex:it" one. This change could easily be performed for the legacy documents in automatic way; moreover the two namespaces could coexist and they might use the same resolution process.

4.4. PROPOSAL FOR THE REGISTRATION

For the above motivations, CNIPA seems to be the most suitable candidate to put forward the request of the official registration for at least two considerations:

- it has an institutional role in standardization activities for PAs in Italy: it is the authority that coordinates the work for defining the standards and that enacts the technical norms and recommendations. Moreover it already maintains central repositories for many NIR services, as register of enacting authorities, norms catalogue for the resolution process, list of nodes with related applicative ports, etc.;

- it has established several international collaborations for technical matters with similar organisations of other countries and participates in several technical boards at European and international level, as European Forum of Official Gazettes, CEN/ISSS (Comité Européen de Normalisation/Information Society Standardization System), etc.

For all these reasons, the final proposal is to charge CNIPA with official IANA registration of "lex" namespace with a basic structure having the following characteristics:

"urn : lex :" <locality> ":" <national-name>

<locality> ::= <country-code> *[;<specification>]

where:

- <country-code> is the ISO 3166 of 2 letters identification code of the country where the measure was issued;

- <specification> are the administrative or geographical sub-structures defined by each country according to its organisation;

- <national-name> is defined in each country by a proper institution, on the basis of a common structure of the type:

<authority> : <measure> : <details> : <annex> @ <version>

It is important that this proposal receives several adhesions from different countries, through the proper institutional organisations, at level of norms production (as Parliamentary, Ministries, regional Councils, etc.) or national / European / international standard bodies. In fact, the application of registration will be more relevant for IANA if supported by a lot of important institutions.

The acceptance of the request will allow the creation of the basic infrastructure for the development of applications based on the URN identifier, that is:

- to insert the main entry point of namespace ("lex.urn.arpa") in the URN root domain ("urn.arpa");

- to activate the primary DNS server for "lex" namespace domain (e.g. c/o CNIPA), pointed from the root via NAPTR (Naming Authority Pointer) record;

- to route the requests, again via NAPTR record, to activated national DNS servers (e.g. "lex:it" for Italy, "lex:br" for Brazil, etc.);

- to address the requests to the proper national resolver, by a decentralization of resolution process through the delegation on particular sub-domains (e.g. "it:stato" for national norms, "it:regione" for regional norms, etc.).

Such infrastructure will produce a generalized benefit to all the applications in the legal field, that is a direct access to legal documents by the URN, in a permanent and conceptual way. This access will be based on the DNS system and will make no more necessary the conversion in other known schemas, as http, wais, etc.

CRONOLEX: A System for a Dynamic Representation of Laws

Javier de Andrés Rivero*, Antonio F. Gómez Skarmeta°
*Researcher of University of Murcia (jandres@dif.um.es)
°Associate Professor of University of Murcia (skarmeta@dif.um.es)

Abstract. In this paper we present the architecture of a system that is being designed for the efficient recovery of Spanish laws based on the metadata structured in XML to allow the definition of a consolidated database to recover the state of a legal norm in a certain date.

Keywords: XML, Recovery, Law, in force, Computer

1. Introduction

The system which we are developing, is a system to manage all the life cycle of a legal norm from the drafting of the norm to the use of the norm by users.

For the system development one of the main tasks was to design a flexible XML structure to be able to represent all the types of legal documents that exist in Spain. The XML structure was captured in a DTD.

The most important property of this XML structure is that all necessary metadata, to indicate the derogations, substitutions, cancellations and integrations that other legal norms have made on the original norm throughout the time, is saved together with the text of the original norm.

The greatest data, of this metadata, are the references to the modifying norm (either complete norm or the article or the specific statement), the date of the update and the section of the norm that is updated.

Onces the XML structure was defined, we developed five modules to resolve the problem of making a consolidated database to recover the state of a legal norm in a certain date.

The modules are:

— Consolidation module

— Search module

— Edition module

— Web module

– Database module

The consolidation module is the most important module because when we consult the state of a legal norm in a certain date is the one in charge of processing the norm and the metadata and, with all this data, it creates a new consolidated version of the norm in the consulting date.

The great benefit of the metadata and this module is that it is not necessary to keep the different versions of the norm throughout the time (because of the changes that other norms make), but the consolidated state of the norm in a certain date is automatically generated.
The consolidation module with the other four modules allows us to manage all the life cycle of a legal norm and to obtain the wished result.

2. Why we use XML?

The advantages that XML offers for document and data management and exchange of information are very well known.

Among the advantages of XML for the legal document marked one it is possible to emphasize:

– **To add the metadata**: The main benefit of XML, for the legal document marked one, is that it keeps by the text that represents the legal document, the necessary metadata to give meaning to that text, therefore the computer can process this document.

– **Hypertextual capacity**: It allows to integrate the connections of the references in the own text, both the internal ones to the document and the external ones to other documents. This capacity is extremely important by the explicit relations that a legal text has.

– **Search facility**: It is possible to integrate easily a search motor that it allows to make functions of precise searches and "semantic" searches functions understanding by "semantic" searches by the meaning of the content of the legal document.

3. Our XML structure

Once we have chosen XML, the first task was to develop a XML structure sufficiently flexible to be able to define all types of legal norms in the Spanish legislation.

This XML structure we have captured in a DTD which has two great parts:

1. The metadata of the norm.

2. The text of the norm.

3.1. THE METADATA OF THE NORM

The metadata of the norm is contained in the tag:

<Metadata> ··· </Metadata>

This tag saves information which is not part of the text of the norm but it is information to identify and describe the legal norm and to indicate all the derogations, substitutions, cancellations and integrations that other legal norms have made on the original norm throughout the time.

It is the part that is updated when other norm modifies (revokes, replaces, cancels or includes) to the norm.

It's composed of:

— Urn[1]: Global identifier of the legal norm.

An example of this is "urn:um:COU954/2002"

The structure of the URN is composed of one prefix of the University of Murcia (um), the abbreviation of the classification of the norm, the number of the norm and the year of the publication of the norm.

— Publication date: Date when the norm is published in a gazette.

— Take effect date: Date when the norm begins to have effect. It can have several for different parts from the norm.

— Approbation date: Date when the norm was approved

---

[1] Uniform Resource Names (URNs) are intended to serve as persistent, location-independent resource identifiers and are designed to make easy to map other namespaces (that share the properties of URNs) into URN-space. Therefore, the URN syntax provides a meaning to encode character data in a form that can be sent in existing protocols, transcribed on most keyboards, etc.

- <u>Gazette</u> where the norm was published.

- <u>Unofficial name</u>: Colloquial name of the norm

- <u>Source of the norm.</u>

- <u>Rank:</u> Legal classification that the norm has.

- <u>Number:</u> Number of the norm.

- Links tags: Links that the norm has with other norms, or with parts of the other norms.

- <u>Derogations tags</u>: Derogations that the norm has suffered by others norms since its publication to nowadays.

- <u>Cancellations tags</u>: Cancellations or annulations that the norm has had, for example by judicial sentences

- <u>Integrations tags</u>: Parts included (passages of text) by other norms.

- <u>Substitutions tags</u>: It represents changes that other norms have made to fragments of text of the norm, throughout the time

The links, derogations, cancellations, integrations and substitutions tags have attributes to indicate the date of the change, the part of the norm that is updated, and the identifier of the modifier norm and these are the tags that help to create the correct norm in a certain date.

By example here we can observe the metadata of "Council Decision of 28_{th} February of 2000" in September of 2006:

```
<MetaInformacion>
 <urn>urn:um:COU185/2000</urn>
 <FechaAprobacion date=''000228''></FechaAprobacion>
 <FechaPublicacion date=''20000228''></FechaPublicacion>
 <FechaVigencia desde=''20000228'' id=''v1''></FechaVigencia>
 <Boletin date=''20000228'' numero=''111''
       tipo=''BOE''></Boletin>
 <Alias>COUNCIL DECISION</Alias>
 <Modificacion id=''m1'' fecha=''20021203''
       parteModificada=''@1.1.2''
       xlink:href=''urn:um:COU954/2002@1.1.1''/>
 <Modificacion id=''m2'' fecha=''20021203''
       parteModificada=''@3.1.3''
       xlink:href=''urn:um:COU954/2002@1.1.2''/>
```

```
<Modificacion id=''m3'' fecha=''20040101''
    parteModificada=''@1.1.2''
    xlink:href=''urn:um:COU161/2004@1.1.1''/>
<Modificacion id=''m4'' fecha=''20040101''
    parteModificada=''@3.1.3''
    xlink:href=''urn:um:COU161/2004@1.1.2''/>
<Rango>Council</Rango>
<Numero>185</Numero>
<IdOrden>EC</IdOrden>
</MetaInformacion>
```

3.2. THE TEXT OF THE NORM

This is the part that saves the text of the norm in a hierarchical form. The tags that compose this part are:

— Head: It is the first tag that saves the text of the norm, saves the head of the legal norm.

— Introduction: Tag where the introduction of the legal norm is structured (also called preamble). It is composed by the "Exhibitions of Reasons" or by a single introduction text.

— Articulate: Tag which represents the articles of the norm. These can be structured in:

Book
   Chapter
   Section
   Subsection
   Article
   Paragraph
   Statement

Only the tags "article", "paragraph" and "statement" are obligatory, the other tags are to represent in a hierarchical way the legal norm.

Each one of these tags has an identifier and has attributes to indicate its take effect date, if it is derogated or it is modified by other legal norm, or if it is cancel by a judicial sentence.

— Resolutions: Part that represents the resolutions that a legal norm may have. There are four types:

- - Additional
  - Temporary
  - Derogation
  - Final

- – <u>End</u>: Final part of the legal norm, it includes the signature and the date.

- – <u>Attachés</u>: This part represents any text which is included at the end of the norm.

4. System Architecture

The system is composed by four modules

4.1. MODULE OF LAW CONSOLIDATION

It is the one in charge of recovering the state of a legal document in a certain date.

The module processes the document XML (that represents the legal norm) and at the same time it creates a new document XML with the state of the legal document at that date.

Its operation is that it processes the metadata of the document, then it verifies if there have been modifications of the legal norm from the date of publication to date that we want to look for.

Besides the original norm, all later norms that substitute, integrate, derogate or cancel the norm are processed, from its take effect date to the concrete date.

At the end of the process we have got a new document XML with the changes that other legal documents (or judicial orders) have made to him.

This new XML document is "a virtual" document (it is not kept in the database), i.e., versions of documents are not created as some of the European projects do (as it happens in the "Norma Project" of Italy).

4.2. XML DATABASE MODULE

This module is the one in charge of keeping all the XML documents that represent the legal norms.

We used a native XML database (XINDICE) because:

1. You needn't transform the document XML in other structure of data.

2. It is not centered on the data, i.e. it does not store atomic data, but it stores documents XML.

4.3. MODULE FOR DOCUMENTS EDITION

This module is the one in charge of transforming the original legal norm into the document XML with the necessary structure.

We can resume this process in this graphic:

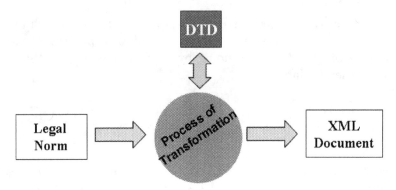

Figure 1.

The legal norm is transformed according to the made DTD and the result is one XML document. When the norm is transformed in XML, it is saved in the database and at the moment the system can use it. Also in this moment, the metadata of the legal norms that the norm modifies is updated. The module is developed as an application Web for the manual introduction of the data. It is a series of forms to introduce all the data in the corresponding tags. An open research line, we are working in, is to make this automatic task.

4.4. SEARCH MODULE OF THE LEGAL DOCUMENTS

We have developed a module to make searches on the contained legal norms in the database. These searches can be made by means of different criteria. The most important searches are the ones for the dates that affect the legal norm as approval date or publication date or take effect date. The criteria can be mixed to make more precise searches. With this module any user can find quickly all the legal norms that he needs to resolve a problem.

5. Conclusions and future work

Within this project, the work of a user is facilitated when he needs to recover the state of a norm at a concrete date, since it is acceded automatically to all the norms that modify a concrete one, and thus he doesnŠt have to do it manually. Besides saving work, it makes errors being reduced because the system is going to consider all the changes that have affected the legal norm from its publication date to search object date. For future works we have two important research lines

1. The improvement of the created applications, mainly in the automatization of the edition module of the legal texts.

2. To extend the defined system in a more generic one which aims at determining, for a certain case, what norms are applicable and what version of these, understanding by version, the state of that norm in a concrete date.

References

Monica Palmirani, "Norma Project", Jornadas sobre técnicas informáticas para la actualización automática del Derecho. Octubre 2004, Murcia.

Javier de Andrés, Juan J. Iniesta, Antonio Gómez, Skarmeta. "XML for the recovery of the Law in force", IAAIL 2005. The Role of Knowledge in e-Government.

Marie-Francine Moens "XML Retrieval Models for Legislation", Berlín Jurix 2004.

Ronald Bourret. XML and Databases. A discussion of the relationship between XML and databases. Includes a discussion of native XML databases.

Hernandez Marín, R., Introducción a la teoría de la norma jurídica, Marcial Pons, Madrid-Barcelona 2002, pp. 442 y ss

C. Biagioli, E. Francesconi, P. Spinosa, M. Taddei, ICAIL 2003, "The NIR Project: Standards and Tools for Legislative Drafting and Legal Document Web Publication".

Provisions modifying provisions and provisions calling for subsequent regulatory acts

A training course organized by the Chamber of Deputies of Italy

Giada Altomare, Emiliana Bassolino, Francesco Carella, Tiziana Federici, Francesco Fratini, Valentina Monnis, Enrico Seta
Italian Parliament - Chamber of Deputies

1. "Project 107"

The research reported hereby has been carried out in close connection with the legal information project of the whole legislation in force, promoted by the article 107 (Act n. 388 of December 23rd 2000).

The Italian project shows a range of difficulties depending basically on two reasons:

— Total number of legal texts enacted since 1861; according to some evaluations this number could amount to 70.000/80.000, whose 22.000 would be in force[1]. In addition, the distinction between regulatory and non-regulatory acts is very difficult.

— Problems of identifying rules effectively in force (not repealed). In fact, the Italian legislator is not compelled to express previous provisions he is going to repeal. Besides explicit abrogation, there are two other ways of repealing provisions, *i.e.* "incompatibility between new and previous provisions" and "new regulation of a subject as a whole" (art. 15 of the Italian civil code preliminary provisions). In both cases (very frequent) repeal is consequent to interpretation of the text.

Summarizing, there are several kinds of difficulties:

a) organizational ⇒ amount of data to be processed

b) juridical ⇒ identification of existing legislation

---

[1] Data obtained from Juranet. Since 1999, this company has been conducting the complete digitalization of Italian official bulletins (*Gazzetta Ufficiale*) published from 1861. Such data base amounts to 430.000 entries (including regulatory and non regulatory acts).

There is also another kind of problem concerning the three institutions directing "Project 107" (which are Italian Government, Chamber of Deputies and Senate). These institutions, however prestigious they are, do not have the power to interpret legal rules (this power is assigned to the Judiciary).

To sum up, this matter consists of:

c) the validity of legal data source ⇒ legislation in force identified in the database "Project 107" is requested to have the maximum level of reliability, but it cannot be the result of an interpretation of legal rules.

2. Project 107: progress report

During the first stage of the project (2001 – 2002):

- **directive bodies** of the project were established (by President of the Council of Ministers Decree January 24th 2003

- **data processing standards** were elaborated: URN (by Public Administration Information Agency (AIPA) circular n. 35 November 6th 2001, published in the *Gazzetta Ufficiale* n. 262, November 10th 2001) and DTX-XML (by AIPA circular n. 40, April 22nd 2002, published in the *Gazzetta Ufficiale* n. 102, May 3rd 2002).

During the second stage (2003-2004):

- All the existing Italian legal data-bases, including private ones, and other in-progress projects, whose aims met those of "Project 1072, **were explored**;

- On this basis a close cooperation with the **Data Elaboration Centre (CED) of the Court of Cassation** was set up;

Finally, during the last 18 months (2005 – June 2006):

- A high level **Legal Advisory Committee** (LAC) representing the three project-leading institutions and the higher Courts has been established. The task of this Committee is – among others - "to define juridical requirements, techniques and methods for the information of consolidated texts" (Committee fourth resolution of March 30th 2005);

- A **XML editor** has been developed by the Research Centre for Juridical Informatics (CIRSFID), based in Bologna, in order to process and mark-up legal texts.

– CED of Court of Cassation has started the **processing of all legal texts** (acts, decrees, etc.) adopted during the XIV Parliament. It will be concluded by December 2006.

With the beginning of XV Parliament, after the general elections of April 9th – 10th 2006, the data-base will be constantly updated.

Therefore, from January 1st 2007 a first part of the normative database will be accessible on a Web site run by the three project-leading institutions.

2.1. RETROSPECTIVE CONVERSION OF PREVIOUS STOCK OF ITALIAN LEGISLATION

The Legal Advisory Committee is developing specific guidelines about the retrospective conversion and the processing of all previous stock of legislation. These guidelines will concern:

a) the selection criteria of both the documents to be included in the database and to be submitted to a complete processing (mark-up and consolidation), and the others (non-regulatory acts implementing normative provisions) to be inserted as notes only;

b) the accuracy level of reporting modifying provisions, in order to retrieve legislation in force;

c) the homogeneous modalities of annotation;

d) the degree of conformity of electronic texts in comparison with versions published in the Official Gazette;

e) functionality of the search engine and ways of data visualization on the Web site;

f) suitability of XML standards (DTD – NIR) related to typologies of documents to insert in the database and to be subjected to the mark-up process.

As regards points b) and c) absolute criteria cannot be adopted, *e. g.*:

a. " Any implicit (not expressed) modification of previous rules will not be considered"

b. " All the modifications (implicit and explicit) will be considered"

Criterion b) could be chosen only theoretically (read following sections).

Criterion a) would supply poor results compared to existing legal data bases. Moreover, implicit amendments frequently modify past rules and, in many cases, the modifying or the repealing effects are well known. So a database which does not take into consideration the implicit modifications would be a poor source of information[2].

Finally, the **LAC will define when and how data base annotations will be requested to indicate implicit amendments** (*Guidelines for Implicit Modifications*).

3. Training Course performed at the Chamber of Deputies

During 2005 some faculties and university research centres asked the Chamber of Deputies to plan a training course for young graduates specialized in parliamentary subjects and drafting.

For 2006, the Chamber focused the traineeship on the analysis of several topics linked to "Project 107".

The traineeship has been performed from January to April 2006. Eleven graduates in Law, Political Science and Sociology, took part in it, monitored by seven Parliament officials and two coordinators of the Legal Advisory Committee (Cons. Ernesto Vozzi and Cons. Antonio Rodinò).

4. Research topic

Research developed around the analysis of four legal texts and survey of all the provisions suitable to modify previous rules. Working method has been determined on the basis of XML marking features and on the perspectives connected with deeper semantic analysis of legal texts. Data gathering involved not only explicit modifications, but above all the implicit ones[3].

Texts analysis has been tackled in view of these goals:
MAIN GOAL ⇒

  a. identifying and annotating every part of the text implying a modification of a previous rule;

---

  [2] This solution has already been excluded by resolution 08/03/2004 of the Steering Committee of "Project 107".

  [3] Explicit and implicit modifications have been defined "direct links" among rules.

b. classifying modifications according to the "*Taxonomy of modifying provisions to build up legal texts in force*", by CIRSFID (September 2005).

The implementation of point a) was more difficult than point b), because of the large variety of cases found inside texts and subsequent different approaches in order to identify them. Difficulty in implementing point a) is the following:

recognizing an implicit modification implies knowledge and check of the whole legal framework affected by new provisions.

This problem could be actually solved only by a highly specialized activity.

In addition, even if it could be possible to find all relevant previous provisions, recognizing implicit modifications might often come from an interpreting activity (which is not duty of data base operators).

Hence, there is a second goal:

PRACTICAL GOAL ⇒

a) testing what kinds of problems the LAC will have to tackle in order to define – by means of guidelines – the accuracy level of data gathering and models of annotation regarding provisions implicitly modifying other provisions (letter *b)* in section 3).

b) reporting research results to be **transmitted** to the LAC.

Another issue of this topic deals with **provisions calling for subsequent regulatory acts** (see section 6.3) which produce **indirect links** among rules, worth being noted.

5. Research results

5.1. TYPOLOGIES OF MODIFICATIONS

The final report (composed of more than fifty pages and four attachments) highlighted several important issues to be submitted to LAC members and other subjects in charge of deciding the processing strategy regarding previous legislative stock.

Firstly, the number of provisions modifying other provisions is much higher than what expected by parliamentary officials[4].

Secondly, the final report underlines that legislators are seldom used to

---

[4] Trainees compared data collected with those contained in two data bases (De Agostini and Juranet), observing a wide quantity gap, especially for older

explicitly indicating modifications. So, explicit modifications represent just a small part of all the modifications found during the traineeship. Because of this, it was considered appropriate to divide normative references (relationship between two provisions) in three main "categories" according to their different degree of completeness:

- **explicit references**, *i.e.* where the legislators identify the modified provision very punctually (number and date of the legal document, article, paragraph and, where necessary, its further parts);

- **partly explicit references**, *i.e.* the ones which contain just some of the identifying details of the provision effectively modified (for instance, number and date of the legal document, but not the article) or even those indicated through their generic denomination only (such as "financial act of 2005", "budget act of 2002", etc.);

- **implicit references**, that's to say those where there is no mention of the modified provisions.

Since an XML editor software aimed at processing and marking explicit modifications already exists, traineeship focused on cases of **"partly explicit modifications"** and **"implicit modifications"**.
The first ones didn't reveal any particular problem, thanks to the details indicated by the legislator or to their denomination. They are common inside the most recent documents of the four sample texts processed.

Actually, some cases apparently classifiable as partly explicit modifications turned out to be explicit, instead. In fact, lack of indication of the modified provision can be an intentional choice of legislators to modify - by means of one new provision only- the whole previous act, in any part relevant to the case. In such situations the fairest solution seems to be the mark-up of modification as "explicit", inserting a normative reference with regard to the entire document (making a note on its epigraph), because of extreme difficulties in identifying specific modified provisions.

5.2. PROPOSAL FOR A CLASSIFICATION OF IMPLICIT MODIFICATIONS

Research of implicit modifications, on the contrary, required an hard effort that has been carried out via internet, private data bases (De Agostini and Juranet) and, especially for older acts, legislative official

---

provisions. For instance, as to Act December 30th 1991, n. 412, the annotations inserted by the workgroup of "traineeship 107" were more than a hundred whilst the ones contained in De Agostini and Juranet data bases are both around twenty.

collection.

The utmost heterogeneity of implicit modifications led the working-group to formulate a **classification**, based upon the following **criteria**:

— Certainty degree about the identification of modified provisions;

— Certainty degree of results completeness (*e.g.* reconstruction of the "regulatory sequence");

— Certainty degree about the qualification assigned to modifications.

In the light of these criteria all implicit amendments have been categorized as follows:

— **type A**: high degree of certainty in identifying modified provisions, as well as the regulatory sequence;

— **type B**: partial or uncertain identification of modified provisions and/or reconstruction of regulatory sequence;

— **type C:** partial or uncertain identification of modified provisions and/or reconstruction of regulatory sequence, as well as uncertain qualification of modifications;

— **type D:** great uncertainty about identification of modified provisions and – of course – of regulatory sequence (it would be useful to apply to experts of specific areas).

The final report contains a complete classification of **fifty-eight** implicit provisions modifying other provisions.

Since "Project 107" is also aimed at simplifying and reorganizing existing legislation, and considering the high degree of uncertainty of the two last categories, modifications types C and D might be used by the Legal Advisory Committee for the achievement of "better regulation" project (a database not public, accessible only by the institutional bodies entrusted with "regulatory reorganization").

5.3. Provisions calling for subsequent regulatory acts

The expediency of connecting (by means of specific notes) the calling provisions with the subsequent issued acts is of great interest, owing to the characteristics of the Italian legal system. The same target of "in-force legislation" (as expressed in article 107 of law n. 388 of 2000) would not be achieved if similar relations were ignored.

Nevertheless, the difficulties, both theoretical and practical, arisen on this regard have been - even in this case – more than they were expected to be, and the variety of situations found has been very high. To begin with, three categories of call for a subsequent acts have been created:

— implementing - executing acts (which complete the contents of the calling provision);

— acts through which tasks and functions assigned by the calling provision are exercised;

— acts which constitute a condition to the actual application of the calling provision.

Unfortunately, these categories don't provide a quick and univocal standard for a general rule (exclusion/inclusion principle) to be applied to the whole previous stock of legislation. In fact, they cannot be defined according to "objective" parameters, since they come from an inductive reasoning hinging on the interpretation of the "function" of the analysed act. Therefore, the idea of finding formal principles to quickly recognise the nature of a called act arose during the course: this would help to univocally decide which acts should always be inserted (according to a specific rule) in the data-base, regardless of substantial aspects.

The study of scholars' writings on this topic shows the great variety of opinions expressed about it. Considering that according to the "Project 107" all regulatory acts should be inserted in the data-base, part of the course was devoted to the identification of criteria allowing to distinguish regulatory from non-regulatory acts. On the other hand, it was made an attempt to define a method - although approximate, being the subject quite problematic – to select, among non-regulatory acts, those that could be all the same inserted in the data-base (in this regard it might be useful to read the short work about the most frequent and relevant non-regulatory acts that can be found in the Italian legal system, such as agreements, circulars, ordinances, often tightly related to laws or regulations). In this context, the LAC might evaluate the possibility of prescribing the insertion of all abstract act, as well as of concrete and general ones.

As a result of the analysis of the two above-mentioned aspects it was found that it would be possible to select criteria to establish when an act has a regulatory or a non-regulatory nature, since scholars' writings and constitutional jurisprudence give some indication in this regard. Yet, neither the formers nor the latter are helpful to work out the second kind of problems.

5.4. OTHER RELEVANT ISSUES

Other issues pointed out to the Committee are the following:

- **implicit modifications inside novels.** A complete legal data processing would entail analysis of implicit modifications contained in novels as well (it would be necessary to test if the editor used by CED of Italian Court of Cassation is programmed for that);

- **rules of procedure**: legal texts often refer to this kind of rules or to "basic" rules. An exhaustive reconstruction of every modification of a given subject would also require the mark-up of these rules. In addition, it would be useful to mark other similar rules, *i. e.* interposed provisions referring to institutions suppressed by the modifying provision, and provisions of consolidation acts, or of any other "basic" act, even though no more in force;

- **drafting**: it would be advisable to lay down new drafting rules in order to adapt them to XML mark-up of legal texts. So, normative documents could be automatically processed. Anyway, the drafting issue, because of its complexity, requires more specific research.

Legal Consolidation formalised in Defeasible Logic and based on Agents.

Régis Riveret, Monica Palmirani, Antonino Rotolo
C.I.R.S.F.D, University of Bologna,
via Galliera 3, 40100 Bologna, Italy
{rriveret, palmiran, rotolo}@cirsfid.unibo.it

Abstract. Updated legal corpora have been indicated by the European Union as fundamental to eDemocracy, and member states looking to set up eGovernment initiatives are acting on that input. However, the usual automation of legal consolidation presents shortcomings, namely, the collapse of temporal dimensions and local views of normative systems. This paper presents solutions to these shortcomings by providing the formalisation in logic of an appropriate legal temporal model and an investigation of the use of the multi-agent paradigm.

Keywords: Consolidation, knowledge representation and reasoning, agents.

1. Introduction

The need to obtain updated legal corpora has been indicated by the European Union as fundamental to eDemocracy, and member states looking to set up eGovernment initiatives are acting on that input. However, collections of digital legal documents managed within information systems open the way to the automation of legal consolidation so that human users, such as jurists and citizens, and non-human users, such as software agents, can access the updated version of legal provisions. However, usual legal consolidation modules tend to present serious shortcomings, namely, (i) the collapse of the temporal dimensions of force, efficacy and applicability into a flat model, so the modifications are applied to the legal documents in a wrong time sequence with respect to legal principles; (ii) they tend to have a local view of the normative system, failing to get a global view, so they risk producing an incoherent normative system; (iii) they do not deal with conditional modifications; (iv) they are not proactive, in the sense that they do not take initiatives to detect modifications that have not been factored into consolidation.

As a remedy to these drawbacks, we present in this paper a system for managing the process whereby the documents in a normative system get consolidated. These shortcomings are overcome by providing a legal temporal model (Palmirani and Brighi, 2003) that respects legal principles and that is formalised into logic to permit automatic reasoning, and by investigating the use of the multi-agent paradigm in such a way as to allow proactivity and a larger view of the normative system.

The temporal model is briefly presented in Section 2. Its logical expression is presented in Section 3. Finally, the use of the multi-agent paradigm is investigated in Section 4.

2. The Legal Temporal Model

The temporal model allows us to give an accurate account of the dynamics of norms over time and therefore to manage legal consolidation consistently with legal principles. This model (Palmirani and Brighi, 2006) is briefly presented here.

First, we will introduce some terminology. A legal system is defined as a set of documents fixed at a defined time t and which have been issued by an authority and whose validity depends on rules that determine, for any given time, whether a single document belongs to the system. Formally:

$$LS(t) = D_1(t), D_2(t), D_3(t), ...D_m(t)$$

where $m \in \mathbb{N}$, D_i denotes documents and t is a fixed time in a discrete representation. A normative system, in turn, takes the documents belonging to a legal system and organizes them to reflect their evolution over time. A normative system should therefore be more precisely defined as a particular discrete time-series of legal systems that evolves over time. In formal terms:

$$NS = LS(t1), LS(t2), LS(t3), ...LS(tj)$$

where $j \in \mathbb{N}$. The passage from a legal system to another legal system is effected by normative modifications (besides persistence), and these can be of different sorts. A taxonomy of modifications can be defined according their effects, which we divide in four main categories (Palmirani and Brighi, 2006): (i) textual changes that intervene when a law is repealed, replaced, integrated or relocated; (ii) changes of scope consequent on derogation, extension, or interpretation; (iii) temporal changes that impact on the date of force, the date of efficacy, or date of application of the destination norm (the entire act or a part of it, such as an article or a paragraph); (iv) normative-system changes that apply not only to specific documents but to the normative system considered in its entirety. A modification is initiated in a text called *active* norm and produces its effect on another text, a receiving text called *passive* norm. The reference to the passive norms may be incomplete or insufficiently clear, and that makes it necessary to have a distinction between *explicit* and *implicit* modifications according as the reference(s) to the passive norm(s) is accurate and complete (explicit change) or not (implicit change).

As any other legal provision, a modification can be seen as a conditional statement. Accordingly, a modification has three temporal dimensions, these being attached to the conditions, to the effects, and to the overall conditional. These temporal dimensions refer, then, to the efficacy, applicability, and force of the provision, respectively. Furthermore, one has to consider the time of observability of the normative system. Consider a law X of 2001 nullified in 2005: The change affects the entire normative system because the legal text is removed from the system as if it had never been there in the first place (ex-tunc removal). The same would happen with a temporary law decree that does not pass into law, or with a retroactive abrogation, or with an interpretation of a law that comes in as the authentic reading of it (Guastini, 1998)(Pagano, 2001). The peculiarity of system changes shows up when we query the system to retrieve information from it: if today (e.g., 2005) we ask for all the laws in force in 2001, law X will not turn up and the system will look as if that law had never been in force in the first place. But if we enter the query as if we were in 2001, when the annulment had not yet occurred, law X will show up as being in force, and the entire system will reflect that fact. This difference depends on the temporal point of view from which we query the system and this refers to the time of observability of a normative system.

3. Model Representation

The application we are working on is designed to provide practitioners with documents for consolidation, all while giving advice backed by proof of correctness. Advice is provided anytime a modification is detected that has not yet been factored into consolidation. Advice and proofs are generated by inference mechanisms that comply with legal principles. The input is the normative information contained in the system and is encoded in an expressive logic, namely, in Temporal Defeasible Logic (TDL) which is an extension of Defeasible Logic (DL). TDL has proved useful in modelling temporal aspects of normative reasoning, such as temporalised normative positions (Governatori et al, 20005); in addition, the notion of a temporal viewpoint-the temporal position from which things are viewed-allows for a logical account of

norm modifications and retroactive rules (Governatori et al, 2005). DL
and TDL are briefly presented below.

3.1. DEFEASIBLE LOGIC

The legal temporal model points out the importance of uncertainty due
to the addition of new premises that can invalidate formerly derivable
consequences. This means that consolidation must proceed on the basis
of non-monotonic reasoning. In fact, the reasoning used in consolidation
forms part of the wider realm of legal reasoning, which too is deemed
to be non-monotonic (Sartor, 2005). Non-monotonic reasoning is supported by a number of non-monotonic logics. Among these, DL (Nute,
1987)(Nute, 94)(Antoniou et al., 2001) is based on a logic programming-
like language and it is a simple, efficient but flexible non-monotonic
formalism capable of dealing with many different intuitions of non-
monotonic reasoning. An argumentation semantics exists (Governatori,
2004) that makes its use possible in argumentation systems (Verheij,
2005). DL has a linear complexity (Maher, 2001) and also has several
efficient implementations (Bassiliades et al., 2004).

A Defeasible Logic theory is a structure $D = (F, R, \prec)$ where F
is a finite set of facts, R a finite set of rules, and $\prec$ a superiority
relation on R. Facts are indisputable statements, for example, "Bob
is a minor," formally written as $minor(bob)$. Rules can be strict, defeasible, or defeaters. Strict rules are rules in the classical sense; whenever
the premises are indisputable, so is the conclusion. An example of a
strict rule is "Minors are persons," formally written as $r1: minor(X) \rightarrow$
$person(X)$. Defeasible rules are rules that can be defeated by contrary
evidence. An example of a defeasible rule is "Persons have legal capacity"; formally, $r2: person(X) \Rightarrow haslegalcapacity(X)$. Defeaters are
rules that cannot be used to draw any conclusion. Their only use is to
prevent some conclusions by defeating some defeasible rules. An example of this kind of rule is "Minors might not have legal capacity," formally
expressed as $r3: minor(X) \rightsquigarrow \neg haslegalcapacity(X)$. The idea here is
that even if we know that someone is a minor, this is not sufficient
evidence for the conclusion that he or she does not have legal capacity.
The superiority relation between rules indicates the relative strength
of each rule. That is, stronger rules override the conclusions of weaker
rules. For example, if $r3 \succ r2$, then the rule $r3$ overrides $r2$, and we
can derive neither the conclusion that Bob has legal capacity nor the
conclusion that he does have legal capacity.

Given a set R of rules, we denote the set of all strict rules in R by R_s, the set of defeasible rules in R by R_d, the set of strict and defeasible rules in R by R_{sd}, and the set of defeaters in R by R_{dft}. $R[q]$ denotes the set of rules in R with consequent q. In the following $\sim p$ denotes the complement of p, that is, $\sim p$ is $\neg p$ if p is an atom, and $\sim p$ is q if p is $\neg q$. For a rule r we will use $A(r)$ to indicate the body or antecedent of the rule and $C(r)$ for the head or consequent of the rule. A rule r consists of its antecedent $A(r)$ (written on the left; $A(r)$ may be omitted if it is the empty set), which is a finite set of literals; an arrow; and its consequent $C(r)$, which is a literal. In writing rules we omit set notation for antecedents.

Conclusions are tagged according to whether they have been derived using defeasible rules or strict rules only. So, a conclusion of a theory D is a tagged literal having one of the following four forms:

$+\Delta q$ meaning that q is definitely provable in D.
$-\Delta q$ meaning that q is not definitely provable in D.
$+\partial q$ meaning that q is defeasibly provable in D.
$-\partial q$ meaning that q is not defeasibly provable in D.

These different notions of provability come of use here because they enable the system to label a suggestion as stronger or weaker depending on the kind of proof associated with it. Provability is based on the concept of a derivation (or proof) in D. A derivation is a finite sequence $P = (P(1),..., P(n))$ of tagged literals. Each tagged literal satisfies some proof conditions. A proof condition corresponds to the inference rules that refer to one of the four kinds of conclusions we have mentioned above. $P(1..n)$ denotes the initial part of the sequence P of length n. In this paper, conditions for $\pm\Delta q$, which only describe forward chaining of strict rules, are omitted due to lack of space. We state below the conditions for defeasibly derivable conclusions:

$+\partial$: If $P(i + 1) = +\partial q$ then either
    (1) $+\Delta q \in P(1..i)$ or
    (2) (2.1) $\exists r \in R_{sd}[q] \forall a \in A(r) : +\partial a \in P(1..i)$ and
        (2.2) $-\Delta \sim q \in P(1..i)$ and
        (2.3) $\forall s \in R[\sim q]$ either
            (2.3.1) $\exists a \in A(s) : -\partial a \in P(1..i)$ or
            (2.3.2) $\exists t \in R_{sd}[q]$ such that
                $\forall a \in A(t) : +\partial a \in P(1..i)$ and $t \succ s$.

$-\partial$: If $P(i + 1) = -\partial q$ then
    (1) $-\Delta q \in P(1..i)$ and
    (2) (2.1) $\forall r \in R_{sd}[q] \exists a \in A(r) : -\partial a \in P(1..i)$ or

(2.2) $+\Delta\sim q \in P(1..i)$ or

(2.3) $\exists s \in R[\sim q]$ such that

    (2.3.1) $\forall a \in A(s) : +\partial a \in P(1..i)$ and

    (2.3.2) $\forall t \in R_{sd}[q]$ either

        $\exists a \in A(t) : -\partial a \in P(1..i)$ or $t \not\succ s$.

Informally, a defeasible derivation for a provable literal consists of three phases: First, we propose an argument in favour of the literal we want to prove. In the simplest case, this consists of an applicable rule for the conclusion (a rule is applicable if its antecedent has already been proved). Second, we examine all counter-arguments (rules for the opposite conclusion). Third, we rebut all the counter-arguments (the counter-argument is weaker than the pro-argument) or we undercut the (some of the premises of the counterargument are not provable).

3.2. TEMPORAL DEFEASIBLE LOGIC WITH VIEWPOINTS

Defeasible Logic allows us to deal with incomplete information but as such does not provide any natural means to deal with temporal dimensions as exposed in the legal temporal model (see Section 2). Temporal Defeasible Logic with viewpoints (Governatori et al., 2005) is an extension of Defeasible Logic to deal with temporal aspects. It deals importantly with temporal viewpoints to reflect the time of observability from which the normative system is comsidered. Temporal aspects are integrated by two means.

First, we introduce temporal coordinates that allow us to temporalise literals and rules. A temporal coordinate is a concatenation of pairs of the form $[t, x]$ where t is an instant of time which is an element of a totally ordered discrete set of instants of time $Temp = \{t1, t2,...\}$ and $x \in pers, trans$ indicates whether the element occurring in the scope of the temporal qualification is persistent ($pers$) in time or not ($trans$). For example, $[1970, pers]$ and $[t + 18, trans]:[1970, pers]$ are temporal coordinates.

A temporalised literal is an expression of the form $l{:}T$ where l is a literal and T is a temporal coordinate. Intuitively, the meaning of a temporalised literal $l{:}T$ is that l holds at the coordinate T. For example, $major(bob):[1973, pers]:[1968, pers]$ means that Bob is major in 1973 (and later) from somebody reasoning in 1968 (and later). Similarly, a temporalised rule is an expression of the form $r{:}T$ where r is a rule and T is a temporal coordinate. An example of a temporalised rule is:

$$(r: \ born(X):[t, trans] \rightarrow major(X):[t + 18, pers]):[1970, pers]$$

This rule formalises the provision in force in 1970 and later that somebody get its majority at 18 years old.

Time labels allow us to deal formally with the different temporal dimensions in the legal domain. The time labels associated with the antecedents of a legal rule, with the consequents, and with the overall rule can respectively be interpreted as the time of *efficacy*, *applicability*, and *force* of the represented legal provision.

Temporal calculi are driven by the operations of temporal extension, temporal reduction, temporal diminution and temporal progression of coordinates. These operations, as defined and explained below, allow us to compare coordinates.

A temporal extension consists in the extension of a temporal coordinate of a certain length into a new coordinate with a higher length. Whereas temporal extensions are acknowledged to be necessary, their forms are less certain and are subjects of many proposals. For our purposes, one can distinguish two proposals. The first understands temporal extension by the concatenation of the temporal pair $[0, pers]$ with a temporal coordinate. For example, the coordinate $[5, pers]:[20, trans]$ can be extended to $[5, pers]:[20, trans]:[0, pers]$. The second proposal captures temporal extension by the concatenation of the temporal pair $[t, pers]$ with a temporal coordinate of the form $T:[t, x]$. For example, the coordinate $[5, pers]:[20, trans]$ can be extended to $[5, pers]:[20, trans]:[20, pers]$. We propose thus two definitions of temporal extensions in order to represent the proposals.

DEFINITION 1.   *A temporal extension of a temporal assertion $\gamma{:}T$ is the operation concatenating the pair $[0, pers]$ with the temporal coordinate T.*

DEFINITION 2.   *A temporal extension of a temporal assertion $\gamma{:}T$ is the operation concatenating the temporal pair $[t, pers]$ with a temporal coordinate of the form $T{:}[t, x]$.*

While our setting allows us to deal with these two definitions, it is worth emphasing that one using the logical framework has to commit to a unique form of extension.

A temporal reduction is the complement of extension in the sense that it consists in the reduction of a temporal coordinate of a certain length into a new coordinate with a lower length. Since there exists two proposals of temporal extension, we propose thus two definitions of temporal reductions:

DEFINITION 3. *A temporal reduction of a temporal assertion γ:T is the operation that reducts a temporal coordinate of the form T:[0, pers] into a temporal coordinate T.*

DEFINITION 4. *A temporal reduction of a temporal assertion γ:T is the operation that reduces a temporal coordinate of the form T:[t, x]:[t, pers] into a temporal coordinate T:[t, x].*

Note that one that has committed to the first (second) definition of temporal extension has to commit to the first (second) definition of temporal reduction. Extensions and reductions are mathematical devices allowing for comparison between coordinates that do not have initially the same length. Using temporal extensions and reductions, coordinates can then be brought into relation to each other by way of the equality operator $=$. At the first sight, that two coordinates $[t_{i1}, x_{i1}]$:....:$[t_{in}, x_{in}]$ noted T_i and $[t_{j1}, x_{j1}]$:....:$[t_{jn}, x_{jn}]$ noted T_j are equals, i.e. $T_i = T_j$, means they have same length and that each pair $[t_{ik}, x_{ik}]$ equals $[t_{jk}, x_{jk}]$, that is $t_{ik} = t_{jk}$ and $x_{ik} = x_{jk}$. For example, consider the coordinates $[5, pers]$:$[0, trans]$ noted $T1$ and $[5, pers]$:$[0, trans]$ noted $T2$, then one can state that $T1 = T2$. One may, moreover, say intuitively that $[5, pers]$:$[0, pers]$ and $[5, pers]$ are also equals since one can make a temporal extension of the later into $[5, pers]$:$[0, pers]$.

DEFINITION 5. *Let $T_i = [t_{i1}, x_{i1}]$:....:$[t_{in}, x_{in}]$ and $Tj = [t_{j1}, x_{j1}]$:....:$[t_{jn}, x_{jn}]$ be two temporal coordinates. T_i equals T_j (noted $T_i = T_j$) if there exists either a temporal extension or reduction or none of these, of T_i into the form $[t_{j1}, x_{j1}]$:....:$[t_{jn}, x_{jn}]$ such that each pair $[t_{ik}, x_{ik}]$ equals $[t_{jk}, x_{jk}]$, that is $t_{ik} = t_{jk}$ and $x_{jk} = x_{jk}$.*

Another temporal operation called temporal diminution consists in substituting a pair of the form $[t_i, pers]$ with a pair $[t_f, trans]$. For example, by temporal diminution, a temporalised assertion a:$[5, pers]$:$[20, pers]$ becomes a:$[5, pers]$:$[20, trans]$.

DEFINITION 6. *A temporal diminution of a temporal assertion γ:T is the operation allowing the substitution of a pair in T of the form $[t_i, pers]$ with a pair $[t_f, trans]$.*

A temporal progression of a temporal assertion is the operation that allows us to "slip" the assertion from an initial coordinate to a new coordinate. For example, the temporal literal a:$[5, pers]$:$[20, trans]$ can progress to a:$[10, pers]$:$[20, trans]$. Temporal progressions are constraints as follows: a pair of the form $[t_i, trans]$ cannot progress while a pair of the form $[t_i, pers]$ can only progress to another pair $[t_f, pers]$ such that $t_i < t_f$.

DEFINITION 7. *A temporal progression of a temporal coordinate T is the operation that substitutes a pair in T of the form $(t_i, pers)$ by a pair $(t_f, pers)$ such that $t_i < t_f$.*

If two coordinates T_i and T_f are such that T_i can progress to T_f then we can write it $progress(T_i, T_f)$.

DEFINITION 8. *Let T_i and T_f, be two temporal coordinates. We have $progress(T_i, T_f)$ if there exists a combination of temporal extensions, reductions, diminutions and progressions from T_i to T_f.*

For example, we can state $progress([5, pers], [10, pers]:[20, trans])$ since the coordinate $[5, pers]$ can be extended into $[5, pers]:[0, pers]$, progressed into $[10, pers]:[20, pers]$ and finally be dismunished into $[10, pers]:[20, trans]$. However, we cannot state $progress([5, trans], [10, pers]:[20, trans])$, because it does not exists any combination of temporal operations from $[10, trans]$ to $[10, pers]:[20, trans]$.

Based on the notion of temporal progression, we define the operator $<$ that allows us to compare coordinates that are not similar.

DEFINITION 9. *Let $T_i = [t_{i1}, x_{i1}]:...:[t_{in}, x_{in}]$ and $T_j = [t_{j1}, x_{j1}]:...:[t_{jn}, x_{jn}]$ be two temporal coordinates. T_i strictly precedes T_j (noted $T_i < T_j$) if by substituting any pair of the form $[t_{ik}, trans]$ by a pair $[t_{ik}, pers]$ to form T_i', one can state $progress(T_i', T_f)$.*

For example, consider $T_1 = [5, trans]:[5, pers]$ and $T_2 = [10, trans]:[10, trans]$. If one substitute any pair of the form $[t_{ik}, trans]$ by a pair $[t_{ik}, pers]$ in T_1 to form $T_1' = [5, pers]:[10, pers]$, then one can state $progress(T_1', T_2)$. Hence, $T_1 < T_2$.

The second step towards the integration of time to DL in order to properly model the temporal aspects in normative systems is the expression of normative modifications. Normative modifications are functions that take as input a rule to modify and return as output the rule modified. Thus the function $m(r_1:T_1):T_2$ returns the rule obtained from r_1 as such at time T_1 after the application of the modification corresponding to the function m and the result refers to the content of the rule at time T_2.

Given this basic notion of modification, we can define some specific rule-modifications. We will limit ourselves to substitution and annulment, but other temporal and textual modifications can be captured similarly. Suppose r is a generic defeasible rule such as $(r: a_1:T_{a1}, \ldots, a_n:T_{an} \Rightarrow b:T_b):T_r$.

- $substitution(r{:}T, x'_1{:}T'_1/x_1{:}T_1, \ldots, x'_m{:}T'_m/x_m{:}T_m){:}T_s$ says that we operate at T_s a substitution which replaces some temporalised literals $x_i{:}Ti$ in the antecedent or consequent of r with other literals $x'_i{:}T'_i$. The new version of r will hold at T_s. For example, $substitution(r{:}T_r, c{:}T_c/a_1{:}T_{a1}){:}T_s$ returns $(r{:} c{:}T_c, a_2{:}T_{a2}, \ldots, a_n{:}T_{an} \Rightarrow b{:}T_b){:}T_s$.

- $annulment(r{:}T){:}T_{an}$ says that $r{:}T$ is annulled at T_{an}. The function $annulment(r{:}T_r){:}T_{an}$ returns the empty rule $(r{:}\perp){:}T_{an}$.

Rule modifications oblige us to deal with new conflicts, namely conflicts between modifications. For example, a substitution $substitution(r{:}T,'_1{:}T'_1/x_1{:}T_1, \ldots, x'_m{:}T'_m/x_m{:}T_m){:}T_s$ and an annulment $annulment(r{:}T){:}T_{an}$ are in conflict if $T_s = T_{an}$.

The formalism we have introduced allows us to have rules in the head of rules, thus we have to admit the possibility that rules are not only given but can be derived. Accordingly we have to give conditions that allow us to derive rules instead of literals. Then we have to extend the notation $R[q]$ to $R[\gamma{:}T]$ where γ is an assertion, that is either a literal or a rule. Given a set of rules R and a set of rule modifiers $M = \{m_1, \ldots, m_n\}$, then $R[r{:}T_r] = \{s \in R, C(s) = r{:}T_r\}$ gives the set of rules whose head results in the rule $r{:}T_r$ after the application of the rule modifier; and $R[\sim r{:}T_r] = \{s \in R, C(s) = m_i(r{:}T_r)\}$ gives the set of rules that modify $r{:}T_r$.

A temporal defeasible theory is a structure $D = (Temp, F, R, \succ)$ where $Temp$ is a discrete totally ordered set of instants of time, F is a finite set of temporalised literals, R is a finite set of temporalised rules, and $\succ$ is the usual superiority relation on R. As in standard DL, we denote the set of all strict rules by R_s, the set of defeasible rules by R_d, the set of strict and defeasible rules by R_{sd}, and the set of defeaters by R_{dft}. Orthogonally to these distinctions of strict, defeasible rules and defeaters, we will assume a discrimination between rules that can be modified and rules that cannot be modified. The set of non modifiable rules is noted R^{perm} ($perm$ as permanent). A rule that cannot be modified is labelled by a pair x^{perm} where x the identifier of the rule and the symbol $perm$ indicates the non-modifiability of the rule. An example of non-modifiable rule is $(r1^{perm}{:} a{:}[2, pers] \Rightarrow b{:}[1, trans]){:}[1, pers]$

A conclusion of a theory D is a tagged temporal assertion having one of the following forms:

$+\Delta\gamma{:}T$ meaning that $\gamma{:}T$ is definitely provable in D.

$-\Delta\gamma{:}T$ meaning that $\gamma{:}T$ is not definitely provable in D.
$+\partial\gamma{:}T$ meaning that $\gamma{:}T$ is defeasible provable in D.
$-\partial\gamma{:}T$ meaning that $\gamma{:}T$ is not defeasible provable in D.

Provability is based on the concept of a derivation (or proof) in D. A derivation is a finite sequence $P = (P(1),..,P(n))$ of tagged literals. Each tagged literal satisfies some proof conditions, which correspond to inference rules for the four kinds of conclusions we have mentioned above. Let γ be an assertion, namely either a literal or a rule.

$+\Delta$: If $P(i+1) = +\Delta\gamma{:}T$ then
$\quad$(1) $\gamma{:}T_i \in F \cup R^{perm}$ and $progress(T_i, T)$, or
$\quad$(2) $\exists r{:}T_r \in R_s^{perm}[\gamma : T_\gamma]$ and $progress(T_\gamma, T_r)$,
$\qquad$(2.1) $+\Delta r{:}T_r \in P(1..i)$, and
$\qquad$(2.2) $\forall\gamma{:}T_\gamma \in A(r{:}T_r), +\Delta\gamma{:}T'_\gamma \in P(1..i)$ and $T'_\gamma = T_\gamma{:}T_r$.

$-\Delta$: If $P(i+1) = -\Delta\gamma{:}T$ then
$\quad$(1) $\gamma{:}T_i \notin F \cup R^{perm}$ and $progress(T_i, T)$, and
$\quad$(2) $\forall r{:}T_r \in R_s^{perm}[\gamma{:}T_\gamma]$ and $progress(T_\gamma, T_r)$,
$\qquad$(2.1) $-\Delta r{:}T_r \in P(1..i)$, or
$\qquad$(2.2) $\exists\gamma{:}T_\gamma \in A(r{:}T_r), -\Delta\gamma{:}T'_\gamma \in P(1..i)$ and $T'_\gamma = T_\gamma{:}T_r$.

A temporalised assertion $\gamma{:}T$ is definitely provable $(+\Delta)$ if it belongs to the set of unmodifiable rules or facts, or there exists a unmodifiable temporal rule $r{:}T_r$ whose consequent is $\gamma{:}T_\gamma$ with $progress(T_\gamma{:}T_r, T)$ such that 2.1) the rule itself is provable and 2.2) applicable. To prove that a definite conclusion is not possible we have to show that all attempts to give a definite proof of the conclusion fail. Notice that the inference conditions for negative proof tags are derived from the inference conditions for the corresponding positive proof tag by applying the Principle of Strong Negation.

Here is an example for the proof conditions for strict derivations of literals.

$Temp = \mathbb{N}$
$F = \{a{:}[2, pers]\}$
$R^{perm} = \{(r_1^{perm}{:} \ a{:}[2, pers] \rightarrow b{:}[1, trans]){:}[1, pers]$
$\qquad\quad (r_2^{perm}{:} \ b{:}[1, trans] \rightarrow q{:}[3, pers]){:}[2, pers]\}$
$\prec = \varnothing$

Suppose we want to know whether $+\Delta q{:}[4, pers]{:}[4, pers]$, i.e., whether q strictly holds at 4 and later, when we consider the evidence and rules that hold at 4 (the time at which we consider the derivation). The only fact in F makes the r_1 applicable and so we obtain, by means of the persistence of r_2, $+\Delta b:[1, trans]:[2, pers]$. This makes r_2 applicable and, since r_2 and its conclusion are persistent, we obtain $+\Delta q:[4, pers]:[4, pers]$. One of the preconditions for strictly applying a rule is that it is strictly derivable: notice that all rules used for derivations are strictly provable, as they belong to the set of non-modifiable rules R^{perm}.

We now turn our attention to defeasible derivations, that is, derivations giving a temporal assertion $\gamma:T$ as a defeasible conclusion of a theory D. Defeasible provability $(+\partial)$ consists of three phases. In the first phase, we put forward a supported reason for the temporal assertion that we want to prove. Then in the second phase, we consider all possible attacks against the desired conclusion. Finally in the last phase, we have to counter-attack the attacks considered in the second phase.

$+\partial$: If $P(i + 1) = +\partial\gamma:T$ then either

(1) $+\Delta\gamma:T \in P(1..i)$ or

(2) (2.1) $\exists r:T_r \in R_{sd}[\gamma:T_\gamma]$ and $progress(T_\gamma:T_r, T)$,
$\qquad$ (2.1.1)$+\partial r:T_r \in P(1..i)$, and
$\qquad$ (2.1.2)$\forall\gamma:T_\gamma \in A(r:T_r)$,
$\qquad$ $+\partial\gamma:T'_\gamma \in P(1..i)$ with $T'_\gamma = T_\gamma:T_r$; and
$\quad$ (2.2) $-\Delta\sim\gamma : T \in P(1..i)$, and
$\quad$ (2.3) $\forall s:T_s \in R[\sim\gamma:T_\gamma]$, $T_\gamma:T_r \leq T_{\sim\gamma}:T_s \leq T$,
$\qquad$ $+\partial s:T_s \in P(1..i)$, either
$\qquad$ (2.3.1) $\exists\beta:T_\beta \in A(s:T_s)$, $-\partial\beta:T'_\beta \in P(1..i)$ and
$\qquad$ $T'_\beta = T_\beta:T_s$, or
$\qquad$ (2.3.2) $\exists w:T_w \in R[\gamma:T_{w\gamma}]$, $T_{\sim\gamma}:T_s \leq T_{w\gamma}:T_w$, and
$\qquad$ $progress(T_{w\gamma}:T_w, T)$, and
$\qquad$ $w:T_w \succ s:T_s$ if $T_{\sim\gamma}:T_s = T_{w\gamma}:T_w$, and
$\qquad\qquad$ (2.3.2.1) $+\partial w:T_w \in P(1..i)$, and
$\qquad\qquad$ (2.3.2.2) $\forall\chi:T_\chi \in A(w:T_w)$,
$\qquad\qquad$ $+\partial\chi:T'_\chi \in P(1..i)$ and $T'_\chi = T_\chi:T_w$, and
$\quad$ (2.4) $\forall r \in R, +\partial r:T_r \in P(1..i)$, $-\partial m(r:T'_r):T_m$, $T_m \leq T$, $T'_r \leq T_r$.

Let us illustrate this definition. To show that $\gamma:T$ is provable defeasibly we have two choices: 1) We show that $\gamma:T$ is already definitely provable; or 2) we need to argue using the defeasible part of D as well. In particular, we require that there must be a strict or defeasible rule $r:T_r$ with head $\gamma:T_\gamma$ and $progress(T_\gamma:T_r, T)$ which can be applied (2.1). But now we need to consider possible attacks, i.e., reasoning chains in support of $\sim\gamma:T$. To be more specific: to prove $\gamma:T$ defeasibly we must show that $\sim\gamma{:}T$ is not definitely provable (2.2). Also (2.3) we must consider any rule $s{:}T_s$ which has head $\sim\gamma{:}T_{\sim\gamma}$ with $T_\gamma{:}T_r \leq T_{\sim\gamma}{:}T_s \leq T$ (note that here we consider defeaters, too, whereas they could not be used to support the conclusion γ; this is in line with the motivation of defeaters given earlier) which is known to be proved $(+\partial s{:}T_s)$. Basically, each such rule $s{:}T_s$ attacks the conclusion $\gamma{:}T_\gamma{:}T_r$. For $\gamma{:}T$ to be provable, each such rule $s{:}T_s$ must be counterattacked by a rule $w{:}T_w$ which has a head $\gamma{:}T_{w\gamma}$ with $T_{\sim\gamma}{:}T_s \leq T_{w\gamma}{:}T_w$ and $progress(T_{w\gamma}{:}T_w, T)$ with the following properties: $w{:}T_w$ must be defeasibly proved (2.3.2.1) and applicable (2.3.2.2). Note that if $T_{\sim\gamma}{:}T_s = T_{w\gamma}{:}T_w$ then $w{:}T_w$ must be stronger than $s{:}T_s$. So each attack on the conclusion $\gamma{:}T$ must be counterattacked. Finally, any rule $r{:}T_r$ that have participated to the derivation of $+\partial\gamma{:}T$ should not have been modified before T (2.4).

Here is an example for the proof conditions for strict derivations of literals.

$Temp = \mathbb{N}$
$F = \{a{:}[10, trans]\}$
$R_{perm} = \{(r_1{:} \ a{:}[t, trans] \Rightarrow b{:}[t, pers]){:}[0, pers]$
$\qquad\qquad (r_2{:} \ b{:}[t, trans] \Rightarrow c{:}[t, pers]){:}[50, pers]$
$\qquad\qquad (r_3{:} \qquad \Rightarrow annul(r1{:}[0, pers]){:}[0, trans]){:}[100, pers] \ \}$
$\prec = \oslash$

Suppose we want to know whether $+\partial c{:}[50, pers]{:}[60, pers]$. The fact $a{:}[10, trans]$ makes the rule $r_1{:}[10, pers]$ applicable, and we have $+\partial r1{:}[10, pers]$ so we can derive $+\partial b{:}[10, pers]{:}[10, pers]$, and by temporal persistence $+\partial b{:}[10, pers]{:}[50, pers]$. This later result makes the rule $r_2{:}[50, pers]$ applicable, and we have $+\partial r2{:}[50, pers]$ hence we can derive $+\partial c{:}[10, pers]{:}[50, pers]$ and temporal progression $+\partial c{:}[50, pers]{:}[60, pers]$. Suppose now that we want to know whether $+\partial c{:}[50, pers]{:}[120, pers]$. The fact $a{:}[10, trans]$ makes the rule $(r_1{:} \ a{:}[t, trans] \Rightarrow b{:}[t, pers]){:}T_{r1}$ applicable, and we have $+\partial r1{:}T_{r1}$ with $T_{r1} < [0, pers]{:}[100, pers]$ (because we can derive $+\partial annul(r1{:}[0, pers]){:}[0, trans]{:}[100, pers]$, see condition 2.4 of the proof conditions), so we have $+\partial b{:}[t_b, pers]{:}T_{r1}$ with $[10, trans]{:}Tr1 \ [t_b, pers]{:}T_{r1} < [0, trans]{:}[100, pers]$. This later result makes the rule $r2{:}T_{r2}$ applicable with $T_{r2} \geq [50, pers]$ and we have $+\partial r2{:}T_{r2}$. Hence we can derive $+\partial c{:}[t_c, pers]{:}T_{r2}$ with $[10, trans]{:}T_{r1} \leq [t_c, pers]{:}T_{r2} < [0, pers]{:}[100, pers]$. Now, since we want to know whether $+\partial c{:}[50, pers]{:}[120, pers]$, substitute tc by 50 and T_{r2} by $[120, pers]$. These values do not verify $[t_c, pers]{:}T_{r2} < [0, pers]{:}[100, pers]$, thus one cannot derive $+\partial c{:}[50, pers]{:}[120, pers]$.

3.3. DIGITAL REPRESENTATION

Logic allows us to express normative knowledge and reason on it. However, it requires being associated to a digital representation so that applications can process the knowledge. In other words, pieces of information contained in legislative documents have to be represented, marked up using any appropriate digital language.

The legislative documents to be consolidated are inserted in the system using dedicated editors, such as Norma-Editor (Palmirani, 2000), that make it possible transform normative documents on the basis of a common XML representation language compliant with the NormeinRete project standards (Circolare 35) (Circolare 40). As has been argued in (Brighi 04)(Palmirani et al., 03), the semantic markup of normative references enables intelligent agents to reason and provide advice in consolidating documents. The concepts on which agents make their decisions are defined in ontologies written in OWL or in any other XML syntax. An OWL ontology of modifications has been defined (Palmirani and Brighi, 2003).

On the other hand, whatever the format of a hypothetical legal-knowledge interchange language built on emerging Semantic Web languages (such as XML, RDF, and OWL) or any other format to facilitate the interaction between legal knowledge systems, a translation into the knowledge-representation format internal to the system can be provided. Such translation can be implemented using XSLT as a translation tool.

4. The Model Architecture

The application we are working on is designed to provide practitioners with documents for consolidation with advice backed by proofs of correctness. This section explains the motivation of a multi-agent architecture for the application, investigates briefly some issues concerning the cooperation of agents, and finally presents an overview of the system.

4.1. MOTIVATION OF MULTI-AGENT ARCHITECTURE

Due to the distributive nature of a normative system, and in order to preserve single administration autonomy and technological/organisational independence (Mecella and Batini, 2001)(De Santis et al., 2005), a fully distributed solution is required. And because the consolidation process is about bringing into relation the information distributed over different elements, the solution has to be such as to allow advanced cooperation among these distributed elements. Furthermore, the normative environment is under constant change consequent on normative modifications that occur unpredictably, which makes the evolution of the normative system unpredictable, too. Consequently, the application needs to be easily scalable, flexible, and adaptive to the unpredictable evolution and heterogeneity of the normative environment, i.e., the application should be able to integrate new information in the process. This means that consolidation requires autonomy, that is, the application relies only scarcely on the prior knowledge of its designer, and largely on new information coming in from the normative system. Moreover, a normative modification occurs by an active provision that modifies a passive provision. So the application needs reactivity (i.e., a capacity to reflect the passive provisions of modifications) as well as proactivity (i.e., a capacity to reflect the active provisions of modifications). Finally, there are many different sources of normative knowledge, different processes of norm production, and different kinds of users, and this heterogeneity makes it necessary to have an interoperable system. Interoperability is usually ensured by meeting certain standards, such as XML. To sum up, the goal of supporting consolidation, coupled with the distributed and heterogeneous nature of the normative environment, requires distributed and standards-based technologies enabling proactivity, scalability, and autonomy as well as advanced cooperation among distributed elements.

There are three basic models for distributed applications: the client/server model, the peer-to-peer model, and the agent-based model. The client/server model makes a distinction of roles between its distributed elements, namely, servers and clients. Usually, servers are reactive, in that they cannot act on their own initiative to communicate with a client; they handle most of the capabilities and must provide stability (they cannot appear and disappear, for example). In contrast, clients can take initiatives (they can take the initiative of communicating with a server but cannot communicate directly with one another); they have few capabilities, and they are allowed to appear and disappear. The client/server architecture is the most widespread architecture of legal applications on the Web. In a peer-to-peer architecture, instead, nodes can function as both servers and clients at any time, depending on the role node acts in. The agent-based model makes no such distinctions of roles. Agents are software paradigms that are proactive (they can take initiatives) and social (they can communicate using high-level protocols); they can be endowed with artificial intelligence and so can reason, adapt to new situations, and act autonomously, without human guidance. Moreover, agents facilitate the design of applications that manage the complexity of a domain (here, the normative system). Indeed, as the complexity of a system arises from the interactions between the elements of the system, agents facilitate their representation and the implementation of their interactions. Finally, the integration of agents using step-by-step procedures allows scalability and flexibility.

So, in view of the requirements specified above and of the technologies available, the agent-based model appears to be the one best suited to handle the characteristics of a dynamic normative system.

4.2. COOPERATION AMONG AGENTS

Agents may not have enough expertise and resources (each one has a partial view of the normative system), so they need to cooperate to exchange information, and vice versa (they need to exchange information to cooperate). In multi-agent settings, the exchange of information is usually done using either direct or indirect message-passing. Typically, direct message-passing refers to the exchange of messages directly between agents using agent communication languages and protocols, while indirect message-passing relates to the exchange of messages indirectly between agents via centralised artefacts such as blackboards. Since a centralised solution is little coherent with administrative federalism, our choice has been for agents to exchange information using direct message-passing. In a direct message-passing setting, messages are written in an Agent Communication Language (ACL). Most of the work done in ACL's is based on the theory of speech acts, so that messages are usually conceived as speech acts. Eventually, agent cooperation may require more than one-shot utterances, i.e., the exchange of a complex series of messages. This can be effected through the use of protocols determining which speech acts can be used at various points in conversation. One can wonder what types of interactions hold between the bodies of a legal system. Or, in technical terms, what are the relevant speech acts and protocols? One may appreciate a set of speech acts and protocols that is isomorphic with the set of real interactions taking place between the bodies of a legal system.

For our purposes, we need both information dialogues and argumentation dialogues. Information dialogues define the content of utterances as essentially propositional, with different speech acts, such as assertive or interrogative. Argumentation dialogues allow agents to exchange arguments, justify themselves, and persuade other agents. The dialogues involve agents putting forward arguments for or against propositions together with justifications for the acceptability of these arguments.

4.3. OVERVIEW OF A MAS APPLICATION

The MAS is designed to support users in consolidating legislative documents by providing advice proactively and autonomously on the basis of the semantic representations contained in the text and the behaviour built into the agents. The system should support users in carrying out some main tasks as follows:

— Detecting proactively and autonomously (a) any events that modify the normative system; (b) the conditions that modifications are dependent on; (c) any inconsistencies that a modification may bring to the normative system; (d) any antinomies; (e) any anomalies, as when a modification is modified; and (f) events that result in a double negation, as when an abrogation is abrogated.

— Giving advice aimed at consolidating documents.

— Providing proofs that the conditions for a consolidation to be effective hold.

If a modification is found to be effective, the information is routed to the user. The user might be sceptical, asking whether this modification can be trusted, and particularly whether all the conditions that produce a valid modification are verified. The agent thus undertakes to provide proof of validity for the modification. The proof is then presented in a user-friendly manner to the practitioner, who can thus check whether a modification is valid or invalid, and who is then responsible for following the advice or not (depending on whether the modification was found to be valid or invalid). If the user accepts the suggestion, a new consolidated version of the passive document is produced, and the entire normative system shall be properly updated.

This MAS application is particularly efficient in verifying the conditions to which a modification is subject in the normative system, so that we can (upon verification) launch proper events and produce updated law in real time. Finally, this way of processing the Semantic Web content embedded in legislative documents enables us to manage the normative system as made up of different agents. These agents can simulate the dynamicity of the normative system, which can react properly to modifications on the basis of behaviours designed to mimic mental attitudes (Boella and van der Torre, 2003).

5. Conclusion

This paper is part of an ongoing effort in Computer Sciences and Law to provide appropriate models, representation of legal reasoning, and computer science paradigms to deal with the dynamics of normative systems. We argued that our solution overcome the main shortcomings of traditional legislative information systems by the formalisation in logic of an adequate temporal model, and by an investigation into the use of the multi-agent paradigm. The expected result is the improvement of the automation of legal consolidation.

References

Studio di fattibilitá per la realizzazione del progetto "Accesso alle norme in rete". *Informatica e Diritto* No. 1, 2000.

Antoniou, G., D. Billington, G. Governatori and M. Maher. Representation results for defeasible logic. *ACM Transactions on Computational Logic*, 2(2):255-287, 2001.

Bassiliades, N., G. Antoniou and I. Vlahavas. DR-DEVICE: A defeasible logic system for the Semantic Web. In PPSWR04. Springer, Berlin, 2004.

Boella, G. and L.W. N. van der Torre. Attributing mental attitudes to normative systems. In Proceedings of the 2nd International Joint Conference on Autonomous Agents and Multiagent Systems (AAMAS'03), ACM Press, 942-943, 2003.

Boella, G. and L.W. N. van der Torre. Permissions and obligations in hierarchical normative systems. In Proceeding of the 9th International Conference on Artificial Intelligence and Law (ICAIL'2003), ACM Press 109-118, 2003.

Brighi, R. An Ontology for Linkups between Norms. In Proceedings of the 15th International Workshop on Database and Expert Systems Applications (DEXA'04), IEEE Computer Society, 122-126, 2004.

Circolare 22 aprile 2002 n. AIPA/CR/40, Formato per la rappresentazione elettronica dei provvedimenti normativi tramite il linguaggio di marcatura XML. Gazzetta Ufficiale n. 102, 3 May 2002.

Circolare 6 novembre 2001 n. AIPA/CR/35, Assegnazione dei nomi uniformi ai documenti giuridici. Gazzetta Ufficiale Serie generale n. 262, 10 November 2001.

De Santis, L., C. Lupo, C. Marchetti and M. Mecella. The x-Leges System for Legislative Document Exchange. In Proceedings of the 3rd International Workshop on Legislative XML, I Quaderni n. 18, November 2005.

Governatori, G., M. Maher, D. Billington, and G. Antoniou. Argumentation semantics for defeasible logics. Journal of Logic and Computation, 14, 5: 675-702, 2004.

Governatori, G., M. Palmirani, R. Riveret, A. Rotolo, and G. Sartor. Normative Modifications in Defeasible Logic. In Marie-Francine Moens, editor, Jurix'05: The Eighteenth Annual Conference. IOS Press, Amsterdam 2005.

Governatori, G., A. Rotolo, and G. Sartor. Temporalised normative positions in defeasible logic. In Anne Gardner, editor, Procedings of the 10th International Conference on Artificial Intelligence and Law, pages 25-34, ACM Press, 6-10, 2005.

Guastini, R. Teoria e Dogmatica delle fonti. Giuffrè, Milano, 1998.

Maher, M. Propositional Defeasible Logic has Linear Complexity. TPLP 1(6): 691-711, 2001.

Mecella, M. and C. Batini. Enabling Italian E-Government through a Cooperative Architecture. In A.K. Elmagarmid, W.J. McIver Jr. (eds.): Special Issue on Digital Government. IEEE Computer, vol. 34, no. 2, pp. 40-45, 2001.

Nute, D. Defeasible reasoning. In Proc. 20th Hawaii International Conference on Systems Science. IEEE Press, 470-477, 1987.

Nute, D. Defeasible logic. In Handbook of Logic in Artificial Intelligence and Logic Programming, D. Gabbay, C. Hogger, and J. Robinson, Eds. Vol. 3. Oxford University Press, Oxford, 353-395, 1994.

Pagano, R. L'arte di legiferare. Giuffrè, Milano, 2001.

Palmirani, M. and R. Brighi. Time Model for Managing the Dynamic of Normative System. EGOV 2006: 207-218

Palmirani, M., R. Brighi, R. and M. Massini. Automated Extraction of Normative References in Legal Texts. In Proceeding of the 9th International Conference on Artificial Intelligence and Law (ICAIL'2003), ACM Press, 105-106, 2003.

Palmirani, M. Norma-System. In the series "Filosofia, Informatica, Diritto", Bologna, Clueb, 2000.

Sartor, G. Legal reasoning. Springer, 2005.

Verheij, B. Virtual Arguments. On the Design of Argument Assistants for Lawyers and Other Arguers. T.M.C. Asser Press, The Hague, 2005.

Provisions as legislative elements: Annotations to Biagioli's Theory

Harald Hoffmann* , Friedrich Lachmayer°
*METADAT GmbH, Vienna, Austria
°University of Innsbruck, Austria

Abstract. Biagioli's theory of legal provisions classifies the semantic elements of legal acts. He requests the legists to implement an equivalence between formal legal elements and semantic legal elements (the provisions), desirably with a 1:1 relation. The authors of this contribution expand on this approach by differentiating between the legal and the documentalistic system. Of course, in the case of authentic electronic publication both systems will merge again. To lay systematic grounds for this differentiation this contribution develops a formal notation of the legal and documentalistic systems and suggests an abstract visualisation.

Keywords: Provisions, Ex-ante, Ex-post, XML, Legal system, Documentalistic system.

1. Terminology

This contribution uses the following terms, grouped in 3 legislative layers. To outline these layers the following tables use 2 lines for representing the legal and the documentalistic view and 3 columns for describing the terms:

Table I. **Top layer**. The top legislative layer is the **system layer** (SYST).

Notation	Term	Examples
$SYST_{leg}$	Legal system	Authentic publication
$SYST_{doc}$	Documentalistic system	Legal information system

Table II. **Middle layer**. The middle legislative layer is the **product layer** (PROD). A product in the legal sense is a **legal act**, e.g. a legal source (constitution, law, statutes, decisions, and others like treaties). A product in the documentalistic sense is a **document**. Both, legal act and documents, may be summarised by the term **legal information**.

Notation	Term	Examples
PROD_{leg}	Legal product	Legal act like constitutions, laws, statutes, decisions, treaties
PROD_{doc}	Documentalistic product	Document like the §-document of RIS (the Austrian Rechtsinformationssystem)

Table III. **Bottom layer**. Products are based on **elements**, representing the bottom layer.

Notation	Term
ELEM_{leg}	Element of a legal product
ELEM_{doc}	Element of a documentalistic product

Table IV. **Bottom layer** including Biagioli's view. Biagioli emphasizes that there are two kinds of legal elements: **formal** and **semantic elements**. Using an abstract point of view he interprets the legal semantic elements as "**legal provisions**" (e.g. a norm, a permission, a reference)[1]

Notation	Term	Examples
$ELEM_{leg}$	Element of a legal product	
$ELEM_{leg-form}$	Formal element of a legal product	§ of the Law
$ELEM_{leg-sem}$	Semantic element of a legal product	Provision
$ELEM_{doc}$	Element of a documentalistic product	

Table V. **Bottom layer** including Biagioli's and the authors' view. This paper suggests to use the same distinction between formal and semantic elements for classifying the documentalistic elements, following the approach taken in RIS, the Austrian Rechtsinformationssystem. RIS uses documentalistic elements (formal and semantic ones), called "**categories**". The formal elements (like the RIS-category §) prevail. There are only a few semantic elements (e.g. time of validity). The reason for this unbalance lies in the current definition of the production processes of legal documents in Austria.

Notation	Term	Examples
$ELEM_{leg}$	Element of a legal product	
$ELEM_{leg-form}$	Formal element of a legal product	§ of the Law
$ELEM_{leg-sem}$	Semantic element of a legal product	Provision
$ELEM_{doc}$	Element of a documentalistic product	
$ELEM_{doc-form}$	Formal element of a documentalistic product	Procedural and syntactical elements like category "§"
$ELEM_{doc-sem}$	Semantic element of a documentalistic product	Semantic elements like category "time of validity"

---

[1] In the provision theory a reference is intended as an argument of provisions, not as a provision itself.

Table VI. **Bottom layer, XML view**. In Austria, eLaw exclusively uses XML to organise the legislative workflow and the authentic electronic publication. Similarly, RIS uses XML for archival and publication or will do so in the near future. It should be noted, however, that both systems emphasize the procedural and syntactical aspects. Therefore, eLaw does not and RIS does not generally map semantic elements; both concentrate on formal ones.

Notation	Term	Examples
$ELEM_{leg}$	Element of a legal product	
XML $<ELEM_{leg-form}>$	Formal XML element of a legal product	Austria: eRecht elements Italy: ITTIG approach
XML $<ELEM_{leg-sem}>$	Semantic XML element of a legal product	Austria: practically not existing Italy: ITTIG approach
$ELEM_{doc}$	Element of a documentalistic product	
XML $<ELEM_{doc-form}>$	Formal XML element of a documentalistic product	Austria: RIS elements Italy: ITTIG approach
XML $<ELEM_{doc-sem}>$	Semantic XML element of a documentalistic product	Austria: few RIS elements Italy: ITTIG approach

All types of elements may be mapped to XML.

Because of the dominance of XML the contents of Table V is now mapped to XML, resulting in → Table VI. This mapping to XML implies an additional principle: The elements $ELEM_{leg}$ are used in the process of creating law (a workflow process)[2], $ELEM_{doc}$ in the process of document archival and retrieval.

The Austrian approach differs from that of Biagioli who includes mapping of semantic elements to XML. The focus of Biagioli's approach for using provisions is to do this mapping already in the legislative phase of drafting legal texts, using a set of tools elaborated by ITTIG. One of

---

[2] In the Italian Law Making Environment (LME) this is the authentic way to describe $ELEM_{leg}$, during the drafting process, using XMLeges and metaEdit software jointly. In practice the provision model, combined with concepts models, can be applied also ex post by a documentalist, using metaEdit web based software. Later, a third way will be to use a semantic based Editor and to draft the text guided by models.

the advantages of this approach is its completeness: It supports formal and semantic elements, in the legal and the documentalistic system, including the transfer between both systems, using a common set of metadata.

The theoretical part of this concept of legal provisions represents an avant-garde achievement in the international scientific community. The practical part of this concept describes the next steps of the evolution of legislative workflows and legal information systems.

Based on this abstract introduction the remainder of this paper will expand on these principles, considering other aspects. Hypothesis is that legal and documentalistic systems will merge and that meta data, in the context of harmonisation and standardisation, will play an important role, for Europe in particular.

2. Mapping between formal and semantic elements

Note: The following figures show the term XML only, meaning a short notation for XML <ELEM$_{leg-form}$>, XML <ELEM$_{leg-sem}$>, XML <ELEM$_{doc-form}$> and XML <ELEM$_{doc-sem}$>.

The starting point for a societal model of law is the citizens communicating in their everyday language. Common law uses this language.

Law as a legal speech act is different: it is an application of the professional language of a lawyer. This language is rather prescriptive than descriptive as it addresses a professional audience. It therefore is difficult to understand for a citizen.

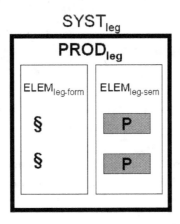

Figure 1.

The professional juridical language uses formal elements like groupings to express laws, resulting in **formal structures**. Additionally,

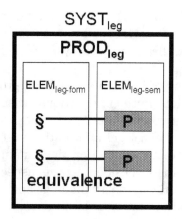

Figure 2.

there are semantic elements, the provisions P (Fig. 1), resulting in
semantic structures.

Biagioli's theory of legal provisions deals with the semantic structures of law. There are families of semantic elements, including normative provisions, deontic structures, institutional and procedural semantics. Biagioli maps these structures to the formal structures of laws,
postulating an equivalence between the elements (Fig 2).

The question is: How to map? A straightforward answer is to map
a semantic element like a norm to a formal one like a paragraph. Biagioli recommends a 1:1 relation avoiding e.g. norms spread over several
paragraphs[3].

This recommendation is an example for the structured approach
which Biagioli's Theory suggests. This approach uses formal or semantic
elements to be applied by those people responsible for the drafting of
laws, the legists. This approach aims at cultivating legislative reasoning.

3. Mapping between elements of a legal and a documentalistic system

In addition to Biagioli's formal-semantic duality this paper expands
on a second duality, the duality of the legal and the documentalistic
system: Ideally, documentalists and legists achieve the same semiotics
with different means (Fig. 3).

The documentalists create documents with legislative information
describing the laws. Therefore their language is rather descriptive than

---

[3] **See 2 - Formal and functional profiles of the law structure**

prescriptive as it addresses a wide audience. It therefore is easy to understand for a citizen.

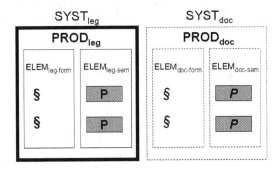

Figure 3.

The question is how to map the elements. **Mapping of formal structures** is well established. However, there are different approaches: The formal structure of a document may correspond (1) to a law as a whole (as in the legal information system of Lower Austria and Vienna), (2) to a single article (RIS uses the terms paragraph [§] for article, and §-document for the corresponding document), (3) to a grammatical paragraph (as used by Dietmar Jahnel for documenting the Austrian constitutional law) or (4) to other elements, even to single letters.

Mapping the structures of the professional and prescriptive language of a lawyer to the verbose and descriptive language of a documentalist means **mapping of semantics**. This mapping is more difficult, in particular if it needs human interaction e.g. by adding remarks or explanations (semantic value).

4. Mapping elements to XML

Any structure may be mapped to a technical structure like XML. In the case of legal information, a structure consists of formal and semantic elements, which both may be mapped to XML.

If correctly done, mapping always takes place towards XML, never back from XML to the structural elements. Therefore, the role of XML should not be overestimated: XML is just a technology, and technologies are interchangeable. However, there are two reasons why XML is important: (1) It is an Internet standard and (2) it is designed for machine-machine communication. Because of (1) it received high acceptance and is widespread in use, and because of (2) it is well suited for automating the handling of legal information, in particular in workflow systems, one of the workhorses of the backoffice of e-government.

When introducing XML then usually the first step is to map the formal elements to XML elements (Fig. 4). Why is this usually the first step? Because it is largely a technical issue only, avoiding discussions regarding semantics which often are highly political.

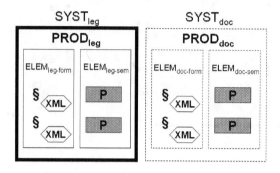

Figure 4.

In Austria, this first step has been done, first by introducing "**categories**" as formal elements some 20 years ago. At that point of time RIS was a host based application used for the archival and retrieval of legal information but not for its production. To introduce XML was an evolutionary process, with its last achievement being the XML based authentic publication of federal law with the beginning of 2004. In contrast, eRecht started as an XML based workflow system from the beginning, building on the RIS experience and its categories in particular.

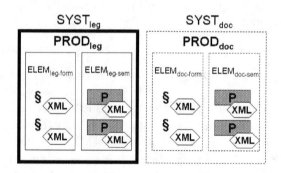

Figure 5.

Mapping semantic elements to XML elements (Fig. 5) usually is a second step only. Why? (1) Traditional publishing of legal information (e.g. a law) does not require much "semantic enrichment", if any. Therefore, the number of semantic elements in the legal system might be negligible. (2) Traditionally mapping the languages of legists and documentalists happens outside of the process of publishing legal information. Therefore, the number of legal elements in the documentalistic system might be negligible as well. Not much is left which needs to be mapped to XML.

In contrast to both traditions, Biagioli requests (1) the introduction of a not-negligible number of semantic elements (the "**provisions**") and (2) their availability in the legal system. This means they have to be generated "ex ante" - during the process of producing legal information. Now there is something which is to be mapped to XML.

5. Ex ante - ex post

XML as an enabler of workflow implies a process view of both the legal and the documentalistic system: The first corresponds to the process of **production of legal information**, the second to the processes of **archival and retrieval of legal information**. This process view is the major reason behind having introduced two closely interlinked systems in Austria: **eRecht** (the XML based production system for legal information, or more precise, for federal law) and **RIS** (the Rechtsinformationssystem for publishing and retrieving federal law documents, amongst other legal information).

Aiming at a specific type of legal information (e.g. a law) the production process requires the "**ex ante**" availability of templates (defining the structure) and styles (defining the layout of formal elements). Using XML, templates are called "**style sheets**". Specific formal elements of a template are the "**categories**" of RIS (Fig. 6). Specific semantic elements of the template may be Biagioli's "**provisions**". They both require the input of metadata during the production process. Adding this metadata as soon as available still is called "**ex ante**".

Figure 6.

Semantic elements usually are not part of a structure which is defined an "ex ante", as it depends on the semantics of the legal information

which elements make sense and, therefore, are needed. Therefore semantic elements usually are added "**ex post**" and "**ad hoc**", and at
the same time they are loaded with metadata. "Ex post" may be under
responsibility of the documentalists, or, if already outside of the system,
under responsibility of the private sector.

"Ex post" is like an afterthought by a third party. Even if an afterthought creates value it nevertheless never is authentic. Therefore
Biagioli requests the provisions to be available "ex ante", either in the
template or "ad hoc" when needed, to be loaded with metadata "ad hoc"
when needed as well.

Technically, there is no argument which opposes this request. However, discussions might be expected because "ex ante" now is under the
responsibility of the legists.

6. Merging legal and documentalistic system

Mapping between elements between a legal and a documentalistic system was already covered. It should be noted, however, that XML is a
purely technical structure (a syntax). It does not bridge the difference
between the structure a legist is using for mapping law ("Legislative
XML") and the structure a documentalist is using for documenting law
("Documentalistic XML"). Furthermore, as XML is syntax only it does
not bridge semantic differences at all.

To be able to overcome these differences, to map legal and documentalistic system and finally to merge both systems in one document it is
necessary to put a meta level on top of both systems (Fig. 7).

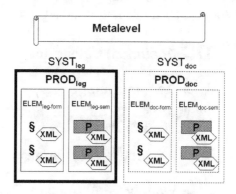

Figure 7.

This meta level may include legal thesauri, semantic networks, legal
ontologies, deontic logic, as well as legal theory. A taxonomy of legal
terms is a minimum needed for legislative XML.

At the end of the production process legal and documentalistic information is merged into a document which is published and archived in the documentalistic system. No matter how good the mapping between legal and documentalistic system was - so far the document is a weak speech act with low authority as it is not law.

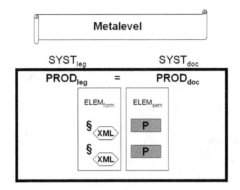

Figure 8.

Authentic publication was introduced in Austria with the beginning of 2004. Now the document became a strong speech act - it became law. Mapping and finally merging formal elements and structures only, with the semantic structures being minimal, any deficiencies of mapping between elements of the legal and the documentalistic system were eliminated by "legal mystery" (Fig. 8).

Biagioli requests to include semantic elements. This means that also the semantic elements have to be mapped and finally merged in the published document. As a result, mapping must take place between legal and documentalistic information as well as between formal and semantic elements, arriving at a double merged structure (Fig. 9).

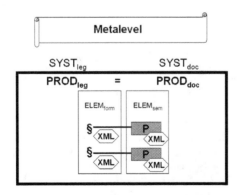

Figure 9.

For this double merged structure both the rules of the legal as well as the documentalistic system apply, based on a common meta level of formalised abstract models. Work for the legists and the documentalists will merge, too.

7. Conclusions

Legal systems are not just hierarchical - static but procedural - dynamic as well. The legislative workflow has a dimension of time which has an influence on the creation of legal and documentalistic metadata. In particular, the importance of "ex ante" - "ex post" will increase. The authors have positive experience with formal "ex ante" metadata and support Biagioli's proposal to include semantic metadata, in particular if they are created "ex ante". Of course, implementation of this approach requires the availability of suited tools during the production process and a redesign of the guidelines of legal techniques. The authors watch the following trends:

The first is the merge of legal and documentalistic systems for the production of professional products.

The second is an emphasis on the differentiation of both systems. One obvious example is the transformation of a pure documentalistic system into a support system for citizens, speaking their language and giving straightforward answers to their questions.

Therefore, the goal is to bridge the approach of legal and documentalistic systems with those of e-government.

References

Discussion of the authors with Carlo Biagioli during V Legislative XML Workshop, 14-16 June 2006 - San Domenico di Fiesole (Florence - Italy).

Carlo Biagioli, Lorenzo Bacci, Enrico Francesconi, Fabrizio Turchi (ITTIG-CNR, Florence), Amedeo Cappelli (ISTI-CNR, Pisa) *Law-Making Environment. Perspectives.* In Proceedings of V Legislative XML Workshop, San Domenico di Fiesole (Florence - Italy), 14-16 June 2006.

Friedrich Lachmayer (University Innsbruck), Harald Hoffmann (METADAT GmbH) *Legal and Documentalistic Subelements - Remarks on Biagioli's Concept of Legal Provisions.* In Proceedings of V Legislative XML Workshop, San Domenico di Fiesole (Florence - Italy), 14-16 June 2006.

Carlo Biagioli, Istituto di Teoria e Tecniche dell'Informazione Giuridica (ITTIG) - Consiglio Nazionale delle Ricerche (CNR), Italy. *Towards self explaining texts through analytical metadata.* In Proceedings of III Legislative Workshop, Furore (Amalfi - Italy), 06-08 April 2005.

Bundeskanzleramt (BKA), Austria. *Administration on the Net - An ABC Guide to E-Government.* Brochure, January 2006.

Legal-RDF Vocabularies, Requirements & Design Rationale

John McClure
http://www.Legal-RDF.org

Abstract. This is a rationale covering certain recommendations I've made about the design of an international standard for the exchange of legislative documents during my presentation, *Legislative-XHTML – Integrating ECMA Script & RDF*, to the V Legislative XML Workshop. This paper focuses on the scope of data models needed for open and de-centralized legislative document annotation. These data models are used when naming text words, phrases, and numeric and currency amounts in a document. Automated extraction of this information – the ultimate aim of legislative document exchange – is argued to be best accomplished using a document exchange standard that is built upon the Resource Description Framework (RDF) rather than XML Schema. Electing RDF implies strongly that annotating XHTML, Version 2.0 documents is the proper medium for standardized exchange.

Keywords: annotation, semantics extraction, RDF, OWL, XHTML, ECMA, C#

1. Introduction and Background

Often the simple bromides (*adapt and grow the installed base*) can apply as much to development of standards for annotation of legal documents as to application development. Understanding the 'installed base' in this context involves examining who will be responsible for annotation and the tools they will apply to the legal text. In the U.S., private market research indicates that while authors of legal passages have little interest in interrupting themselves to (almost mechanically) name strings and blocks of text within their prose, they nevertheless do understand the usefulness of doing so, e.g., pseudo-intelligent wizard-bots can then be introduced to their desktop. Instead, paralegals in corporate, legislative publishing, and academic settings are the prime candidates to become the professionally-trained cadre of official annotators necessary for a standard legal vocabulary to achieve a critical mass yielding social and economic benefits far beyond its initial cost. Due specifically to the text-processing nature of the task, users will be fully aware of the annotation vocabulary – so it must be naturally expressive while also simple to understand (and debug), it must be as comprehensive as the text content annotated, and it must be structured to cater to cascading name-selection menus. Finally, the vocabulary's architecture must allow large-scale controlled customization by vocabulary users.

Legislative and other legal documents are now published on the Internet using just one mark-up language: HTML. To maximize the standard's adoption rate, annotation should proceed against this particular base of documents (albeit after first converting the HTML document to its XML cousin, XHTML). Strategies that envision an XML-based document mark-up legal vocabulary are unrealistic in view of the costs and difficulties that accrue when an organization replaces its current technologies. Instead, the alternative described here integrates well with the installed base of documents and tools by defining a global attribute that can be embedded onto any XHTML element – such as the <span> element in Figure 1 – during annotation of a block of narrative text, or phrase, word, or numeric text, occurring in the XHTML document.

```
<span about='somePublisher' x:property='PublisherTitle.1.eng'>
THE COUNCIL OF THE EUROPEAN UNION</ span>
```

Figure 1. **Simple annotation within an XHTML document**

The standard's architecture should incorporate the capabilities of semantic analysis tools and network databases tuned for semantic data structures. A survey of reasoning tools on the web shows for instance a definitive use of the Web Ontology Language (OWL) and the Protégé-based development platform – important arguments against development of an annotation standard based on an XML Schema or ancient DTD. Only by adhering to the Resource Description Framework (RDF) can deployment of reasoning wizard-bots to desktops of annotators and authors be possible on a wide basis.

Figure 2 is an example of RDF's familiar alternating pattern of upper- and lower-case element names, with id's place on the upper-case elements. This figure translates the mark-up shown in Figure 1 to an XML representation. Note the default lower-case <has> element has been placed between the upper-case elements that represent nodes, or resources, within one's description.

```
<rdf:Description about='somePublisher'>
   <has>
   <PublisherTitle rdf:ID='PublisherTitle.1'
      eng='THE COUNCIL OF THE EUROPEAN UNION'/>
   </has>
</rdf:Description>
```

Figure 2. **Translation of Figure 1 to Legal-RDF, as serialized XML**

In the RDF, all XML entities contain 'statements of fact' implicitly, as in Figure 2, or explicitly, as in Figure 3; a *statement* being the conventional grammatical concept of a subject, predicate, and object. Legal-RDF defines a <u>small</u> set of predicates – just the tenses of the verbs *to-have* and *to-be* – that starkly contrasts with typical RDF predicate-naming practice, which is to concatenate a verb with a noun, for instance, *hasTitle*. Several advantages occur using the Legal-RDF approach of defining predicates that are verbs-only. Chief among these is that object-property naming practices adopted by international standards organizations (typically required to be concatenated nouns or qualified nouns only) can be accommodated without change. Secondarily, the Legal-RDF approach supports block/phrase/word name-selection menus, a key tool needed by annotators and authors of legal documents. Typical RDF naming practices (such as *hasTitle*) would be more difficult to accommodate with cascading menu implementations.

Figure 3 shows that Figure 2 is composed of two RDF statements. Explicit statement specifications such as Figure 3 allow linguistic models to reflect the statement's context, voice, aspect, *et al* to be recorded and used in semantic analyses.

```
<rdf:Statement>
   <rdf:subject resource='somePublisher'/>
   <rdf:predicate resource='has'/>
   <rdf:object resource='PublisherTitle.1'/>
</rdf:Statement>
<rdf:Statement>
   <rdf:subject>
     <PublisherTitle rdf:ID='PublisherTitle.1'/>
   </rdf:subject>
   <rdf:predicate resource='eng'/>
   <rdf:object>
     <rdf:Literal    value='COUNCIL    OF    THE    EUROPEAN
UNION'/>
   </rdf:object>
</rdf:Statement>
```

Figure 3. **Standard reification of document content, as serialized XML**

Figure 4 presents an optimization of these statements. Use of a <verb> property for a *Statement* that is distinct from the <predicate> property has eliminated the now-redundant *Statement* and *PublisherTitle* resources. The <predicate> property remains a pointer to an *ObjectProperty* instance, but one whose name is a <u>noun phrase</u> that concatenates the names of the classes that are referenced by the *domain* and *range* properties of the <predicate> property. Another type of noun-phrase typically represented by noun-oriented predicates, are those whose name concatenates an adjective, adverb, or participle with a noun, *e.g.*, *FirstArticle*.

```
<rdf:Statement xml:id='PublisherTitle.1.eng'>
  <lgl:model resource='someURI'/>
  <rdf:subject resource='somePublisher'/>
  <lgl:verb resource='has'/>
  <rdf:predicate resource='PublisherTitle'/>
  <rdf:object>
    <rdf:Literal value='COUNCIL OF THE EUROPEAN UNION'/>
  </rdf:object>
</rdf:Statement>
```

Figure 4. **Legal-RDF content reification, as serialized XML**

As can be seen, noun-oriented predicates contrast markedly with typical RDF predicate-naming practice (*e.g.*, *hasTitle*). When predicate-verbs can be separately specified, verb tenses can be semantically exploited to easily express, for instance, that the publisher in Figure 4 <had> a different title. Semantic distinctions between <has>, <had>, <willHave>, <mayHave> and <mustHave> can be easily developed, as well as negatory expressions such as <mayHaveNot>.

2. Vocabulary Models

Figure 4 above also shows Legal-RDF's <model> property, a mechanism for associating resources with named sub-graphs of nodes in a universal directed acyclic graph, a common feature in network schemas. Often each model URI is then physically implemented as the name of a "Statements" table within a relational database. [Note: the default value of the <model> property is the URI of the XML entity in which the statement appeared.]

Annotation of narrative legal documents requires a number of vocabularies to be minimally available to semantic wizard-bots and to users during name-selection menu navigation. These vocabularies, described below, are each framed as a model that contains class- and property-name definitions. [Note: a model technically has *Arc* instances, a superclass of *Statement*, however a default model can be specified as a container for all statements about a resource for which a model is not specified.]

2.1. SEMANTICS MODEL

Basic to wizard-bots is a controlled vocabulary for concepts of information representation. Due to Legal-RDF's orientation, RDF's *Statement*
model is refined for the needs of annotating legal documents found in
managerial, judicial, electoral, and personal contexts. Several legally-
significant types of statements have been identified, for example *Condition, Definition, Fact, Hypothesis, Negation, Permission, Prohibition,
Requirement,* and *Warning,* that are found within most legal documents.

Statements occur in either a narrative context (a set of statements
made by a single speaker) or in a conversation (more than one speaker).
Sub-types of the *Conversation* class may then convey semantics applicable to analysis of the conversation's statements. Refinements of the *Conversation* class should include low-level definitions of service-oriented
peer-architectures.

Context is an important attribute of a statement. According to Wordnet, context is "discourse that surrounds a language unit and helps
to determine its interpretation; the set of facts or circumstances that
surround a situation or event" and is therefore relevant to the needs
of semantic wizard-bots. Context can be modelled using a dramatic
performance as a base, and then associating context with the speaker
of the statement. Since one principle of modelling is to reflect the real
world to the maximum extent possible, it's reasonable that the sum of
social interactions is a dramatic production. Six elements are involved
with a performance: its actors and their roles, its scenes with their
props, and its dramas that convey its themes. A semantic distinction
can then be naturally made between scripts for the performance versus
the actual record of the performance.

The greatest usefulness of modelling context relative to a 'performance' is that a powerful communicative analogy is used to convey
subtle relations among the model's components with the goal of creating
a rich semantic environment for wizard-bots.

Finally, a Semantics model needs to include a relationship to the
basic indexing categories standardized by the Dublin Core in order to
preserve RSS-based publish-and-subscribe implementation options. A
common set of indexes allows the development of more generic, resource-
only aware, software applications.

2.2. LINGUISTICS MODEL

Basic wizard-bots perform neighbor text/phrase analyses to facilitate
(and automate) the annotation process as much as possible. These
wizard-bots need to grammatically parse blocks of text to sentences,
sentences to clauses, clauses to phrases, and phrases to individual words

and other types of tokens. This process can associate text with any of 429 language classes provided by the model, for example, *EnglishText* is a class having a text-property named *eng*.

A Linguistics model is also used when parsing names of terms that are defined in the vocabulary, that is, class and property names. For instance, the name *PublisherTitle* is typed as a *NounPhrase* whose constituent nouns, adjectives, and adverbs can be further characterized for efficient processing by wizard-bots. A further significance of parsing camel-case and other concatenated phrases is that multi-lingual idiomatic dictionaries naturally emerge which can be referenced together with word-sense dictionaries such as Wordnet.

2.3. STATISTICS MODEL

Many assisted-annotation systems auto-select numeric quantities found within the text. A Statistics model is needed to define an extensive controlled vocabulary of (1) names of statistical quantities and calculated expressions including base types for percentages and rates (2) units of measurement applicable as a quantity or to a quantity and (3) numeric datatypes standardized by W3 XML Schema and used as the foundation for all other classes defined in the model. A database of units of measurement is associated with this model.

2.4. ECONOMICS MODEL

Assisted-annotation systems auto-select amounts of currency parsed from narrative text – identifying currency amounts within a document normally carries a high organizational priority. An Economics model defines an extensive vocabulary of economic measures including currency-based flow rates. These measures can be categorized into 18 types of currency amounts, from *CapitalAmount* and *ChargeAmount* through *WealthAmount* and *WithdrawalAmount*.

2.5. POLITICS MODEL

A model is needed to describe the political and legal context(s) in which a document is to be interpreted; legal documents constantly references resources that are instances of classes in these models. A Politics model is responsible for defining the relationships between a *Government*, *Nation,* and *Law* including dependent classes such as domestic, civil, and criminal roles that an *Actor* may perform.

2.6. DOCUMENT MODEL

A Document model needs to adopt the grammatical paragraph model
that is being introduced by the forthcoming XHTML, Version 2.0.
Among its many problems, the current XHTML version lacks the regular structure of document divisions, sub-divisions, sections, sub-sections,
paragraphs, lines, and tables now being enforced by XHTML, Version
2. A Document model also needs to integrate Extensible Stylesheet
Language (XSL) concepts – page-set, page, and header and footer –
due to their common use and textual references within legal documents.
Each styling directive defined by the Cascading Stylesheet Language
(CSS) is also needed to be part of the Document model to assure lossless
transformations among input and output formats.

2.7. ASPECTS MODEL

Aspect-oriented programming (AOP) techniques demonstrate the utility of separating concrete classes from 'mix-in' classes. Mixin-classes
identify the capabilities and the states that can be associated with new
classes added-in by a user to a foundation of classes. Many object-
properties and text-properties normally defined for concrete classes can
profitably be more properly associated with mixin-classes. Applications
that are programmed to manipulate the properties of mixin-classes
instead of concrete classes are (more) immune to changes in the hierarchies of concrete classes, a key requirement of a standard for annotation
of legal documents.

For instance, the mixin *BillableThing* can be used to type any resource one may want; by doing so, the resource's *BillingAddress* property only then is applicable. If the resource is not billable, then there
is no need to access any properties related to the *BillableThing* mixin
capability class.

Numerous resources transition between numerous transient states
that may be concurrent, sequential, or hierarchical, for example, a
Human begins life as an *ImmatureThing* but ultimately becomes a *Ma-
tureThing* – these two classes, and their subclasses, can be enumerated
values for the *Maturity* of a resource.

A third group of mixin classes in an Aspect model addresses past-
participle qualifiers within a class-name, for example, *BilledThing* is a
subclass of the *QualifiedThing* class, while *BillableThing* subclasses the
QualifiableThing class. At the same time, the *BilledThing* class subclasses the *BillableThing* class, a formulation reflecting the key axiom
that all billed-things are, by definition, billable-things. This design allows properties often associated with a process (*e.g.,* a billing process)
to be partitioned between classes that represent the capability of in-

stances to be subjected to the process (*e.g., BillableThing*) and those classes that represent the state to which instances, once subjected to the process, have then transitioned.

2.8. ACTORS MODEL

An Actors model contains concrete classes for individuals and groups of persons, companies, governments, and organizations. Actors perform roles in the context of many performances, refining their behaviour according to their context and experience and the scripts applicable to the performances.

Every *Actor* is either a *Human* or a *Group*. A *Human* is a subclass of a *Person* so that a *Corporation* may also be a legal *Person*. A *Person* is further categorized with demographic and industrial associations. A *Group* is subclassed with *Organization, Family, Nation,* and other species of *Human* and *Person* collections. An *Organization* subclass is *Institution,* then further categorized as *PrivateInstitution* (a *PrivateThing*) or *PublicInstitution* (a *PublicThing*). A *Corporation* is a *PrivateInstitution,* while a *Government* is a *PublicInstitution.*

2.9. ROLES MODEL

A *Role* is the general category for vocabulary terms that denote workroles (occupations), legal roles, and family-life roles. The occupations hierarchy in a Roles model should incorporate and refine as necessary occupational-title classification schemes available from government sources. Domestic, civil, and criminal roles are defined by a Politics model.

2.10. SCENES MODEL

A *Scene* is the general category for locations (and eras), that is, time and place. The *Location* class is divided into *Land* and *Facility.* Subclasses for *Facility* can be derived largely from the facilities referenced by the North American Industrial Services Classification, involving its definition of a "business establishment". However, these facility types are usefully organized with categories from national real estate industry sources.

An *Atlas* is a key resource (instance database) associated with this model. Additionally, generic era-based calendars are associated with this model.

2.11. PROPS MODEL

A *Prop* is the general category for products and for types of legal property. The *Product* hierarchy can be derived from the North American Industrial Product Classification. *Property* includes personal and real property; of note is that *IntellectualProperty* subtypes items that are creative artifacts, for instance, the *Ontology* class.

2.12. THEMES MODEL

A Themes model allows the incorporation of topic maps that are applicable to a certain industry or activity. These topics all concern conceptual non-concrete classes. For instance, *Justice* and *Injustice* classes are subtypes of the *Theme* class, meaning that instances of 'Injustice' can be identified and described using the normal RDF mechanisms.

2.13. DRAMAS MODEL

A Dramas model provides the framework for describing discrete acts and open-ended activities that occur during a performance. This category is for definitions of *Act* and *Activity* classes as subclasses of the *Event* class. To be consistent with the RDF, each *Event* subclass is named by a noun-phrase, *e.g., AbrogationEvent, AdjudicationEvent, AgreementEvent,* and so on. Each of these *Event* classes has subclasses representing discrete events or open-ended related activities, *e.g., AgreementAct* and *AgreementActivity*. Every *Activity* naturally contains its coordinate *Act* as one of the acts that can occur during the *Activity, e.g.,* an *AgreementActivity* concludes with an *AgreementAct* (which can be followed by postlude acts). Certain classes defined in the base Semantics model, *e.g., Agreement* as a subclass of the *Statement* class, are referenced by the *Act* class, *e.g.,* a property of *AgreementAct* is named *AgreementStatement* whose range is an *Agreement*.

2.14. SCRIPTS MODEL

A Scripts model contains definitions of specific forms that are completed manually or by machine. A *Script* is a set of recorded statements. For instance, a *DriverLicense* contains the name of the driver, expressed as *LicenseeName* or perhaps as *DriverName*, but that name is not the name of a 'property' of the form. Rather, the name (*DriverName)* is the name of a property of a *Person* who is the *Licensee* who is a subject of the form. A *Scripts* model addresses the kind and content of statements that are to be present in instances of a completed form, are optional, and are disallowed.

2.15. SUMMARY OF MODEL REQUIREMENTS

Table I. **Summary of references applicable to proposed models**

Model	*References*
Semantics Model	ISO Topics, W3 RDF, Dublin Core, DAGs
Linguistics Model	ISO Languages, Reed-Kellog, W3 SWBP Wordnet
Statistics Model	W3 XML Schema, SI Units of Measure
Economics Model	ISO Currencies, Federal forms, industry glossaries
Politics Model	U.N. glossaries and membership data
Aspects Model	Aspect Oriented Programming
Document Model	W3 XHTML, W3 CSS, W3 XSL-FO
Actors Model	North American Industrial Service Classification
Roles Model	U.S. and Canada Occupations Classifications, North American Industrial Service Classification
Scenes Model	U.N. atlases and calendars, Real estate standards, North American Industrial Service Classification
Props Model	North American Industrial Product Classification
Themes Model	Industry topic maps
Dramas Model	North American Industrial Service Classification
Scripts Model	W3 Xforms, ECMA Languages

3. Conclusion

Minimal support for the annotation of legal documents suggests that a broad general-purpose vocabulary of classes and properties is needed. The class-names and property-names defined in this vocabulary are used to annotate blocks of text, sentences, phrases, words, and numeric amounts, that is, to name the text content within the legal document. Automated information extraction – a prime goal of a standard for the exchange of legal documents – may then proceed with reference to a vocabulary that addresses the information requirements of wizard-bots and user interfaces manipulating the extracted information.

Achieving the most successful standard for the exchange of annotated legal documents – one that imbeds annotation directly into published documents – seems to require XHTML versions of the legal document to be the base for the standard. Alternative design approaches that envision publishing XML representations conforming to one or more XML Schemas or DTDs, though attractive in some regards, unfortunately are short-sighted in that they do not consider the needs of semantic analysis tools nor the character of the existing base of legal documents, and may lead to a future of more complexity and less access to legal information by the general public and legal practitioners.

Multilingual Conceptual Dictionaries Based on Ontologies

Gianmaria Ajani*, Leonardo Lesmo°, Guido Boella°, Alessandro
Mazzei°, Piercarlo Rossi*
*Dipartimento di Scienze Giuridiche, Università di Torino - Italy -
gianmaria.ajani@unito.it. p.rouge@inwind.it
°Dipartimento di Informatica, Università di Torino - Italy -
{lesmo,guido,mazzei}@di.unito.it

Abstract. This paper introduces a new tool called "Legal Taxonomy Syllabus".
This is a ontology based tool designed in order to annotate and recover multi-lingua
legal information.

Keywords: Multilingual Legal Ontologies

1. Introduction

The legal orders of the EC Member States are currently on the verge of
further convergence of their respective private law - a process which is
strongly influenced and directed by European primary and secondary
legislation.

Several researches in the field of European law are currently targeting
the identification of similarities and differences, common principles and
concepts within national and European legal institutions. A EU legal
terminology is however required to properly represent the European
concepts and differentiate them from those of Member States (European
Commission, 2003a; European Commission, 2004).

1. That is a priority identified by the European Commission: "rewrit-
ing legal texts" is necessary "to render them more coherent and understandable" (European Commission, 2003b), in order to enhance a
uniform interpretation of EU law in each national legal system. Terminological fragmentation causes lack of internal and external coherence
in European law, especially where the impact of EU legislation is significant such as in a subject matter like consumer protection (European
Commission, 2001). The internal coherence is hindered by the potentially legal uncertainty resulting from inconsistent definitions of EU
legal terms and from the contradictory use of legal terms within different
sectoral legislative interventions (see EC Directives on consumer law,
like Timeshare, Distant Contract, Unfair terms, and so forth).
The external coherence is frustrated by the differences in legal conceptualisations that may import the "result of Member State transposition
which has itself added unnecessary, complicated, detailed or excessive

provisions" (European Commission, 2003b). This is the case of Directives that need to be implemented by national statutory instruments.
The implementation of a Directive may not correspond to its straight
transposition in a national law and may be subject to further interpretation. Thus a same legal concept can be expressed in different ways
in a Directive and in the transposition law. For example, in Directive
99/44/EC, the concept corresponding to the English word "reasonably"
is translated into Italian with "ragionevolmente" in the language of the
Directive, and with "con ordinaria diligenza" in the Italian transposition law. We can define this problematic issue as a sort of extra-EU
polysemy. This implementation process is problematical, since it leads
to use a different terminology in the EU legislation and in the national
legislation.

Moreover, the terminological fragmentation is considered by the European Commission as an obstacle to "developing more user friendly access
to consult and use Community law" (European Commission, 2003b).
Consider for example EUR-Lex, a wide portal providing access to all
the official legal documents of the European Union, though with the
paradox that, in order to obtain a full coverage, it limits the complete
accessibility to legal documents, particularly for the needs of lawyers.

Reporting too large instances for each query without comprehensible
classifications for the expectances of national jurists and practitioners
hinders the applicability of EUR-Lex for most legal uses in the Member
States' legal orders. Where the searched legal terms do not properly
correspond to the given legal terms in the EUR-Lex database, the
queries submitted by the lawyers become enlarged to ordinary language
or full text access with several limitations in the possibility of managing
such an amount of data.

2. The criteria for a comparison of legal concepts among different
legal systems deal with the question of what legal concepts are and of
which is their relation with the terms representing them. It is clear that
the problem of the legal concepts which sometimes emerges from the
terminological transposition of the Directives is wider and constitutive
of the European legal order, where several national legal systems with
their own traditions have been converging in a new European order that
does not substitute them but interplays with them.

This state of affairs represents an opportunity to demonstrate how
information technology can prevent the problem of knowledge representation known as conceptual misalignment.

In fact, the difference in terminology sometimes corresponds to a
difference in meaning and sometimes does not. Moreover, some legal
traditions prefer to use different terms for different concepts while others
do the opposite. Unfortunately, that problem is underestimated in the

process of drafting European law and implementing it in national instruments as well as in the classification systems of main European legal database, such as EUR-Lex. So, the German phrase "Klar und verständlich", used in several Directives on consumer law, is ambiguous between the concepts denoted in Italian respectively by "chiaramente", "chiaro e comprensibile" and "inequivoco", but in the Italian language version of the same Directive that difference is not traced back.

One tool which might help to increase European terminological consistency taking into account the problem of knowledge representation is the Legal Taxonomy Syllabus which has already set off two years ago by the Department of Computer Science of the University of Turin specialised in ontology for the web domain, legal ontology and AI studies on law, which cooperates with the main groups of research on this topic in the international context, such as the LOA, Laboratory for Applied Ontology of Italian CNR, CIRSFID at the University of Bologna, and so forth.

Such tool has been developed to support the Uniform Terminology project (Rossi and Vogel, 2004), in the overall collaboration with the Law Department of Turin, specialised in comparative and European law and involved in several substantial researches funded by the Commission on: a) legal terminology, like the Uniform Terminology for European Private Law - EU Fifth Framework Program - "Improving Human Potential" (http://www.uniformterminology.unito.it); b) common frame of reference, like the Joint Network on European Private Law - EU Sixth Framework Program "Network of Excellence" (http://www.copecl.org).

Legal Taxonomy Syllabus is designed as an open-access database linking European terms with national transposition law and also linking terms horizontally (i.e. between national legal orders). It provides full text reference of relevant EU and Member States' legislation. The database includes related case law and short commentary notes by national scholars where this is necessary to describe differing legal doctrine. As a starting point, the Legal Taxonomy Syllabus covers consumer law with national law references limited to France, Germany, Italy, Spain and the UK. The Legal Taxonomy Syllabus could be useful for lawyers, translators, legislators and scholars: the tool may help legislators to enhance terminological coherency already at drafting stage of legal acts. The cross-reference features enable lawyers to search for relevant case law in other Member States by a one-click method. Unlike a dictionary, the Legal Taxonomy Syllabus does not only provide translators with a proper translation but provides the respective legislative context of each term.

The database can also help scholars to perform cross-sector analyses on the use of legal terms and concepts, integrating with the ontologies the classification systems employed by existing database, which are oriented towards the multilingualism terminology but only in one dimension, that of the European Union; or which are structured on the subdivisions and sections of the European Treaty that have no relevant connection with the classifications implied in the legal discourse within the Member States.

What seems important to us is to introduce the Legal Taxonomy Syllabus system among the developed tools, as a new way to properly manage the diverseness of EU law. The treatment of legal terminology adopts a mixed descriptive-prescriptive terminological application to the corpora constituted by the European legal documents. In this way, prior to improving the consistency of the EU terminology, the research is focused on the understanding of such a terminology within the Member States, highlighting the matter of polysemy and amphibology of the terms used in a same language (such as French) at the European level and at the national level of France or Belgium.

2. From terms to ontologies: the Legal Taxonomy Syllabus system

The tool that we propose is based on a clear distinction between the notions of "legal term" and "legal concept". The basic idea is that the basic conceptual backbone consists in a taxonomy of concepts (ontology) to which the terms can refer to express their meaning. One of the main points to keep in mind is that we do not assume the existence of a single taxonomy covering all languages. In fact, it has been convincingly argued that the different national systems may organize the concepts in different ways. For instance, the term "contract" corresponds to different concepts in common law and civil law, where it has the meaning of "bargain" and "agreement", respectively argued (Sacco, 1999; Pozzo, 2003).

Consequently, the Legal Taxonomy Syllabus includes different ontologies, one for each involved language plus one for the language of EU documents. Each language-specific ontology is related via a set of "association" links to the EU concepts, as shown in fig.1.

2.1. POLYSEMY AND TRANSLATIONS

Although this picture is conform to intuition, in the Legal Taxonomy Syllabus it had to be enhanced in two directions. First, it must be observed that the various national ontologies have a reference language. This is not the case for the EU ontology. In fact, a given term in, say,

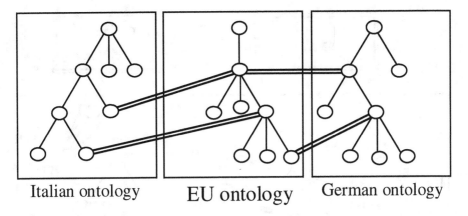

Italian ontology   EU ontology   German ontology

Figure 1. Relationship between ontologies. The thick arcs represent the inter-ontology "association" link.

English could refer either to a concept in the UK ontology or to a concept in the EU ontology. In the first case, the term is used for referring to a concept in the national UK legal system, whilst in the second one, it is used to refer to a concept used in the European directives. This is one of the main advantages of the Legal Taxonomy Syllabus. For example "Klar und verständlich" could refer both to concept "De379" (a concept in the German Ontology) and to concept "EU882" (a concept in the European ontology). This is the Legal Taxonomy Syllabus solution for facing the possibility of a correspondence only partial between the meaning a term has in the national system and the meaning of the same term in the translation of a EU directive.

This feature enables the Legal Taxonomy Syllabus to be more precise about what "translation" means. It puts at disposal a way for asserting that two terms are the translation of each other, but just in case those terms have been used in the translation of an EU directive: within the Legal Taxonomy Syllabus, we can talk about direct EU-translations of terms, but only about indirect national-system translations of terms. The situation enforced in the Legal Taxonomy Syllabus is depicted in fig.2, where it is represented that: The Italian term Term-Ita-A and the German term Term-Ger-A have been used as corresponding terms in the translation of an EU directive, as shown by the fact that both of them refer to the same EU-concept EU-1 In the Italian legal system, Term-Ita-A has the meaning Ita-2 In the German legal system, Term-Ger-A has the meaning Ger-3 The EU translations of the directive is correct insofar no terms exist in Italian and German that characterize precisely the concept EU-1 in the two languages (i.e the "associated" concepts Ita-4 and Ita-5 have no corresponding legal terms)

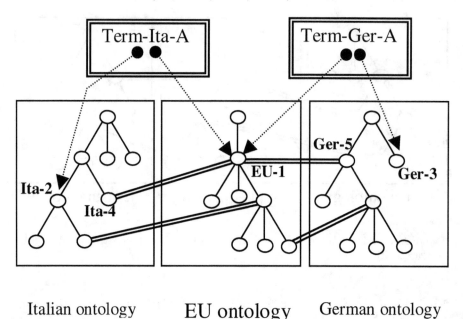

Italian ontology   EU ontology   German ontology

Figure 2. Relationship between ontologies and terms

A practical example of such a situation is reported in fig.2, where we can see that The ontologies include different type of arcs. Beyond the standard is-a (linking a category to its supercategory), there is also a purpose arc, which is self-explanatory The dotted arc represent the reference from terms to concepts Some terms have links both to a National ontology and to the EU Ontology (In particular, "Withdrawal" vs. "Diritto di Recesso" and "Difesa del Consumatore" vs. "Consumer Protection"). The last item above is especially relevant: note that this configuration of arcs specifies that: 1. "Withdrawal" and "Diritto di Recesso" have been used as equivalent terms (concept EU-2) in some European Directive. 2.In that context the term involved an act having as purpose the some kind of protection of the consumer 3.The terms used for referring to the latter are "Consumer Protection" in English and "Difesa del Consumatore" in Italian 4.In the British legal system, however, not all "withdrawals" have this goal, but only a subtype of them, to which the code refers to as "Cancellation" (concept Eng-3). 5.In the Italian legal system, the term "diritto di recesso" also refers to a kind of "risoluzione" (concept Ita-3).

All of this seem to correspond neatly to the conception of terminology that is currently accepted by the scholars in comparative law. For instance, it can safely be stated that the term "diritto di recesso" as used

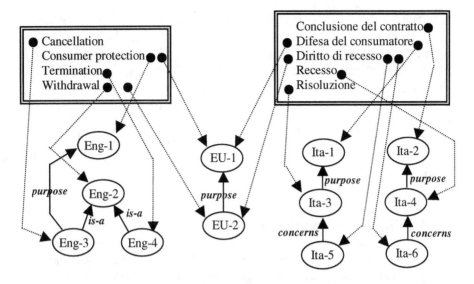

Figure 3. An example of interconnections among terms

in consumer law directives (i.e. the right of a consumer to withdraw from a contract) does not correspond to an existing legal concept in the Italian legislation. Moreover, the right of withdrawal appearing in EU directives also differs from the doctrine with the same label of the British system.

2.2. The Legal Taxonomy Syllabus knowledge base

This complex scenario shows how the traditional top-down approach to the development of legal ontologies (Visser and Bench-Capon, 1998) is not flexible enough. Usually, ontologies are built starting from very general concepts which are then specialised in more detailed concepts. Moreover most ontologies are oriented to a single national tradition. In this process the knowledge engineers risk not to take into account the interpretation process of the legal specialists on the real multilingual data. These ontologies aim at modelling the legal code but not the legal "doctrine", that is the work of interpretation and re-elaboration of the legal code which is fundamental for transposing EUD into national laws.

In the development of the ontologies described in the previous section, we propose to follow the approach of the "Uniform terminology project" (Ajani et al., 2005). As a first step, terms are collected in a database together with the legal sources where they appear, in order to identify the concepts. Then, for each EU language, the set of concepts is organized in an ontology which can be different for different legal traditions. This reconstruction work is done by legal experts rather than knowledge engineers. In this phase the result is a light-weight ontology rather than an axiomatic one. Only relations among terms are identified without introducing restrictions and axioms. The function of these ontologies is to compare the taxonomic structure in the different legislations, to provide a form of intelligent indexing and to draw new legal conclusions.

In a second phase, a knowledge engineer can reorganize the ontology and integrate it with a top-level well-founded ontology like DOLCE (Gangemi et al., 2002).

3. Accessing to the Legal Taxonomy Syllabus

Even if many tools for the construction of ontologies are available (e.g., Protegè), we had to design a new development system based on the constraints of being *distributed* and *user-friendly*. As described in Section 2, the central step of the legal concepts annotation is performed by legal experts from different countries rather than knowledge engineer. As a consequence, the Legal Taxonomy Syllabus has been designed by using a very simple client-server web application[1]. The ontology framework has been inspired by the Gene Ontology project (http://www.geneontology.org/), from which it inherits the logical and graphical representation. The tool has two levels of use.

In the first level the web interface makes available to the legal expert a friendly way to introduce data about terms and concepts. At this level, the tool aims at providing the expert with a support in her/his activity of term comparison, Fig. 4. In other words, instead of using a standard database interface, the expert can specify the correspondences among terms found via the manual inspection of EU directives or ECJ decisions (or in national legislation and case-law) in a controlled way and save in an ontology structure the result of her/his analysis.

The second level is devoted to a user who wants to retrieve the documents related to a given legal term. At this level, Legal Taxonomy Syllabus acts as the desired extension of a standard legal database (cf. "EUR-Lex", see below), by enabling the user to find the relevant documents taking into account the complex net of semantic correspondences that characterize the relationships between legal terms at the international level (Fig. 5).

The importance of such two levels of use has ever not been stressed sufficiently. As pointed out in jurisprudence and European law litera-

---

[1] The web server has been implemented by using a WAPP (Windows, Apache, PostgreSQL, PHP) platform.

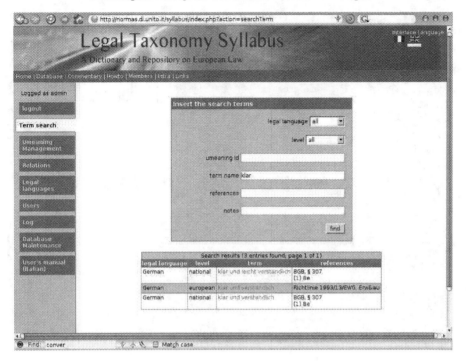

Figure 4. A screenshot of the Legal Taxonomy Syllabus interface for navigation and update of the ontologies.

ture (Patterson, 1996; Gerven, 2000), the classification schemes of legal objects (such as the distinction between rights *in rem* and rights *in personam* with the reference to the time-share property) does not exist externally to the legal domain and exists only because the legal science deems it does. The principle of consensus (the intentional use of the majority of scholars operating within the relevant discipline) and not only the interoperability may foster the ontological knowledge at the level of legal domain. Consequently, if many classification schemes are adopted in several legal orders the ontology should take all into account before refining them.

3.1. Towards XML format

From technological point of view, the Legal Taxonomy Syllabus knowledge is stored in a relational database, i.e. in a number of SQL tables. As we have pointed out in the previous section, the database structure used in the Legal Taxonomy Syllabus is a descendant of the structure used by the Gene Ontology database. Gene ontology project includes a number of programs that allows us the transformation from the SQL

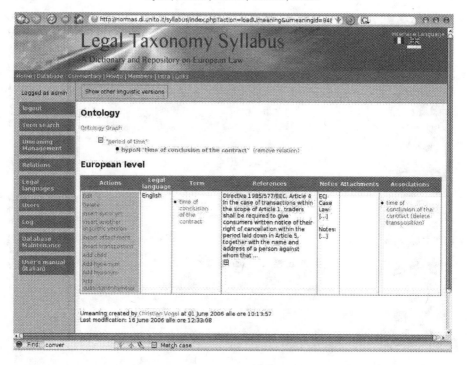

Figure 5. A screenshot of the Legal Taxonomy Syllabus interface for searching a legal term.

tables into a number of formats. In particular these program allow the conversion into the OWL format. Anyway there are a number of differences between the Legal Taxonomy Syllabus and the Gene ontology tables, e.g. the latter do not take the concept-term distinction into account. In the next future work we intend to modify the programs provided by Gene ontology project in order to work fine with the Legal Taxonomy Syllabus SQL relational schema. The modification has to account for three critical issues deriving from the term-concept distinction: 1. one single term can correspond to a number of distinct concepts. 2. one single concept can correspond to a number of distinct terms belonging to the same language. 3. one single concept can correspond to a number of distinct terms belonging to different languages.

4. Conclusion and future development

There is a number of works that consider the theoretical issues related to the construction of legal ontologies (McCarty, 1989; Stamper, 1991; Breuker et al., 1997). In particular the framework presented in

(Kraligen, 1997) is a frame-based system that classify the legal facts. A basic component of this system is the *legal concept description*, i.e. Kralingen proposes a distinction between a legal term and a legal concept similar to the distinction that we have adopted in Legal Taxonomy Syllabus. From a practical point of view, there are two projects that are related in someway to the Legal Taxonomy Syllabus. The "EURLex" system (http://europa.eu.int/eur-lex/) is a web portal that interfaces a number of databases in order to access a wide collection of legal documents produced by the EU. However, in order to obtain a full coverage, EURLex limits the complete accessibility to legal documents, particularly for the needs of lawyers. Each query, even when using boolean search, reports too large instances without comprehensible classifications for the expectances of national jurists and practitioners, and thus hinders the applicability of EUR-Lex for most legal uses in the Member States' legal.

"Eurovoc" (http://europa.eu.int/celex/eurovoc/) is a web application that accesses a number a multilingual thesauri. The main point of this project is the splitting of the legal terms into two sets: the *descriptor* and *non-descriptor*. A non-descriptor legal term can be always be mapped into a descriptor legal term that has the same meaning. Moreover, the basic hypothesis is that each descriptor can be translated straightforwardly into the official languages of the EU. In contrast to the Legal Taxonomy Syllabus, the main purpose of Eurovoc is the information extraction. Indeed, the sparsness problems related to the *bags of word* techniques can be reduced by replacing the non-descriptor with the corresponding descriptor. However Eurovoc does not distinct between a legal terms and a legal concepts, and cannot resolve easily the problems related to the polysemy.

"LOIS" Project (http://www.loisproject.org) aims at extending EuroWordnet with legal information. Whilst the final goal of LOIS is to support applications concerning information extraction, the Legal Taxonomy Syllabus we propose herein is concerned with the access of human experts to the EU documents.

In this paper we have described the Legal Taxonomy Syllabus. The actual ongoing phase of this project involves the collections of the legal terms and legal concepts by a group of legal experts belonging to a number different countries (in particular Italy, England, Germany, Spain, France). In the next work we intend to release new tools to allow the conversion from the SQL tables, used by the Legal Taxonomy Syllabus database, into the OWL format.

Acknowledgements

The Legal Taxonomy Syllabus project has been partially funded by the Uniform Terminology project (www.uniformterminology.unito.it, Contract n. HPRN-CT-2002-00229).

References

G. Ajani and M. Ebers, editors. *Uniform Terminology for European Contract Law.* Nomos, Baden Baden, 2005.

J. Breuker, A. Valente, and R. Winkels. Legal ontologies: A functional view. In *Procs. of 1st LegOut Workshop on Legal Ontologies*, pages 23–36, 1997.

European Commission. Green Paper on EU Consumer Protection. *Communication from the Commission to the European Parliament and the Council*, COM(2001)(531), 2001.

European Commission. More Coherent European Contract Law, An Action Plan. *Communication from the Commission to the European Parliament and the Council*, COM(2003)(68 final), 2003a.

European Commission. Updating and simplifying the Community acqui. *Communication from the Commission*, COM(2003)(71 final), 2003b.

European Commission. European Contract Law and the revision of the acquis: the way forward. *Communication from the Commission*, COM(2004)(651 final), 2004.

A. Gangemi, N. Guarino, C. Masolo, A. Oltramari, and L. Schneider. Sweetening ontologies with dolce. In *Proceedings of EKAW*, pages 21–29, 2002.

W. Van Gerven. Of rights, remedies and procedures. *Common Market Law Review*, pages 501–536, 2000.

V. Kraligen. A conceptual frame–based ontology for the law. In *Procs. of 1st LegOut Workshop on Legal Ontologies*, pages 15–22, 1997.

L.T. McCarty. A language for legal discourse: Basic features. In *Proc. of Second International Conference on Artificial Intelligence and Law*, 1989.

D. Patterson. *Law and Truth.* Oxford University Press, 1996.

B. Pozzo. Harmonisation of european contract law and the need of creating a common terminology. *European Review of Private Law*, 6:754–767, 2003.

P. Rossi and C. Vogel. Terms and concepts; towards a syllabus for european private law. *European Review of Private Law (ERPL)*, 12(2):293–300, 2004.

R. Sacco. Contract. *European Review of Private Law*, 2:237–240, 1999.

R.K. Stamper. The role of semantics in legal expert systems and legal reasoning. *Ratio Juris*, 4(2):219–244, 1991.

P.R.S. Visser and T.J.M. Bench-Capon. A comparison of four ontologies for the design of legal knowledge systems. *Artificial Intelligence and Law*, 6:27–57, 1998.

An OWL Ontology of Norms and Normative Judgements

Rossella Rubino*, Antonino Rotolo*, Giovanni Sartor°

*CIRSFID, Alma Mater Studiorum - Università di Bologna
Via Galliera, 3, I-40121 Bologna, Italy
°Law Department, European University Institute
Via Boccaccio, 121 I-50133 Firenze,Italy

Abstract. In this paper we present an OWL ontology of fundamental legal concepts developed within the ESTRELLA European project. The ontology includes the basic normative components of legal knowledge: deontic modalities, obligative rights, permissive rights, liberty rights, liability rights, different kinds of legal powers, potestative rights (rights to produce legal results) and sources of law. Besides the taxonomy the ontology comprises also the semantic relations between the concepts. The aim of the paper is that the proposed ontology may be useful for semantic access to digital legal information and for the representation of legal knowledge.

Keywords: ontology, OWL, legal concepts

Introduction

In this paper we shall provide an OWL ontology of fundamental legal concepts introduced in (Sartor, 2006) with the twofold aim of clarifying the basic normative components of legal knowledge and of contributing to enable semantic access to digital legal information.

The ontology has been developed under the European project ESTRELLA[1] which aims to develop and validate an open, standards-based platform allowing public administrations to develop and deploy comprehensive legal knowledge management solutions, without becoming dependent on proprietary products of particular vendors. The main technical objectives of the ESTRELLA project are to develop a Legal Knowledge Interchange Format (LKIF), building upon emerging XML-based standards of the Semantic Web, including RDF and OWL, and Application Programmer Interfaces (APIs) for interacting with LKIF legal knowledge systems.

The formal language chosen to express this first version of our ontology is OWL-DL (Smith et al, 2004)[2], which is an OWL version directly translatable into Description Logic and for which there are

---

[1] ESTRELLA - The European project for Standardized Transparent Representations in order to Extend Legal Accessibility (IST-2004-027665) http://www.estrellaproject.org/

[2] http://www.w3.org/TR/2004/REC-owl-guide-20040210/

several inference engines. The ontology has been developed using the OWL Plugin of the Protégé ontology editing tool.

According to (Sartor, 2006), the set of fundamental legal concepts includes, besides the usual deontic modalities (*obligation, prohibition* and *permission*), other notions like the following: *obligative rights* (rights related to others' obligations), *permissive rights, erga-omnes rights, liberty rights, liability rights,* different kinds of *legal powers, potestative rights* (rights to produce legal results) and *sources of law.*

Of course, we also need some more general concepts such as those of an *agent* and an *action* which an agent can perform, or again, the concept of a *situation* which an agent can create. In this paper we assume that these concepts can be imported from top and core ontologies such as DOLCE[3] ontology, LRI-core[4] ontology and so on.

This paper is structured as follows. In Section 1 we give a taxonomy of the fundamental legal concepts introduced in (Sartor, 2005; Sartor, 2006) along with their definition. In Section 2 we describe in more detail the structure of the ontology in terms of classes and properties. For space reasons full OWL code is not provided here but it can be requested to the authors. Finally, conclusions and future work are drawn in Section 3.

1. A Taxonomy of Legal Concepts

A first classification of legal concepts, as depicted in Figure 1, includes two main classes: *Norms* and *Normative judgements.* In the following

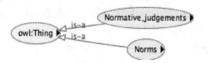

Figure 1. Relationships among main legal concepts

subsections we will analyze these "macro-concepts" and how they can be further classified.

1.1. NORMATIVE JUDGEMENTS

A normative judgement is the propositional constituent expressing a normative fact and can be classified (see Figure 2) into the following kinds:

---

[3] http://www.loa-cnr.it/DOLCE.html

[4] http://wiki.leibnizcenter.org/open/index.php/LRI_Core

- *evaluative*, which indicates that something is good or bad, is a value to be optimised or an evil to be minimised (for example, "human dignity is value", "participation ought to be promoted");

- *qualificatory*, which ascribes a legal quality to a person or an object (for example, "x is a citizen", "x is an intellectual work", "x is a technical invention");

- *definitional*, which specifies the meaning of a term (for example "x means y" or "by x it is meant y");

- *deontic*, which imposes the obligation or confers the permission to do a certain action (for example "x has the obligation" or "x has the permission to do A");

- *potestative*, which attributes powers (for example "a worker has the power to terminate his work contract");

- *evidentiary*, which establishes the conclusion to be drawn from certain evidence (for example "it is presumed that dismissal was discriminatory");

- *existential*, which indicates the beginning or the termination of the existence of a legal entity (for example "the company ceases to exist");

- *norm-concerning judgements*, which state the modifications of norms such as abrogation, repeal, substitution, and so on.

In the following we will analyze in more detail the concepts of deontic judgements and potestative judgements.

1.1.1. *Deontic judgements*

A deontic judgement expresses the fact that a certain content is qualified by deontic modalities, such as typically obligation, prohibition and permission.

Deontic modalities: *permissive judgements* and *obligative judgements* (see Figure 3). Deontic concepts can be reduced to those of obligation and permission. Classically, prohibition is defined in terms of the notion of obligation (**OBL¬**). We shall not consider here the distinction between weak (or negative) permission, consisting in the non-derivability of a prohibition, and strong permission, equivalent to the explicit negation of a prohibition.

Basic deontic modalities (*Basic Obligative* and *Basic Permissive*) correspond the standard deontic qualifications in deontic discourse.

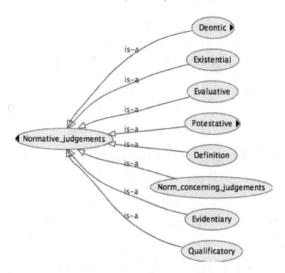

Figure 2. A taxonomy of normative judgements

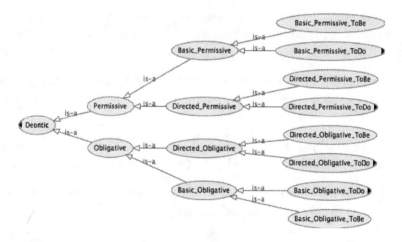

Figure 3. A taxonomy of deontic normative judgements

They are also called undirected deontic modalities, as no explicit reference is made to any subject which may be the beneficiary of the deontic qualification.

Basic deontic modalities can be further classified into *ought-to-be* and *ought-to-do* judgements: the former express deontic qualifications whose content are states of affairs without necessarily mentioning actors or actions bearing relations with such states of affairs; the latter may be interpreted as expressing deontic qualifications of explicit actions. Although in many cases ought-to-be statements can be reframed as ought-to-do statements, it is quite controversial that this can be done in general and ought-to-be statements are often made when it is not known who will have the responsibility of realising the state of affairs though it is known that somebody has this responsibility.

An example of normative judgement involving an undirected ought-to-be qualification is the following: "The balance of a bank account ought to be non-negative".

An example of normative judgement involving an undirected ought-to-do qualification is the following: "Everybody has the obligation to pay taxes".

Normative judgements stating directed deontic modalities, that is *Directed Obligative* and *Directed Permissive*, indicate the beneficiaries of the deontic qualifications specified in such judgements.

We distinguish two ways in which such an indication can take place: either the deontic qualification holds towards specified individuals, in which case we speak of an individualised qualification, or it holds towards everybody, in which case we speak of an erga-omnes qualification.

An example of normative judgement involving a directed erga-omnes ought-to-be qualification is the following: "In the interest of the every Italian citizen traffic ought to be reduced".

An example of normative judgement involving a directed individualised ought-to-do qualification is the following: "In the interest of Mr. Jones, Ms. Smith has the obligation to pay him one thousand euros".

An example of normative judgement involving a directed erga-omnes ought-to-do qualification is the following: "In the interest of the owner everybody is forbidden to use his/her property without his/her consent".

We represent the distinction between individualised deontic qualification and erga-omnes deontic qualification through the values assigned to the property **towards**, which will concern individually named agent in the case of individualised judgements, and the all agents in the case of erga-omnes judgements. We will see the properties of each class in the next section.

Directed obligative ought-to-do are also called *obligative rights*. k has the obligative right that j does A iff it is obligatory, towards k, that j does A. An example of obligative right is "it is obligatory, towards Mary, that Tom pays 1,000 euros to John".

Another type of obligative rights are the *exclusionary rights* which concern the prohibition against performing certain inferences (against reasoning in certain ways), or against using certain kinds of premises for certain purposes, in the interest of a particular person. This is especially the case with anti-discrimination rules. For instance, in many legal systems employers are prohibited from adopting any decision having a negative impact on their employees on the basis of race or sex, and this prohibition, though also serving some collective purposes, is primarily aimed at promoting the interest of the employees in question.

Let us now specifically consider how we can conceptualise the difference between directed ought-to-do deontic judgements having a positive or a negative content (see Figure 4), that is, concerning actions
or omissions. Both obligations and permissions can be divided into
positive and negative according to whether they concern an action or
an omission.

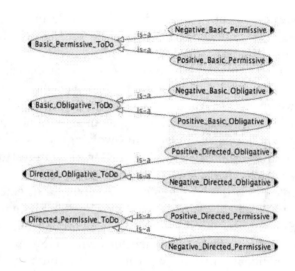

Figure 4. A taxonomy of positive and negative judgements

Directed negative permissions constitute what is also called *privilege*
in the Hohfeldian language (Hohfeld, 1913; Hohfeld, 1917): j has a
privilege towards k, with regard to action A, iff it is permitted towards
k that j omits to do A.

Always following Hohfeld, we may use the less controversial expression *noright* to express that one does not have the obligational right that
another does a certain action, that is, to denote the situation when the
latter is permitted towards the former to omit that action. Therefore,
we can say that k has a noright that j does A iff j is permitted, towards
k, to omit A. Let us make an example both for privileges and norights.
Assume for instance that Mary, a writer, has made a contract with
Tom, a publisher, and has committed herself to write a novel for him.
Mary's privilege would consist in the Mary having permission towards
Tom not to write the novel, a normative situation which could also be
described as Tom's noright that Mary writes the novel.

Positive and negative permissions, as showed in Figure 5, are merged into the concept of *faculty* (for instance, by saying that a woman has the faculty of wearing a miniskirt when going to work, we mean that it is permitted both to wear it and not to wear it).

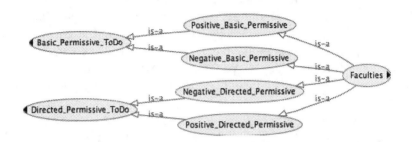

Figure 5. A taxonomy of faculties

When, for the benefit of a person, this person is both permitted to perform and to omit an action – that is, when the action is facultative – we can say that he or she has a *liberty right* with regard to that action. This notion can be further developed according to the fact that others (or the government) may have, always in the interest of that person, a prohibition to prevent the facultative action, and they may even have the obligation to provide means for its performance. This leads us to distinguish three kinds of liberty rights: a mere liberty right, a negatively protected liberty right, and a positively protected liberty right.

In general we speak of a right to characterise the situation where a normative judgement is intended to benefit a particular person.

According to this notion of a right, the directed obligations of agent j for the benefit of agent k can be viewed as k's right, namely as k's obligative right towards j. The negation of a directed obligation is a directed permission. However, it counts as a right, namely, a *permissive right*, only when such negation is aimed at benefitting the author of the permitted action.

Another notion of a right is that of *liability rights*. That j has a liability right concerning k's action A means that if k performs the permitted action A then k will have to perform another action B for the benefit of j. For example, consider a copyright regime when one is permitted to reproduce a protected work, but the author is entitled to a royalty for the reproduction of his or her work. In this case we have a normative connection between a permitted action and an obligation of the agent, to the benefit of another.

However for us this kind of legal position represents a conditional, namely, a norm, rather than a normative judgement.

1.1.2. *Potestative judgements*

Potestative judgements concern the attribution of powers. The first level of our classification (see Figure 6) includes the categories *Hohfeldian powers, enabling powers* and *declarative powers*: the first covers any action which determines a legal effect, the second only cases when the law aims at enabling the agent to produce the effects in this way, the third the case when the effect is produced through the party's declaration of it.

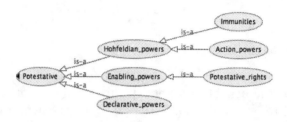

Figure 6. A taxonomy of potestative judgements

In more detail we say that **j** has the declarative power to realize **A** to mean that if **j** declares **A**, then it is legally valid that **A**. For example, if **x** has the declarative power to terminate **y**'s obligation towards **x** to do then if **x** declares that **y**'s obligation towards **x** finishes, then it is legally valid that this obligation finishes.

The second Hohfeldian square includes immunities, action powers, subjections (the normative position that Hohfeld denotes as liability), and disabilities.

Immunities. **k** has an immunity towards **j** with regard to the creation of position **Pos** in the head of **k**, exactly if is not the case that **j** has that power.

Action powers. An action-power consists in a generic power to produce a legal effect through an action determining it.

Subjections. That **k** is in a state of subjection towards **j**, with regard to normative position **Pos**, means that **j** has the abstract enabling-power of determining **Pos** in the head of **k**. For instance, debtor **k** is subject to creditor **j** in relation to **j**'s power of freeing **k** from **j**'s obligation.

Disabilities. **j** has a disability towards **k**, with regard to the creation of position **Pos** exactly if it is not the case that **j** has the abstract enabling power of creating **Pos** in the head of **x**.

A special kind of enabling powers, called *potestative rights*, can be distinguished, that is powers which are meant to benefit the holder of the power. For example, if **y** does not belong to anybody, then **x** has the potestative-right to start **x**'s ownership of the animal, by capturing **y**.

1.2. OTHER POSSIBLE CLASSIFICATIONS

Our model does not exhaust all possible classifications of norms and of their components. For instance we could consider the antecedents of conditioned norms, and introduce the traditional classification between juridical fact, acts (facts relevantly determined by humans), and declarations of will or intentions.

In this way we might also characterise the notion of a *source of law*, by which we mean any fact that embeds normative propositions and makes them legally valid by virtue of such an embedment. Some sources of the law are events (like the issuing of a high court decision), while others are state of affairs (like the practice of a custom or a result declaration).

1.3. NORMS

Norms are propositions stating normative judgements. Norms can be unconditioned, that is their judgement may not depend upon any antecedent condition (consider, for example. the norm "everyone has the right to express his or her opinion"). Usually, however, norms are conditioned. We distinguish conditioned norms into *rules*, which make a normative judgement dependent upon defeasibly sufficient conditions or *factor links*, which make a normative judgement dependent upon contributory conditions.

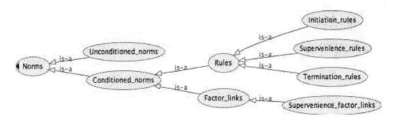

Figure 7. A taxonomy of norms

As showed in Figure 7 rules can be distinguished in:

- *initiation rules*, that is, rules stating that a certain normative proposition starts to hold when the rule's conditions are satisfied. An example is "if one causes a damage, one has to compensate it";

— *termination rules*, that is, rules stating that a normative proposition ceases to hold when the rule's conditions are satisfied. An example is "if one pays a debt, the obligation terminates";

— *supervenience rules*, that is, rules stating that a normative proposition holds as long as the conditions are satisfied. An example is "if one is in a public office, one is forbidden to smoke".

As we said factor-links make a normative judgement dependent upon contributory conditions: in this case the condition favours the judgement, but it does not determine it, not even defeasibly. It seems to us that factor links usually are of the supervenience kind, and thus we will include only this option in our ontology. For example "if a work has educational values, this favours the conclusion that it is covered by free use" is a supervenience factor link since the conclusion is favoured while the condition (the work has educational values) holds.

2. The Ontology Structure

Besides taxonomy, an OWL ontology usually provides a description of concepts in terms of classes and properties (Noy and McGuinness, 2001). The word concept is sometimes used in place of class. Classes are a concrete representation of concepts. Therefore, all the concepts examined in the previous section constitute classes organized into a superclass-subclass hierarchy (the taxonomy) already described. Subclasses specialise ('are subsumed by') their superclasses. For example, as depicted in Figure 1, the `Norms` class and the `Normative judgements` class are subclasses of the `Thing` class that is the class which contains everything (everything is a thing).

Features or attributes of a class are called its properties and normally, because of inheritance, properties are defined for the highest class in the hierarchy to which they apply. The *domain* of a property is the class of objects the property can be applied to, while the *range* defines the values the property can take. In OWL, a clear distinction is made between two types of properties (Antoniou and van Harmelen, 2004): `owl:ObjectProperty`, which relate objects to other objects, and `owl:DatatypeProperty`, which relate objects to datatype values.

The `conditioned_by` property is an `owl:DatatypeProperty` because the domain is the `Conditioned norms` class and the range is the `xsd:String` class.

All other properties are instead `owl:ObjectProperty` and they are:

— the `state` property;

```
<owl:DatatypeProperty rdf:ID="conditioned_by">
  <rdfs:range rdf:resource="http://www.w3.org/2001/XMLSchema#string"/>
  <rdfs:domain rdf:resource="Conditioned_norms"/>
</owl:DatatypeProperty>
```

Figure 8. The `conditioned_by` property

- the `exercised_through` property;

- the `power_holder` property;

- the `concerned` property;

- the `bearer` property;

- the `towards` property.

The `state` property is derived from the definition of norm that is 'Norms state normative judgements'. Indeed, the `Norms` class is the domain and the `Normative judgements` class is the range.

```
<owl:ObjectProperty rdf:ID="state">
  <rdfs:range rdf:resource="Normative_judgements"/>
  <rdfs:domain rdf:resource="Norms"/>
</owl:ObjectProperty>
```

Figure 9. The `state` property

The `exercised_through` property describes the action through which the power is exercised. The `power_holder` is the agent who performs this action. While the `Potestative judgements` class is the domain of both the `power_holder` and the `exercised_through` property, the range is different. Indeed, the `power_holder` property has the `Agents` class as range and `exercised_through` property has the `Actions`[5] class as range.

```
<owl:ObjectProperty rdf:ID="exercised_through">
  <rdfs:range rdf:resource="Actions"/>
  <rdfs:domain rdf:resource="Potestative"/>
  <rdf:type rdf:resource="http://www.w3.org/2002/07/owl#FunctionalProperty"/>
</owl:ObjectProperty>
```

Figure 10. The `exercised_through` property

---

[5] We assume that the `Agents` and the `Actions` class are imported from some top ontology.

```
<owl:FunctionalProperty rdf:ID="power_holder">
  <rdfs:domain rdf:resource="Potestative"/>
  <rdfs:range rdf:resource="Agents"/>
  <rdf:type rdf:resource="http://www.w3.org/2002/07/owl#ObjectProperty"/>
</owl:FunctionalProperty>
```

Figure 11. The `power_holder` property

Similarly to the potestative judgements, we defined two properties for the deontic modalities concerning actions: the `concerned` and the `bearer` properties.

The `concerned` property describes the action permitted or obligatory which is performed by an agent called `bearer`. The domain of the `concerned` property and the `bearer` property is the union of four classes: the `Basic Obligative ToDo` class, the `Directed Obligative ToDo` class, the `Basic Permissive ToDo` class and the `Directed Permissive ToDo` class. The range is the `Agents` class for the `bearer` property and the `Actions` class for the `concerned` property.

```
<owl:FunctionalProperty rdf:ID="concerned">
  <rdfs:range rdf:resource="Actions"/>
  <rdf:type rdf:resource="http://www.w3.org/2002/07/owl#ObjectProperty"/>
  <rdfs:domain>
    <owl:Class>
      <owl:unionOf rdf:parseType="Collection">
        <owl:Class rdf:about="Basic_Obligative_ToDo"/>
        <owl:Class rdf:about="Directed_Obligative_ToDo"/>
        <owl:Class rdf:about="Basic_Permissive_ToDo"/>
        <owl:Class rdf:about="Directed_Permissive_ToDo"/>
      </owl:unionOf>
    </owl:Class>
  </rdfs:domain>
</owl:FunctionalProperty>
```

Figure 12. The `concerned` property

Finally, the `towards` property describes the beneficiary of directed deontic normative judgement. The domain, in this case, is represented by the `Directed Obligative` class and the `Directed Permissive` class while the range is represented by the `Agents` class. This property also enables to represent the distinction between individualised deontic qualification and erga-omnes deontic qualification through the values assigned to the property `towards`, which will concern individually named agent in the case of individualised judgements, and the all agents in the case of erga-omnes judgements.

For each property can be defined relational characteristics such as functionality, inverse functionality, symmetry and transitivity. If some

```
<owl:FunctionalProperty rdf:ID="bearer">
  <rdf:type rdf:resource="http://www.w3.org/2002/07/owl#ObjectProperty"/>
  <rdfs:range rdf:resource="Agents"/>
  <rdfs:domain>
    <owl:Class>
      <owl:unionOf rdf:parseType="Collection">
        <owl:Class rdf:about="Basic_Obligative_ToDo"/>
        <owl:Class rdf:about="Directed_Obligative_ToDo"/>
        <owl:Class rdf:about="Basic_Permissive_ToDo"/>
        <owl:Class rdf:about="Directed_Permissive_ToDo"/>
      </owl:unionOf>
    </owl:Class>
  </rdfs:domain>
</owl:FunctionalProperty>
```

Figure 13. The `bearer` property

```
<owl:ObjectProperty rdf:ID="towards">
  <rdfs:domain>
    <owl:Class>
      <owl:unionOf rdf:parseType="Collection">
        <owl:Class rdf:about="Directed_Obligative"/>
        <owl:Class rdf:about="Directed_Permissive"/>
      </owl:unionOf>
    </owl:Class>
  </rdfs:domain>
  <rdfs:range rdf:resource="Agents"/>
  <rdf:type rdf:resource="http://www.w3.org/2002/07/owl#FunctionalProperty"/>
</owl:ObjectProperty>
```

Figure 14. The `towards` property

property links value a to value b then its inverse property will link value b to value a. If a property is inverse functional then it means that the inverse property is functional. Functional properties are also known as single valued properties and also features. If a property P is transitive, and the property relates value a to value b, and also value b to value c, then we can infer that value a is related to value c via property P. If a property P is symmetric, and the property relates value a to value b then value b is also related to value a via property P.

The `exercised_through` property and the `concerned` property are functional because the action involved is only one. The `power_holder` property, the `bearer` property and the `towards` property are functional because the agent which perform the action or the beneficiary are single agents.

Properties may be enriched with other facets which will be considered in future work.

3. Conclusion and Future work

The ontology presented in this paper represents the first attempt of classifying such type of legal concepts. In the literature, ontologies such as LRI-core examine top concepts such as action, intention, social role, legal action, normative article, and so on. Other ontologies are instead too specific since they consider specific legal domains such as, for example, the intellectual property rights (IPROnto (Delgado et al, 2003)).

In future work we intend to extend the ontology by importing core and top ontologies for main legal concepts and for all the modifications that a norm may have in the time (norms concerning judgements). Moreover, class properties will be specified in more detail as regards disjointedness or equivalence among classes, property cardinality, property restrictions and default values for properties.

Finally, the problems of the expressive power of OWL in representing concepts usually described by using logic formalisms will be analyzed.

Acknowledgements

The work reported here has been partially financed also by the EU projects IST-2004-027968 ALIS, MEXC-2005-024063 ONE-LEX.

References

Antoniou, G. and van Harmelen, F. A Semantic Web Primer *MIT Press*, 2004.

Delgado, J., Gallego, I., Llorente, S. and Garcia, R. IPROnto: An Ontology for Digital Rights Management. 16th Annual Conference on Legal Knowledge and Information Systems, JURIX 2003. *Frontiers in Artificial Intelligence and Applications*, Vol. 106, IOS Press, 2003.

Hohfeld, W. N. 1913. Some Fundamental Legal Conceptions as Applied in Judicial Reasoning. I. Yale Law Journal 23: 16–59.

Hohfeld, W. N.. 1917. Some Fundamental Legal Conceptions as Applied in Judicial Reasoning. II. Yale Law Journal 26: 710–770.

Noy, N. F. and McGuinness, D. L. Ontology Development 101: A Guide to Creating Your First Ontology. Stanford Knowledge Systems Laboratory Technical Report KSL-01-05 and Stanford Medical Informatics Technical Report SMI-2001-0880, March 2001.

Sartor, G. Legal Reasoning: A Cognitive Approach to the Law. *Springer*, Part. 1. Legal Reasoning and Legal Rationality, pp. 1-385: Part. II. Legal Logic, pp. 397–792. Bibliography and references: pp. 793–844.

Sartor, G. Fundamental Legal Concepts: A Teleological Characterisation. *Artificial Intelligence and Law*, to be published.

Smith, M. K., Welty, C. and McGuinness, D. L.   OWL Web Ontology Language Guide. W3C Recommendation 10 February 2004. http://www.w3.org/TR/2004/REC-owl-guide-20040210/

The Lois Project: Lexical Ontologies for Legal Information Sharing

Daniela Tiscornia

Institute of Legal Information Theory and Techniques - Italian National Research Council

Abstract. Semantic metadata are expected to support search engines for legal information retrieval, providing legal knowledge to include into their search strategies. In a wide meaning, semantic metadata are 'all kind of information describing a resource'; this paper focuses on a strict notion of semantic metadata, meaning 'information about content', i.e. 'what the resource is about'. In general standard frameworks such as Dublin Core, this kind of information is expressed by the metadata 'Subject', which carries at least one preferred term from lexical resources as controlled vocabularies or encoding schemes, which are usually defined as hierarchies of terms, usually lacking a purely defined semantics. Starting from an European project recently concluded, this paper presents a methodology for building a multilingual semantic lexicon for law, featuring lexically and legally grounded conceptual representations, to be used either as a source of semantic metadata and as an external tool for cross lingual retrieval. The role played by semantic resources, such as lexical and formal ontologies in improving real access to legal information is analysed and the problems encountered in the methodological steps are outlined.

Keywords: Standards for legal documents, Semantic metadata, Legal ontologies

1. Access to legal content

1.1. THE ROLE OF SEMANTIC METADATA

In many countries public institutions have promoted projects aimed at improving the availability of Public Sector information on the Web and the free access of 'institutional' information. In the specific field of legal information there is a further need to join practical/technical solutions for accessing legal information[1] with a further 'social' perspective of allowing citizen to access in an 'understandable' way legal, mainly legislative data.

Today conceptual search strategies based on keywords are still missing a clear semantics of terms, and this does not allow a conceptual query expansion; therefore, there is no semantic relationship between information needs of the user and the information content of documents, apart from text pattern matching. It is necessary, therefore, to explicit

---

[1] Greenleaf G., *Solving the Problems of Finding Law on the Web: World Law and DIAL, 2000(1) The Journal of Information, Law and Technology (JILT).*

the semantic aspects carefully so that the search is driven by a meta-description, expressed trough semantic metadata, which keeps univocal references to the text, since the non-expert user has no precise idea of what he is looking for, and uses general terms of common language rather than specific legal concepts.

Semantic metadata are expected to support search engines for legal information retrieval, providing legal knowledge to include into their search strategies. In a wide meaning, semantic metadata are 'all kind of information describing a resource': this paper focuses on a strict notion of semantic metadata referring to 'information about content', i.e.: *what the resource is about.* In general standard frameworks such as Dublin Core, this kind of information is expressed by the metadata *Subject,* which carries at least one preferred term from sources as controlled vocabularies or encoding schemes, usually defined as hierarchies of terms, usually lacking a purely defined semantics. A descriptive model of contents may point out both the typologies of regulative functions and the categories of the addressees, and it would allow to overcome linguistic barriers[2].

Building a semantic lexicon for law is not a trivial task, as legal conceptual knowledge is closely related to language use within the legal domain, and therefore, there is, as in other terminological domains, a relatively high level of dependence between legal concepts and their linguistic realization in the various forms of legal language. The problem is even more evident in cross lingual retrieval, where corresponding terms are often absent in different languages but equivalent concepts exist in legal systems.

1.2. LEGAL LANGUAGE AND LEGAL KNOWLEDGE

When examining the legal vocabulary, we encounter two different types of semantic information associated with elements from legal text. On the one hand, there is the ontological structuring in the form of a conceptual model of the legal domain; on the other hand, there is a vocabulary of lexical items that lexicalize concepts (a lexicon), which are not necessarily restricted to the legal domain, and are associated with specific linguistic information (e.g. nouns versus verbs and syntactic preference). Therefore the conceptual model that provides the necessary structure to build a semantic lexicon needs to be integrated by a domain model so as to reflect the peculiarities of the legal domain.

---

[2] Visser P., Bench Capon T, *Ontologies in the Design of Legal Knowledge Systems; towards a Library of Legal Domain Ontologies,* Proceedings of Jurix Conference, 2000.

Law and language are connected in many ways (Sacco 2000). First of all, they have a *similar structure*: each has, at its essence, rules which are constitutive of a system and which ensure its consistency. A second aspect is the *dependency* of law on language, since regulatory knowledge must be communicated, and the written and oral transmission of social or legal rules passes through verbal expression.

In addition, legal language, like legal knowledge, has a *multi-layered structure:* according to Kalinowsky (1965), it consists of the *language of Law* and *language of Jurists*. The former is the language in which legal rules are written: not any linguistic expression in a legal text is a legal term, but every legal term is a linguistic expression. The latter is a meta-language. It is composed of a) the "judge's language" in case law, used to speak about legal rules and about persons and behaviours bounded by legal rules; b) the "language of jurisprudence"(legal literature and legal theory), which puts legal language and judicial interpretation into concepts, to make the structure of the system consistent and systematic[3].

2. Tools: lexical and formal ontologies

2.1. FRON THESAURI TO ONTOLOGIES

Restricted vocabularies are usually defined as hierarchies of terms: "The types of vocabulary for which software tools should provide support include thesauri conforming to ISO 2788, classification schemes of various types, subject heading lists, taxonomies (typically combining the hierarchical properties of classification schemes with the reciprocal relationships and other features of thesauri) and simple authority lists. [...] While a taxonomy is designed to classify things, a thesaurus is designed to help you find the right words or phrases to describe what you are ultimately looking for[4]."

Ontologies are designed to allow computers to really interact with each other, covering all semantic metadata in its wider meaning(e.g.: publication date, authors of paper, journal publishers, publication date, normative references, etc.). On one hand, ontologies can be machine generated from good metadata; on the other, here exposed, good ontologies can enrich semantic metadata.

---

[3] A good example is "negozio giuridico" (juridical act): the term never appears in Italian Legislation, but is crucial in contract law to distinguish contracts from other classes of legal acts.

[4] e-Government Unit of the UK Cabinet Office, Tomatoes are not the only fruit: a rough guide to taxonomies, thesauri, ontologies and the like, April 2005. (http://www.govtalk.gov.uk/schemasstandards/metadata.asp)

One relevant aspect to take in account is the *legacy* problem, as there are several semantic resources already used and distributed over the Internet, and a large amount of legal data (for instance, all the EU documents) already classified according to available thesauri and classification schemes. Re-using and harmonizing existing resources within *a reference ontology* requires to increase the precision of the semantics of the existing relations in thesauri (see sect. 4.1).

In the following it will be described the methodology for the development of a semantic framework that can be used as an extensible and flexible thesaurus in monolingual information retrieval but also as a most complex and rich *reference ontology* for concepts equivalence setting in multilingual environments and for legal knowledge conceptualization.

The building steps will be outlined according to:

— the conceptual model for building a semantic lexicon

— the ontological layers and the role of formal ontologies

— the resources harmonization

— the use of the semantic framework in knowledge representation

2.2. Formal ontologies, semantic lexicons

A formal ontology can be considered a theory about several views (i.e. models) of reality. Formal ontologies have a multi-layered structure: *foundational ontologies* contain domain-independent concepts, relations and meta-properties, which provide ontology builders with a formal semantics, that is, formal ontological distinctions to categorize entities in a domain. A *domain ontology* is populated by concepts, relations and instances extracted in a bottom-up fashion from the domain and consistent with the top-down formal semantics imposed by the upper ontology. In complex domains such as the legal one, a *core ontology* is part of a layered architecture which intends to bridge the gaps between domain-specific concepts and the abstract categories of upper ontologies; it also expresses the basic concepts that are common across a variety of domains, providing a global and extensible model into which data originating from distinct sources or different vocabularies can be mapped and integrated (Doerr et al., 2003).

Semantic lexicons are means for content management which can provide a rich semantic repository Compared to formal ontologies, semantic lexicons, also called *lightweight ontologies*, are generic and based on a weak abstraction model, since the elements (classes, properties, and individuals) of the ontology depend primarily on the acceptance of existing lexical entries. In a lexical ontology, such as WordNet (Fellbaum, 1998), many of the hyper/hyponymy links might be logically inconsistent, as it was designed as a lexical resource and constraints over relations and consistency are ruled by the grammatical distinctions of language.

3. The conceptual model

The multilingual lexicon here presented is currently composed by about 35.000 concepts in five European languages. (English, German, Portuguese, Czech, and Italian, linked by English); it has been created within the European funded project LOIS (Legal Ontologies for Knowledge Sharing, EDC 22161, 2003-2006[5]) extending in a multilingual dimension a semantic lexicon for the Italian legal language, the Jur-WordNet data base.

The methodology is based on an existing de facto standard, the WordNet and EuroWord Net resources, WordNet (Fellbaum 1998) is a lexical database which has been under constant development at Princeton University. EuroWordNet (EWN) (Vossen et al., 1997) is a multilingual lexical database with wordnets for eight European languages, which are structured along the same lines as the Princeton word net (see www.globalwordnet.org).

The conceptual model makes a clear separation between a concept (meaning) and its lexicalizations (words). More precisely:

- each concept is expressed by one or more linguistic expressions (single or multi words) in the same language or in different languages;

- each word can have variant forms (singular, plural, tenses in verbs, abbreviations, etc.);

- each word can have more than one sense, i.e. can express more than one concept. Each *word sense* express one concept only.

In terms of the WordNet framework, a concept is a *synset*, the atomic unit of the semantic net. A synset is a set of one or more uninflected word forms (lemmas) with the same part-of-speech (noun, verb, adjective, and adverb) that can be interchanged in a certain context. For example, {*action, trial, proceedings, law suit*} form a noun synset because they can be used to refer to the same concept. More precisely

---

[5] www.loisproject.org

each synset is a set of *wordsenses*. A synset is often further described
by a gloss, explaining the meaning of the concept. English glosses drive
cross-lingual linking. Synsets are linked on the basis of the following
relations:

Monolingual relations

— words are linked by *lexical* relations: synonymy (included in the notion of synset and rare in the legal lexicon), near-synonym, antonym,
  derivation[6]

— concepts (Synsets) can be related to each other by *semantic* relations, of which the most important are *hypernymy/hyponymy*
  (between specific and more general concepts), meronymy (between
  parts or wholes), thematic *role* (between noun (agent) and verb or
  event- denoting nouns (actions), *instance-of*;

— synsets in the National Legal WN are (or shall be) linked by *gener-
  alization/specialization* relations to the general language modules,
  developed within the *EuroWordNet Project*.

Cross-lingual equivalence relations are made explicit in the so-called
Inter-Lingual-Index (ILI). Each synset in the monolingual wordnets
is linked by equivalence relation with an English synset, which is a
record in the ILI. These relations indicate *complete equivalence, near
equivalence,* or *equivalence as a hyponym* or *hypernym*. The network
of equivalence relations (see fig.1) determines the interconnectivity of
the indigenous wordnets. Language-specific synsets from different languages linked to the same ILI-record by means of a synonym relation
are considered conceptually equivalent.

3.1. THE DOMAIN MODEL

To take into account the distinction between sources of law, in creating the semantic resource, a first nucleus of pilot concepts has been
selected at the general level of doctrine conceptualization, offering a
consolidated reference structure and allowing greater sharing. Concepts,
imported from the Italian legal WordNet (JurWordNet, Tiscornia at al.,
2004) have been identified within the frequency list of Italian Legislation corpus. Their selection was based on the assessment of experts.
Descriptions (glosses) were extracted from legal handbooks.

---

[6] Lexical relation are ruled by Part of Speech (POS) constraints (e.g. synonym
and antonym holds between synset pertaining to the same POS, derivation holds
between noun/verb and adjectives).

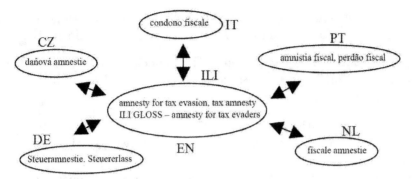

Figure 1. Example of cross lingual link through the ILI

In the second step the emphasis was put on the detection of legislative terminology, i.e. terminology that is specific to the legal domain, as opposed to the abstract conceptualization (often of common sense concepts) above. In order to identify this legislative knowledge, a parallel corpus derived from the European Directives in the consumer law domain was taken into account. Semi-automatic alignment techniques enabled the selection of a multilingual set of legal terms and the automatic generation of a unique *Identifier*. Automatic extraction of legal concepts from national legislation is limited to the consumer law domain.

A further notion of *legal concept* and proper *legal relations* had been added to the conceptual model described above:

- Legal terms were only selected if they had an explicit definition in the text: each definition is assumed to create a *(new) legal concept*.

- Once alignment had been established, *legal equivalence* was assumed and each set of corresponding terms in different languages were automatically linked to one unique identifier.

- an additional legal relation *implemented_ as* defines the link between a European legal concept and its implementation in national legislation.

- As to legal concepts from European legislation, the *Identifier* acts as the Interlingual Index item.

The interrelation between EU and national concepts represents a special case of intra-lingual inter-modular equivalence relation, even if carried out at a mono-lingual level.

According to the two building approaches described, the main module of each national WordNet is composed of:

- an indigenous *lexical data base*, which conceptualizes general language entities pertaining to legal theory and legal dogmatic,

- a *legislative data base,* populated by concepts defined in European and national legislation and structured according to purely legal (supra) national models.

Taxonomic relations can span across the different modules (esp. lexical and national legal) which form a LOIS WordNet: legal concepts (i.e. concepts defined within legal texts) can have hypernyms - as well as near-synonyms - in the lexical database, as legal terms bear specialised meanings which might be different from the meaning of the same words within general language.

With respect to legal concepts from national legislation, the ILI can be automatically generated. If a legal concept from a European directive is implemented in indigenous legislation, and the local legal concepts are deemed (legally) equivalent to their European counterparts, then an equivalence relation between the two local concepts may also be established. In all other cases, the creation of semantic links between local synsets does not necessarily imply the creation of equivalence relations with the ILI, except when concepts from more than one indigenous WordNet coincide, in which case these will all be related to one ILI record. Within this architecture, the semantic structures peculiar to each WordNet will be preserved, and will overlap through the ILI.

External ontologies such as the DOLCE2.1-Lite-Plus + CLO (Gangemi et al., 2005) will structure the ILI concepts, classifying concepts according to explicit and consistent subsumption relations. The ontological level acts as an external ordering principle and subsumption of upper level synset have been manually performed without formalizing conceptual relations derived from legal texts. This external structure supports the management of the semantic/equivalence relations via the ILI in the integration of legislative and lexical/common sense knowledge (see figure 2 for a simplified view on the database structure).

3.1.1. *The role of external ontologies: polysemy disambiguation*
One of the most interesting functions of wordnets (which is usually missing in traditional thesauri) is the disambiguation of *polysemy*. Polysemy (one term has more than one meaning) is expressed by *wordsense* numbering and by the association of one synset to each sense of a polysemic word. As an example, the Italian synset *ordine* (order) has several senses:

ordine_ 1, a command given either in speech or writing by a person or body having the authority to do so;

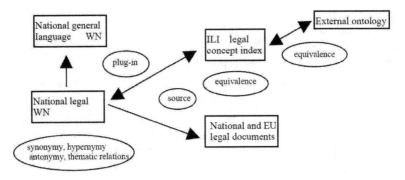

Figure 2. The overall architecture of Lois

ordine_ 2, a group of persons or things which form a separate/independent category, because they share a condition or some particular characteristics;

ordine_ 3, arrangement of separate elements according to specific criteria.

Legal polisemy

A further notion of polisemy detection, implied by the assumption of the constitutive role of legislative definitions is the consistent distinction of degrees of equivalence between contexts in which the word occurs.

The most common situation is the 'apparent polisemy' generated by the integration of the legal and lexical databases, because meanings of the legal concepts are usually more specific than the meanings of corresponding lexical items, and legal senses can display degrees of ontological overlap or even taxonomic ordering. The lexical sense can be considered to be a prototypical description of the concept properties, over which the legislator's definition impose constraint, and therefore it is classified as a hypernym of all legal senses. For instance, from EU Legislation texts, four senses of 'worker' are defined:

worker-1, any worker as defined in Article 3 (a) of Directive 89/391/EEC who habitually uses display screen equipment as a significant part of his normal work.

worker-2, any person employed by an employer, including trainees and apprentices but excluding domestic servants;

worker-3, any person carrying out an occupation on board a vessel, including trainees and apprentices, but excluding port pilots and shore personnel carrying out work on board a vessel at the quayside;

worker-4, any person who, in the Member State concerned, is protected as an employee under national employment law and in accordance with national practice.

The corresponding lexical entry is defined in the lexical part as follows: "a *person who works at a specific occupation*".

Systematic polysemy

Often, sense distinctions do not only concern the history of language, but also interdependent notions used in organizing social reality. For instance, a typical systematic polysemy is that between an institution, a function, and a physical object: the entry *President of the Republic* can indicate a physical person, the constitutional body, or the holder of the state function. Another example, very common in Law, is the systematic polysemy involving both a normative content and a physical entity: the entry *contract* may be conceptualized as a legal transaction, as a physical document, or as an information object. The entry *appeal* can express the sense of a *petition* made to a Judge, and the *written document* of that petition. The entry *office* can express the function and the physical place where the function takes place.

While semantic lexicons can represent simple polysemy, the systematic relations occurring between the different senses cannot be expressed. Rich axiomatic theories like a Core Legal Ontology provide the needed relations to account for systematic polysemy, for example a legal transaction (e.g. the content of a contract) is *expressed* by an information object (e.g. the linguistic encoding of the content of a contract), which is *realized* by a legal document (e.g. the physical object realizing the encoding of the contract). (Gangemi, Guarino et al. 2002).

Separate classes from instances

Ontological characterization also helps the separation of classes from instances. For example, "competent authority" in the EU Directive on data protection is a class; the "*garante per la protezione dei dati personali*" in Italian legislation and the "*Agencia de Proteccion de Dato*" in Spanish legislation are instances. From a multilingual point of view, ontological classes might be even used to enhance comparison between different legal systems, by grouping similar national instantiations of a given class (e.g. the Italian "Camera dei Deputati" and the English "House of Commons" as instances of the ontological class "legal institutions") which might not – due to the *country-dependence* of the legal domain – be perfect equivalents

3.1.2. *Formal consistency checking*

A stronger role formal ontologies could play is to check the consistency of the hierarchical structure and to distinguish language-independent concepts and relations from concepts and relations which are not; in legal term: the *core legal ontology* separates entities/concepts which belong to the general theory of law from concepts proper of national legal systems It intends also to bridge the gap between domain-specific concepts and the abstract categories of formal upper level or foundational ontologies such as DOLCE (Gangemi et al. 2002), transforming lexical relations in formal properties consistent with the top-down formal semantics imposed by the upper ontology.

To check formal consistency checking, all ontologies must be expressed in the same formal language; therefore each lexical resource has been translated in OWL format, according to the word net RDF/OWL Standard approved by the W3C Consortium (working draft June 2006). The word net schema is composed by three main classes:

- Synset: each synset is an instance belonging to one of four disjoint sub-classes (nouns, verbs, adjective and adverbs)

- wordsense: each Wordsens belong to exactly one synset

- word: each Word can be related to one or more wordsenses

Relations between synsets (including Hyponym) and relations between Wordsenses are interpreted as properties. The upper level synsets are linked by sub-class relations to the imported CLO and Dolce ontological classes, thus allowing an ontology-based consistency-checking performed by an external 'reasoner'. Some examples of the results are given below.

The main entities in DOLCE (and consequently in CLO, Core Legal Ontology) are axiomatized, disjoint classes, characterized by meta properties, such as Identity, Unity and Rigidity. As for CLO, the most relevant distinction is between *Roles* (anti-rigid) and *Types*, which are rigid. For example, every instance of a role (e.g. *student, plaintiff, guilty*) can possibly be a non student, not guilty, etc. without loosing its identity. Every instance of a type (e.g. a person) must be a person. A type can play more roles at the same time. For instance, a legal subject (either a natural or artificial person) can be an owner, a tax-payer, or a murderer. In the CLO taxonomy, roles cannot subsume types, and therefore lexical concepts that are anchored to roles should not have hyponyms pertaining to types.

The core ontology also refines automatically created relations from English/ ILI records to lexicon as shown in the examples below:

- *consumer is a* person, *is a* living thing, *is a* physical entity in WN; *is a* social role, *is a* non physical entity in CLO;

- *lease is a* is a contract, *is a* communication, *is a* an abstraction in WN; *is a* contract, *is a* social description, *is a* social concept in CLO.

4. Expanding the lexicon

All over the Lois project development, various methodologies have been applied to populate and structure the lexicon, of which the following are the most important:

- Manual expert translation of a selected bootstrapping set of existing synsets in the Italian legal WordNet (JurWN);

- Manual creation of legal synsets on the basis of authoritative resources;

- Automatic extraction of explicitly defined concepts from legislative text (national and EU);

- Automatic extraction of significant lexical elements from legal text;

- Mapping lexical concepts onto the English WordNet and adopting its hierarchies;

To further expand the domain coverage, a bottom-up strategy will be integrated with a top-down validation. The bottom approach will be based on:

- Automatic extraction of domain concepts and dynamic integration

- Importing and harmonizing existing resources

- Axiomatizing legal definitions

In this context we will focus on the integration of external semantic resources within the structure. This requires the transformation of traditional thesauri into ontologies.

4.1. INTEGRATION WITH TRADITIONAL THESAURI

The most prominent EU thesaurus is *Eurovoc*, a multilingual thesaurus, structured as a set of independent hierarchical trees with inter-lingual relations. To import the Eurovoc *descriptors* (and *non- descriptors*) into the semantic lexicon the Thesaurus relations (*Broader Term, Narrower Term, Used For, Related Term*) will be translated in the WordNet semantic relations.

Tab. I shows the correspondence table.

Form a thesaurus to a WordNet lexicon, relations can be automatically translated; further manual refinements will remove misleading taxonomies, will separate instances from classes and will give a more

Table I. shows the correspondence table

Eurovoc relations	Wordnet relations	*Dolce+CLO properties*
NT/BT	Hyponym/hyper/nym, instance_of, meronym	sub-class-of, instance_of, part-of, member_of
UF	*each term in a synse*	same_as
RT	role, cause	*ontological formal properties*

connotation to the generic *Related term* relation. For instance, see in the figure 3, part of the Eurovoc microthesaurus on *ownership*.

In the taxonomy, *ownership law* (the rules regulating ownership) and *ownership right* (the normative position) are considered synonym; *acquisition of property, division of property, easement, expropriation,* etc. are narrower terms but not proper hyponyms (but legal *events* affecting the normative position of the owner); *land and building* are objects of possession; *law of succession* is hyponym of *ownership law*, but not of *ownership right*.

To achieve a more precise and explicit representation of terms, each descriptor must be assigned to an ontological class and proper relation

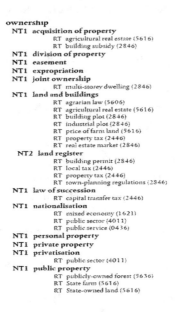

Figure 3. Eurovoc Thesaurus.

must be defined over the ontological classes; to give an example (Tab. II):

Table II.

Onto-class	Concept t(synset)	properties/ relations	Onto-class
Agent (physical agent/ social individual)	natural person, organization, company	*participant_in*	Event/process
Role	owner	*played_by*	Agent
Event/process		*regulated-by*	norm
Event/process	acquisition of property division of property easement expropriation	*affects*	Normative Position/Institutional fact
Normative Position/ Institutional fact	right of pre-emption	*dependent-on*	norm
norm	law of succession	*defines*	role, social individual

The resulting organization is shown in table III.

5. Conclusions

In this paper we have described theoretical, practical and structural aspects of the LOIS multilingual legal knowledge base. This legal knowledge repository contains legal terminology from national and European legislation within the domain of consumer law. It also holds significant lexical, general language concepts that occur in the legal documents. These concepts are interlinked within each language and between languages by means of an extended set of EWN relations.

The structure of the LOIS database allows a user to perform a concept based search for monolingual and cross-lingual legal information retrieval, which uses keywords obtained from query expansion through the structured hierarchies of the legal wordnets and the equivalence relations with the ILI.

Furthermore, the LOIS architecture will allow users to investigate a wide range of legal research issues, such as the comparison of national legal systems through translation, equivalence and ontological structure

Table III.

	ownership, right of accession	
sub-class	personal property joint ownership, private property, public property, real property	sub-class
affected_ by	transfer of property, time-sharing, access to property, privatisation nationalisation, usufruct	gift inheritance
has_ object	land and buildings	agricultural real estate
regulated_ by	law of property, property law, system of property law of succession right of pre-emption	
participant	owner, seller, buyer, landlord, heres	

across the different legal wordnets, the investigation of relations between EU and national legislative documents, and an empirical inventory of the differences between common language meaning and legal meaning. The structure of the LOIS database enhances the interoperability of multilingual legal data, and allows the incremental integration of additional legal information. The role of top-level formal ontology is fundamental in this process. This ontological level not only reinforces the existing structure (polysemy detection, ILI structuring, etc.), but also assists the automatic integration of the database through ontology-building techniques.

In conclusion, the LOIS knowledge base provides a flexible, modular architecture that allows integration of multiple classification schemes, and enables their transformation in enriched semantic metadata.

References

Doerr, M., Hunter, J., Lagoze, C., (2003) Towards a Core Ontology for Information Integration, in Journal of Digital Information, Volume 4 Issue 1, 2003

Fellbaum, C. (ed.) (1998). *WordNet: An Electronic Lexical Database.* MIT Press, Cambridge, Mass.

Gangemi, A., Guarino, N., Masolo, C., Oltramari, A., Schneider, L. (2002), Sweetening Ontologies with DOLCE. In: *Proceedings of EKAW 2002.*

Kalinowsky, G. (1965). *Introduction à la logique juridique.* Pichon & Durand-Auzias, Paris.

Gangemi, A, M.-T. Sagri, D. Tiscornia (2003). Jur-Wordnet, a Source of Metadata
for Content Description in Legal Information. In: *Proceedings of the Workshop on
'Legal Ontologies & Web based legal information management', part of The International Conference of Artificial Intelligence and Law (ICAIL 2003)*, Edinburgh,
June 24, 2003.

Boris Lauser, *AGROVOC: From thesaurus to Ontology Transforming Agrovoc into
a KAON ontology*, Agrovoc Workshop, Rome 2003.

Peters W., Sagri M.T., Tiscornia D., Castagnoli S.(2006), *The LOIS Project* Lerc
2006.

Sacco, R., Il diritto muto, in *Riv.di diritto civile*, 39 (1993), parte I, pp. 689-702.

Sacco, R., Droit et langue. In: *Rapports italiens au XV Congrès international de
droit comparé*, Milano, 1998.

Sacco R., Lingua e diritto, in *Ars Intrepretandi*, Annuario di ermeneutica giuridica,
traduzione e diritto, Milano, 2000.

Vossen, P., Peters, W. & Díez-Orzas, P. (1997). 'The Multilingual design of the
EuroWordNet Database. In: Mahesh, K. (ed.), *Ontologies and multilingual NLP,
Proceedings of IJCAI-97 workshop*, Nagoya, Japan, August 23-29.

Norma-System:
A Legal Information System for Managing Time

Monica Palmirani, Federica Benigni

C.I.R.S.F.I.D, University of Bologna, via Galliera 3, 40126 Bologna, Italy
{palmiran, fbenigni }@cirsfid.unibo.it

Abstract. This paper presents Norma-System, a legal information system developed by CIRSFID (of the University of Bologna) to manage legal resources over time, enabling front-office as well as back-office functions; the system can also ensure legally valid output in agreement with the principles of legal theory. In fact, content-management systems are increasingly being designed for easy management of legal resources, but they often omit to factor into the design the general legal principles on which basis a mere document repository may be made into a legal database proper, capable of presenting legal resources in proper form.

1. Norma-System

Norma-System is a legal information system capable of carrying a document through its entire lifecycle in the course of the lawmaking process at different levels (local, regional, national, supranational), in different languages (multilingual interface), under different legal cultures (for systems of civil law and common law alike), and using different technical standards for representing legal texts, that is, using different Document Type Definitions (or DTDs) and XML schemas - the system is now compliant with the *NormeinRete* DTD 2.0 (Lupo and Batini, 2003) and with the AKOMA NTOSO 1.0 DTD (Akomantoso, 2003).

Norma-System handles all the stages involved in the process of bringing out legal documents (including laws and acts of parliament), these stages consisting in drafting, markup, production, conversion into XML, archiving, updating, retrieval, and Web publication.

From a technical point of view, Norma-System integrates front-office tools (an editor) with back-office tools (DMS, DBMS, a Web portal) so as to manage the entire lifecycle of a legal document. But at the same time, it can serve as a general-purpose content- and document-management system.

1.1. AGREEMENT WITH THE PRINCIPLES OF LEGAL THEORY

The main feature of this legal information system is that built into its ICT design are the main principles of legal theory (lex superior, lex priori, lex specialis), as well as the rules of constitutional law (hierarchy of legal sources, delegation of the legislative power) and those of the judiciary (the rules of legal procedure), thus enabling the ICT design to manage and process legal resources all the while ensuring their legal validity over time.

1.2. A SYSTEM FOR MANAGING, NOT JUST ANY CONTENT, BUT LEGAL INFORMATION

This is specifically a legal-information system for managing the complex relations that obtain over time among the constituents of a normative system. The point, then, is not so much to implement a general-purpose content-management system for the single legal document: it is rather to manage the normative system and the complex relations is sets up among legal sources over time, and to do so in such a way so as to guarantee the integrity of the output, namely, the legal validity of the content produced.

1.3. TESTING ENVIRONMENT

Norma-System can also help the lawmaking process by enabling an ex-ante assessment of the process in a separate environment; in other words, the system makes it possible to test how the normative system will behave when a new act is introduced. This makes it possible to reorder the normative system and to detect in it any anomalies or dysfunctions, thus making it possible to systematize legal resources into bodies of law that are more certain, less fragmentary, and easier to access.

1.4. FEATURES OF NORMA-SYSTEM

Norma-System has two main components, called Norma-Editor and Norma-Server. These two components connect by way of a communication module based on the legacy system and on Web Services technology.

2. Norma-Editor

Norma-Editor is a specialised editor (developed in Visual Basic .NET for Office XP) that runs on top of the Microsoft Word environment and makes it possible to process texts of law, and legal resources generally, by providing the user with tools for drafting these documents, marking them up, converting them into XML, and tagging them with metadata. Norma-Editor is intended for use by practitioners tasked with managing the legal drafting process and the lifecycle of legal documents; but publishers, too, can use it to build legal databases and publish them in official journals or in commercial publications. Norma-Editor enables a number of functions as follows:

1. accompanying the user through the process of producing a legal document from inception, in keeping with the rules of proper legal drafting (legal-drafting module);

2. marking up preexisting legal documents in XML starting from a plan-text file. This function is carried out transparently through a graphical user interface and an automatic parser, so as not to require the user to know any XML (markup module);

3. managing the hierarchy of annexes;

4. automatically recognizing a document's structure, along with its metadata, annexes, and normative references (user-aid module);

5. converting any other input format (HTML, XML, RDF, TXT, etc.) into an XML-compliant format using a selected DTD or XML schema (conversion module);

6. running a semantic check of legal markup (semantic-check module);

7. helping the user consolidate and update in semi-automatic mode legal documents for the construction of the law in force (consolidation module).

Norma-Editor properly manages documents in statute law and case law, and the core project is now being extended to also enable management of other types of documents, such as bills of law, records of debates on the parliament floor, orders of the day and week in parliament, question-and-answer minutes, and commission hansards.

ccompanies the user through the entire lifecycle of a text of law - through all its phases in the lawmaking process. The state diagram below illustrates (in the Unified Modeling Language) the phases a legislative text goes through in the markup process.

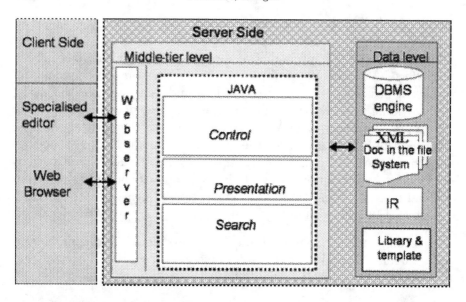

Figure 1. Norma-Systarchi.epsecture

By *markup* is meant the activity of marking up a text with a set of defined tags assigning specific meanings to specific text partitions, thus enriching the text with semantic information (or metadata) that describes it. The markup tool helps the end-user mark up a legal text in a transparent way, that is, without requiring any knowledge of tag set (the DTD or the XML schema) or any knowledge of the technology involved (XML).

Following is a step-by-step illustration of markup activity.

1. Cleanup: The text imported into the Norma-Editor environment is stripped of any preexisting tagging and formatting. Some this preexisting formatting and tagging may help the user detect information useful for markup, so the user has the option of enabling some text recognition before proceeding to the cleanup stage.

2. Detection of tables: Any tables included in the text are marked up. Tables have special formatting, and it is important to detect it before feeding the text to the parser for automatic recognition.

3. Detection of annexes: The main text is split off from any annexes, with the editor managing as well the hierarchy of the annexes (annexes appended to other annexes).

4. Detection of annotations: Any annotations are automatically detected.

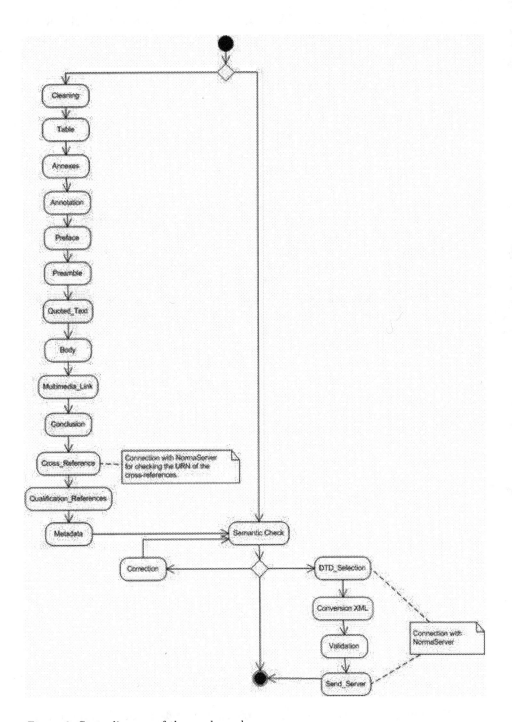

Figure 2. State diagram of the markup phases

5. Markup of the preamble: The heading and the preamble of the legislative text is automatically detected by the parser and manually corrected by the user.

6. Detection of quoted text: Any new text added by insertion or substitution is usually enclosed in quotation marks (e.g., Article 1 Decision 2000/185/EC is hereby amended as follows: 1. in the first subparagraph of Article 1 this "three years running from 1 January 2000 to 31 December 2002" shall be replaced by "four years running from 1 January 2000 to 31 December 2003").

7. Markup of body text: The main partition (or running text) of the document is marked up in automatic or semiautomatic mode.

8. Multimedia links: The legislative document may include multimedia objects, and the editor will manage this kind of link.

9. Markup of closing partitions: Markup of the final parts of the legislative document (signatures, ending clause, date, place, etc.).

10. Markup of normative references: The parser helps the user to automatically detect normative references, by locating such references and detecting the text's structural partitions (document type, date, number) necessary to build a URN (Uniform Resource Name).

11. Qualification of normative references: A specific tool helps the user qualify normative references as being of a certain type. This applies to all normative provisions generally (i.e., any text partition carrying normative meaning), and in particular to modificatory provisions, which are detected and qualified as such in order to enable automatic construction of an updated text.

12. Markup of metadata: The foregoing information enables automatic inference of different kinds of metadata (document type, level in the hierarchy of legal sources, type of act, etc.); other metadata will have to be put into the system manually (examples being the date of entry into force and the modificatory provision's date of application). A graphical interface tool helps the user input several kinds of metadata about the normative provision in question: this includes any ontological classification of the normative provision in line with the LKIF ontology established under WP1.

13. Semantic check: A semantic check will detect any inconsistencies the text may contain from the legal point of view or any departures from the rules of proper legal drafting. The editor produces a report

of any errors or inconsistencies found, thus enabling the user to go back and correct them.

14. Validation: Once the semantic check is carried out (and any inconsistencies set straight), the editor will convert the document from Microsoft Word format to XML and will validate it in keeping with the DTD or XML schema selected by the user. Several reports show any errors in the conversion and validation process, thus aiding the user in correction.

15. Sending package to the server: The final legislative document (complete with annexes and multimedia files) is sent to the server, which will then handle the package for processing and storage.

Norma-Editor needs to coordinate with the server during four different phases of the markup process, while (a) marking up normative references, (b) updating the DTD or XML schema, (c) checking the URN for completeness, and (d) checking to make sure that the text version produced aligns with the rest of the normative system.

2.1. CONSOLIDATION MODULE

The consolidation module helps the end-user update a legislative text. It works in automatic, semiautomatic, and manual mode using the semantic information embedded into the text during the preceding markup stage.

By consolidation, then, is meant the activity of updating a legislative text so that it accurately reflects over time any and all modifications applicable to it. This involves taking all the relevant modificatory legal provisions - both internal to the destination text and external to it - and applying them to that text at the right time (date of modification). The prior markup activity lays the groundwork for consolidation.

The state diagram in figure 3. lays out the main phases of consolidation.

1. Connection with the server to collect the set of documents necessary for consolidation: The editor requests a connection with the server in order to obtain three sets of data, namely, the modifying-document package (main document and annexes), the modified-document package (main document and annexes), and the list of modificatory provisions.

2. Conversion: The editor converts the XML packages in MS Word format and presents them to the end-user. One window shows the text to be modified, and another window the modifying text.

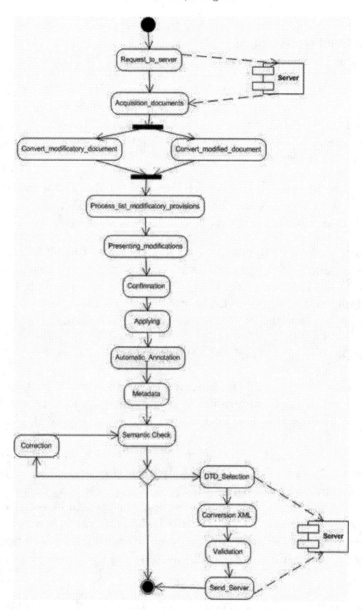

Figure 3. Consolidation state diagram

3. List of modificatory provisions: The editor processes the list of modificatory provisions and lays them out in a user-friendly graphical interface; also, the modificatory provisions are displayed in an order reflecting the temporal sequence in which the corresponding actions are to take effect.

4. Application of the modifications: The editor presents the end-user with the modifications and with tools for applying them to the text to be modified; these tools make it possible to carry out this operation in automatic, semiautomatic, or manual mode.

5. Annotation: Every step in process of applying a modification is automatically tracked and annotated in the text being modified, which will then carry explanatory information about the process itself (thus, for each modification, we will know type of modifying action involved, the name of the modifying document, the text partition of the modified text, and so on).

6. Metadata: The end-user can supply the consolidated text with additional metadata, such as additional keywords facilitating classification.

7. Semantic check, XML conversion, and delivery: The text so consolidated is checked for semantic correctness and is then converted into XML and sent to the server.

Coordination with the server ensures proper execution of three main tasks as follows: (a) importing from the server the exact document set needed for consolidation (with each modifying document being paired to the document to be modified, and all documents being ordered by modification date); (b) importing the list of modificatory provisions, ordered by modification date; and (c) sending to the server the new version of each document in its modified and consolidated form.

3. Norma-Server

Norma-Server is the server side of Norma-System. It is developed in J2EE and handles the following functions:

1. Providing a document repository: All the documents (complete with their lifecycles) are stored in a Document Management System (DMS) based on the Norma-Server file system, a file system for storing XML files along with .doc and multimedia files..

2. Providing a metadata repository: Norma-Server uses a Relational Database Management System (RDBMS) compliant with Structured Query Language (SQL), this makes it possible to store and extract large volumes of metadata and build knowledge-base relations without loss of performance.

3. Managing versioning on the basis of a temporal model: The Database Management System (DBMS) uses metadata specifying a legal document's periods of validity (keeping into account the document's dates of entry into force, efficacy, and application), in such a way as to capture an entire body of documents (or legal system) on the basis of a temporal model. Such temporal and relational storage is specific to the legal domain, and general-purpose versioning (software engineering versioning tools) cannot adequately handle this task. Norma-Server's temporal versioning model manages the entire versioning chain, makes sure the legal systems is coherently represented from legal point of view, and checks for semantic accuracy, so that each of the operations carried out is valid with respect the legal system as a whole (this is done by checking the conditional provisions of modification).

4. Legal reasoning: A reasoning module detects conditional modifications (e.g., "Art. 14 shall only be repealed when Art. 20 comes in force") and uses defeasible logic to represent and manage them. The module checks to see whether the condition to which a modificatory provision is subject has been satisfied (by external or internal events); these findings are then fed to the inferential engine, which on the basis of the argumentation approach uses them to infer new actions and events; and the new knowledge so gained is then presented and explained to the user.

5. Supporting the consolidation process: The server manages the entire consolidation process in keeping with the temporal model represented in the DBMS, and on this basis selects the appropriate documents to be submitted to the end-user for consolidation.

6. Presenting and browsing content through a Web interface: The server displays legal resources in different views presenting, among other things, (a) a legal document's normative chain (i.e., all the modificatory text leading to the modified document's current state), (b) a legal document's versioning chain (i.e., all the versions the document went through), (c) the entire legal system frozen at any given time t, (d) the legal system at a given time y subject to an event occurring at an earlier time x (projecting, for example, what the system would look like if this earlier event gets annulled), (e) the full list of repealed documents, and (f) the relation between a document and its annexes.

7. Searching: The server indexes the textual content (using, for example, the Lucene engine), queries structured data jointly with a full-text temporal model, and extracts the relevant fragment from the

XML document collection. It is essential for a legal-information system to enable management of time along at least three temporal lines, identifying (a) the time when a provision comes into force, (b) time when it comes into operation, and (c) time when it becomes applicable to a concrete case.

8. Semantic Web querying: The server manages the semantic qualifications made to legal documents, making it possible to display such documents in views that show the semantic relationships so specified; this would enable the user, for example, to request all the modifications made by act x at time y.

9. Enabling interactivity with the editor via Web Services; this involves: (a) verifying that normative references are correct (validity of the Uniform Resource Identifier, or URI); and (b) obtaining the correct URI in the event that a normative reference is missing information;

10. Communicating with Norma-Editor to send and receive document packages.

11. Connecting with the legacy system via Web Services: This is an interoperability layer for exchanging (importing and exporting) information and document packages with an external information system or legacy system.

12. Administering functions for managing the server side via a Web interface.

3.1. DOCUMENT-MANAGEMENT MODEL AND TERMINOLOGY

A brief survey of the document-management architecture used by the system will help us better understand the mechanics of the interaction between the system's editor and server components. Let us begin by defining the `LogicUnit` and `DocumentUnit`:

— `LogicUnit`: This is the complete legislative document as it changes over time, consisting of the main or host document (legislative act) along with any annexes, tables, and added annotations and information, plus multimedia, translation, and versioning files.

— `DocumentUnit`: This is the package containing the host document along with annexes, tables, informational documents, and multimedia and translation files, but not containing the versioning file.

Included in the package are MS Word documents, XML documents, and multimedia files, and alternative format files, such as XML documents in PDF format. The `DocumentUnit` will contain a subset called `MinimalDocumentUnit`, consisting of any and all XML documents and multimedia files that belong with it.

We have two main `DocumentUnit` classes depending on the temporal viewpoint from which the unit is viewed, but the model can be extended to include several other classes (such as language and space):

— `Version`: This is a particular kind of DocumentUnit, a child of the parent class DocumentUnit.

— `Original`: This is a particular kind of DocumentUnit, a child of the parent class DocumentUnit.

The components of the `DocumentUnit` are called `NormaFile`, designating any document contained in the `DocumentUnit`. There are four types of `NormaFile` documents as follows:

— `HostDocument`: The main document, marked up in XML and occurring at the top of the document hierarchy.

— `Annex`: An exhibit document linked to the HostDocument. An annex may itself carry an annex, and so on indefinitely, and all file of this type are likewise marked up in XML.

— `Informational`: This is a document that provides information only and does not also specify a norm. It usually occurs as a multimedia file, but it is best for it to also be a text document ready for conversion into the XML format.

— `Multimedia`: This is a file in any format - including PDF, HTML, ZIP, TIFF, JPG - that cannot be converted into XML.

In the model illustrated below, each version of document goes through over time forms a component of the `LogicUnit`, and each is a unique `DocumentUnit` containing a set of `NormaFile` documents. The model makes it possible to keep the legal information system coherent over time and to bring up different views of each version.

3.2. ARCHITECTURE

Norma-Server is organized in four main layers, each corresponding to a `.jar` module as follows:

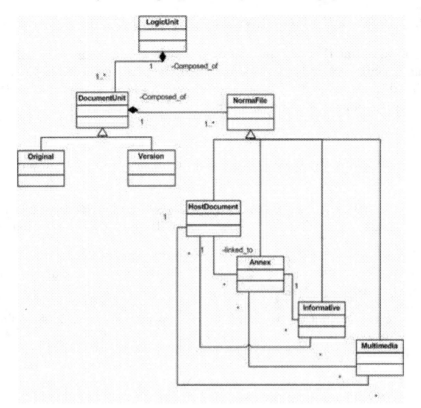

Figure 4. **LogicUnit** classes

- **normabase.jar**: This module serves as the basic object for the other **.jar** modules (these objects including, for example, the **init** and **create** classes).

- **normaapplication.jar**: This module carries out parsing, versioning, communication, DBMS storage, and partial presentation (in future versions, presentation will be extracted and managed in a separate **presentation.jar** module complaint with the Model View Controller pattern)

- **normadms.jar**: This module manages the Document Management System (DMS) and is responsible for Information Retrieval (IR).

- **normaadmin.jar**: This module offers admin tools.

Rendering is effected by way of JSP templates (Java Server Pages) so as to keep the presentation layer independent of the application layer.

3.3. PRESENTATION LAYER

It is essential that the presentation layer be compliant with all the main platforms and browsers and with the technical specifications of the Web Accessibility Initiative (WAI). The layer should enable the following functions and components:

- browsing by document lists;

- presenting the hierarchy between the host document and any annexes and multimedia and informational files;

- navigation across normative references, with tools that provide mapping capabilities for resolving URIs and URIs (even partial ones) into URLs;.

- presenting versioning chains (all the versions a document goes through);

- presenting normative chains (all the normative documents modifying a given document);

- forking the versioning chain, by tracing out the effects of retroactive normative events, namely, events occurring in the present but carrying effects in the past;

- producing lists of the passive (outgoing) and active (incoming) normative references;

- managing annotation and alert mechanisms through the server;

- querying document collection using search tools;

- carrying out temporal searches (retrieving all the documents in force at a given time t);

- carrying out semantic-Web searches (retrieving all the documents that effect a repeal at a given time t);

- full-text searching;

- carrying out structural searches (retrieving all the documents published at time t).

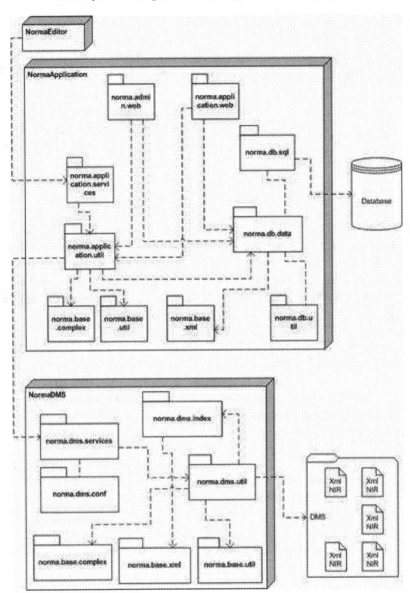

Figure 5. **NormaServer** architecture

3.4. MODULE FOR CONNECTING WITH THE EDITOR

Web Services are written in the Web Services Description Language (WSDL), using the Simple Object Access Protocol (or SOAP) envelopment. Norma-Editor creates new instances through the **New ServiceEditor()** using the **WebReference** class (**.NET** class).

The Norma-Server exports the following Web Services through the `ServiceEditor()` class:

1. `upLoadNDocument(DocumentUnit)`: This Web Service saves the `DocumentUnit` in the Norma-Server (by parsing and then archiving it in the DMS and in the DBMS). The service runs a check on the URI and returns an error message if the `DocumentUnit` already exists in Norma-Server. This Web server is used for three tasks as follows: (a) uploading an original `DocumentUnit`; (b) uploading a `DocumentUnit` version when `NormaFile` versions are uploaded to the Norma-Server; (c) uploading a `DocumentUnit` fork;

2. `upDateNDocument(DocumentUnit)`: This service overwrites the `DocumentUnit` stored in the Norma-Server. This makes for better performance than `DownLoad` and `UpLoad`, and it also helps detect minor errors relative to documents the user has stored locally, with the Web Service returning an error message for any `DocumentUnit` not found in the Norma-Server.

3. `downLoadNDocument(URI@X)`: This service corrects `DocumentUnit` files, which get downloaded for correction from the Norma-Server to the user's local machine. This deletes the `DocumentUnit` from the Norma-Server, and if the document occurs in the middle of a versioning chain, the remainder of the chain, too, is download locally and deleted from the server.

4. `deleteNDocument(URI@X)`: This service deletes selected documents retrieved from the Norma-Server using the editor. This operation is very risky because querying the Norma-Server and deleting a document selected from that query will also delete all the documents forming any versioning chain the selected document may be contained in. Several alert messages caution the user about the risk the operation entails.

5. `downLoadConsCop(modifier_URI@X, modified_URI@Y)`: This service downloads the `DocumentUnit` pairs needed for consolidation.

3.5. WEB SERVICES FOR EXTERNAL INFORMATION SYSTEMS

In order to connect Norma-Server with external information systems it is necessary to implement a layer of web services using SOAP protocol, written in WSDL. Norma-Server uses AXIS library. Norma-Server uses a **queuing mechanism** for collecting all the requests coming from the editor's instances and to pass them to external information system.

The web services that external information system should expose are the following:

1. `StartSession`: This service creates the object from which the other Web Services can be launched, and from which to establish an HTTP session.

2. `QueryURI`: This service will obtain from the repository a list of URIs similar to a given URI, or it will yield the value true if only a single URI turns up matching the parameter specified, a parameter that can also include wildcards for partial matches of URIs that are not well formed. The service returns a SOAP envelope in XML format.

3. `CheckURI`: Checks to see whether or not a given URI is correct, accordingly returning a true or false value.

4. `LoadURI`: Returns a SOAP envelope carrying XML content based on the parameters specified.

5. `SaveDocumentUnit`: In a single atomic operation, this service saves all `NormaFile` documents belonging to the `MinimalDocumentUnit`, all the while managing the coherence and integrity of the transaction.

6. `UpdateDocumentUnit`: In a single atomic operation, this service overwrites all the `NormaFile` documents belonging to a `DocumentUnit`, all the while managing the coherence and integrity of the transaction.

7. `FreezeVersion`: This service freezes an existing versioning chain and, using `SaveDocument`, makes it possible to continue the versioning process, thus building a new chain. When a modification applies retroactively, the versioning chain will have to be forked, with one document version capturing the chain *before* the modification is applied and another document version *after* such application. This yields two versioning chains for the same `DocumentUnit`. If at time X the `DocumentUnit` has the URI `URI@X`, and then an event takes place at time Y (`event_date`) which carries a modification retroactively applicable to the `DocumentUnit` at time Z (`forking_date`), such that $Z < X$, we will end up with two chains as follows: `URI@X;eventdate` and `URI@Z`.

8. `DeleteDocumentUnit`: This service makes it possible to delete all the `NormaFile` documents belonging to a `DocumentUnit` having a

specified URI. This is a high-risk action that, in order to maintain the temporal coherence and integrity of the legal system, uses the specification `@X` to delete all the versions of the `DocumentUnit` occurring after the deletion request is made.

9. `DeleteLogicUnit`: Deletes a `LogicUnit`, similarly to the `Delete-DocumentUnit`, except that the URI is specified using the wide character * (as in URI*), which instructs the system to delete all the `DocumentUnits` in the `LogicUnit`.

3.6. DBMS

The DBMS (Database Management System) has been designed using the least number of tables, so as to make for effective management of the metadata describing the temporal model. The query language is specific to the DBMS engine used. The tables contain, for the most part, metadata describing the versioning chain of each document, and for each version of the document, its time interval, normative references, and annexes, thus making it possible to query the database extracting all the version a document has at a specified time and all the modificatory provisions applicable to any one version.

3.7. DMS

All the `DocumentUnits` used by the Norma-Editor are stored in the server application's file system. The DMS (Document Management System) repository contains the following folders:

- DOC: Stores all MS Word files;

- MAIN: Stores all XML and multimedia files;

- OTHERS: Stores all other formats.

All files are stored in folders named by sequential numbering. This carries the advantage of making it possible to rebuild the entire DBMS working from the collection of documents stored in the DMS. Which in turn makes the system robust, shielding the DBMS from crash or attack episodes.

References

Feasibility study for the project Accesso alle norme in rete. In *Informatica e Diritto*, no. 1, 2000.

Lupo, C. and C. Batini. *A Federative Approach to Laws Accessed by Citizens: The NormeinRete System.* EGOV 2003, Prague, Czech Republic, Springer-Verlag, pp. 413-416.

Palmirani, M. and R. Brighi. *Metadata for the Legal Domain.* In proceedings of the DEXA 2003 conference: A Workshop on Web Semantics. Prague, September 1-5, pp. 105-106. New York: ACM Press, 2003.

Buchanan, B. G. and E. H. Shortliffe. *Rule-Based Expert Systems: The MYCIN Experiments of the Stanford Heuristic Programming Project.* Addison-Wesley Publishing Company, 1984.

Palmirani, M. and R. Brighi. *An XML Editor for Legal Information Management.* In proceedings of the DEXA 2003 conference: A Workshop on E-Government. Prague, September 1-5, pp. 421-429. Berlin, Heidelberg: Springer-Verlag, 2003.

Palmirani, M. and R. Brighi. *Norma-System: A Legal Document System for Managing Consolidated Acts.* In proceedings of the DEXA 2002 conference. Aix-en-Provence, France, September 1-9, pp. 310-320. Berlin Heidelberg: Springer-Verlag, 2002.

Palmirani, M. and R. Brighi and M. Massini. *Automated Extraction of Normative References in Legal Texts.* In proceedings of the ICAIL 2003 conference workshop E-Government: Modelling Norms and Concepts as Key Issues. Edinburgh, Scotland, UK, June 24-28, pp. 95-100. Bologna: Gedit Edizioni, 2003.

Akomantoso, www.akomantoso.org, 16 October 2006.

Standard Models for Legislation –
The Cost of Compliance

Clyde Hatter
Propylon

Abstract. This essay discusses some of the issues that affect the development of standard models for legislation. Although there is wide agreement that legislation interchange standards are a Good Thing, few standards are in use which cross multiple jurisdictions. The essay is not concerned with the merits or demerits of any particular standard, but, instead looks at factors that are significant in determining whether or not a standard is adopted.

It argues that the creation of a legislative standard is complicated by the fact that legislation has multiple consumers and producers, all with differing needs. Reconciling these needs into a single 'model' of legislation which will add value at all stages required for its effective implementation is a tricky problem.

1. A cautionary tale

Legislation in the USA is reasonably similar across states. Similar enough, perhaps, to make the creation of a markup standard for legislation a practical possibility.

However, although there have been attempts to create such a standard, real progress-to-date has been slow. It seems that the issue is less in creating candidate standards, so much as persuading legislatures to take them up.

For example, in late 2004 the goals of the OASIS LegalXML Legislative -Regulatory (LEG-REG) Compliance Technical Committee, were:

to establish a structured information framework that supports the ongoing, timely, proactive delivery of high-quality Legislative-Regulatory Content. It shall further create structured information constructs to support filtering for relevancy and saliency to a particular Consumer's need.[1]

Sadly, by 2005 the Committee had been closed down with the comment:

Everyone can see long-term benefits to having inter-state standards for the document artifacts at least for export or interchange. It was clear from the discussion, however, that there was no near-term realizable benefit that the states participating in the discussion would derive

---

[1] http://www.oasis-open.org/committees/download.php/10542/
ProposeLegRegLegComplience20041203.doc

from participating in the standards effort. States in attendance have developed or are currently engaged in development of artifacts and systems, already incurring the cost of development. Therefore, they did not believe they could convince people responsible for Legislative budget that participation is a priority.[2]

2. What do we mean by a 'standard model'?

A 'standard model' in the sense discussed in this essay refers to an agreed way of representing 'what it means to be a piece of legislation'. Although de facto standards for procedural aspects of the legislative process do exist (e.g. Mason's Manual of Legislative Procedure, Robert's Rules of Order) these do not form the subject of this essay.

More specifically, by 'standard model' we are referring to ways of representing legislation as encoded electronic texts which are documented and which are in the public domain. Although the focus is on XML encodings, many of the issues discussed apply to other syntaxes for text markup.

3. What is an appropriate standard model for legislation?

Legislation is a fluid concept. The 'thing-that-is-legislation' can be measured and described in many dimensions. Some will be obvious to us (such as how the legislation should look when printed), some less obvious (such as the drafter's intention when framing the legislation). Models of legislation are representations one or more of these dimensions. The purpose of such models is to encapsulate information about the legislation that is useful or interesting to us. Ideally the model should allow us to appreciate, understand, manipulate, or make better use of, the legislative text.

The corollary of this argument is that we can make an infinite number of models of a legislative text. None of these models will be objectivity 'correct' as the only viable measure of 'correctness' is *utility* and this utility will vary from consumer to consumer. Does the model do something useful? If so, for whom, and at what cost? Only when the benefits of using the model outweigh the costs of creating and maintaining it does the model become useful. In other words, what is *appropriate* depends upon who you are and what you are seeking to achieve.

---

[2] www.oasis-open.org/committees/download.php/10541/
ProposeLegTCClosure20041203.doc

4. The legislative lifecycle

Legislation represents an attempt to define acceptable and unacceptable forms of social behaviour. It evolves through negotiation between competing interest groups and is encoded and interpreted by diverse individuals and institutions. It attempts to convey precision via the imprecise medium of prose text.

To better understand what *appropriate* means for different producers and consumers of legislation, we must examine the legislative lifecycle — the sequence of processing stages which legislation moves through on its journey from idea to implementation. This lifecycle is summarized in the table below.

Table I.

Stage	Description	Notes
requirement to legislate	The identification and acknowledgment by a legislative body of the need for new legislation.	Usually the result of a political, social or technical imperative.
drafting	The process of writing new legislation.	Requires research of existing legislation which applies to the domain. May involve consultation with interest groups.
consideration	The modification and amendment of the proposed legislation via the parliamentary process.	Requires the management of multiple, potentially conflicting sets of amendments.
enactment and promulgation	The passing of the proposed legislation into law and the public proclamation of this fact.	May include checks for consistency with existing statutes, checks for constitutionality, enrollment into a consolidated code and the announcement and publicisation of the legislation.
implementation and compliance	The creation of regulatory and compliance mechanisms.	Individuals and institutions required to comply with, and enforce, the legislation will need to understand what compliance involves.
jurisprudence	Interpretation of statute law by the courts and the associated body of legal judgments.	Legislation may be challenged or tested via the court in order to ascertain its constitutionality or to confirm or repudiate a particular interpretation of the law

When we examine in detail the various stages of the lifecycle, we can see that, in addition to the base text of the legislation itself, a variety of additional information (so-called *meta-information*) may be required by a particular audience. This information *pertains* to the base text but is not necessarily *part* of the base text. Examples of this additional 'meta-information' are detailed in the paragraphs below.

5. What information is important?

When evaluating whether to proceed with a piece of legislation the proposer must understand the state of existing legislation relating to the subject in question. In addition it may be useful to examine how the subject has been treated historically and how the subject has been addressed in other states.

There are also rules of style and form to be considered. For legislation to be acceptable, it must conform to the editorial, technical and structural rules mandated by the legislature. These rules may be complex. For example, the rules associated with the construction of the long title of a bill may run to several pages in a state's drafting manual.

During the drafting phase, complex legislation may be authored collaboratively, the work split between multiple drafters. At this stage in the lifecycle, the needs of the project manager as well as the individual drafter have to be considered. What is the state of completion of the document? What parts have been, proofed? What organisations have viewed the proofs? What provisions have been reviewed and approved? What outstanding issues remain to be resolved?

In addition to refining the actual text of the legislation the drafters may also need to provide a layer of explanation to inform the individuals who will critique and modify the draft. This layer of explanation may take the form of notes associated with specific provisions or take the form of a separate document.

When the legislation is considered by the legislature, its status and its history become matters of concern. What is the status of the document within the legislative process (initiated, first consideration, withdrawn, etc)? What has been the document's history? How has the document been amended as it passed through the stages of consideration? What is its relationship to other legislation passing through the legislature?

In addition, the process of consideration will require that parts of the document, or amendments to the document be quoted or referenced in other publications (e.g. the Journal, the Debate Record). Operations or processes performed on the document (e.g. ratification by Committee) will be referenced in the various documents of official record.

Promulgation requires that the enacted legislation be published and disseminated. During this phase the publisher of the legislation may have to output the document to a variety of media types, update the text of codified statutes and provide an explanatory commentary. Those bound by the legislation will need to know from where they can obtain official copies of the legislation, when the legislation comes into effect, what existing laws are repealed by the new law and what the mechanisms for enforcement and compliance will be.

It is not enough, of course, to simply publicize the existence of the new law. Effective implementation will involve the creation or modification of existing state or private institutions to ensure that mechanisms exist to monitor and assist with compliance.

To comply with legislation the citizen or institution must know what behaviors are required or permitted. For example, new drug safety legislation may require that a manufacturer modifies the way in which products are labeled and packaged. Institutions must assure themselves that they comply with the law; in order to do this they need to be able to audit activities against the legally mandated requirements.

Finally, despite the best efforts of drafters, a legislative provision may sustain conflicting interpretations. In order to resolve these conflicts legislation will be tested via the judicial system. The court judgments and interpretations associated with the various parts of a legislative document are necessary information for legal practitioners.

6. Problem domains and legislative data models

As the legislation moves through the stages of the lifecycle described above, information requirements vary. Although the requirements at any individual stage may be straightforward, when taken together they form a complicated palimpsest — meaning that our 'standard model for legislation' has the potential to become very complex indeed. If a single, standard model has to support all of these requirements, the requisite complexity may seriously damage its chances of adoption (see A cautionary tale, Section 1).

The tables below summarize the information which *could* be supported by a standard model for legislation. The intention is to give some idea of the complexity of these requirements and the breadth of intellectual problem domains (the classification is intended to be illustrative rather than scientific!) which may need to be addressed.

Drafting

Table II.

Information requirement	Data model implication	Problem domain
how statute relates to the subject under consideration	classification of live statutes by subject-matter	ontology
how the subject has been addressed historically within the jurisdiction	classification of historical statutes by subject-matter	ontology
how the subject has been addressed in other states	classification of external statutes by subject-matter using shared classification system	ontology
conformity to the drafting rules	models of stylistic rules (grammar checkers, controlled vocabularies, spellcheckers, etc) against which text can be validated	heuristics
		validation
conformity to formatting rules	information exists to create correct visual formats	formatting
conformity to technical rules	must contain appropriate printing codes, correct encoding of text, provision numbering sequences	heuristics
conformity to structural rules	models of structural rules (SGML, XML, database schema) against which text can be validated	semantics
	availability of templates and boilerplate text fragments to assist in the creation of the structure	document management
state of completion of the document	taxonomy of drafting operations and associated states	workflow
which parts of the document have been approved and by whom		
what outstanding issues remaining to be resolved		

Drafting

Table III.

Information requirement	Data model implication	Problem domain
intent ('thinking') behind the document and behind individual provisions	ability to comment on legislation, at document and sub-document level (explanatory memoranda, revisor's notes, etc.)	exegesis
sources of information and opinion which are informing the draft legislation	comment fields and links to external and internal information sources	citation
translation	ability to author and display text in multiple languages	hypermedia
		translation memory version control
inclusion of non-text information, diagrams, maps, etc.	reference external entities	transclusion

Consideration

Table IV.

Information requirement	Data model implication	Problem domain
understand status of the document within the legislative process (initiated, first consideration, withdrawn, etc)	metadata, or ability to identify state information within the text of the document	workflow
history of the document (how the document has been amended, and by whom, and it passes through the parliament)	ability to track and engross multiple sets of changes to the document	document management version control
manage proposed amendments to the document		change tracking merging
relationship to other legislation passing through the parliament	ability to map relationships between evolving documents	ontology
requirement to quote or reference document in other publications (e.g. the Journal, the Debate Record).	ability to map information relationships with other document types	ontology
	ability to exchange information across sectional boundaries	interoperability
operations or processes performed on the document (e.g. ratification by committee) will be referenced in the various documents of official record.	ability to map relationships with other legislative actions	ontology

Promulgation

Table V.

Information requirement	Data model implication	Problem domain
where the definitive copy of the legislation resides (e.g. the vellum/linen copy)	document addressing mechanisms	namespaces
from where other 'legitimate' copies of the legislation can be obtained	document addressing mechanisms	namespaces
when the legislation comes into effect	ability to identify enactment dates, sunset provisions, etc.	semantics version control
what existing laws are superseded (repealed) by the new law	ability to identify repealing clauses, etc.	semantics version control
what the mechanisms for enforcement and compliance will be	ability to link to secondary legislation, SIs, rules, regulations, etc.	citation namespaces ontology
publish the document in a variety of outputs	document format which is amenable to repurposing	formatting transformation
update consolidated codes where necessary	ability to understand how legislative text impacts upon consolidated codes	merging version control
publish explanatory commentary where necessary	ability to store and extract comments	exegesis
requirement to maintain the physical or electronic representation of the legislation in a way which preserves the representation as part of the legislature's historical record.	document format which is open and long-lived	data longevity

Implementation

Table VI.

Information requirement	Data model implication	Problem domain
understand the links between the ordinances of the legislation and the various real-world actions which flow from those ordinances.	ability to reference other documents in a hyperlinked repository of information	citation
		hypermedia namespaces ontology

Compliance

Table VII.

Information requirement	Data model implication	Problem domain
understand how individual or institution should behave in order to comply with legislation	ability to reference the legislation from external documents.	citation
		hypermedia namespaces ontology
	ability to add layer of commentary to the legislation	exegesis
	ability to retrieve all legislation relevant to a particular industry segment	ontology
understand law at a particular date	understand what version of the law was current a particular point-in-time	amendment
		document management version control

Jurisprudence

Table VIII.

Information requirement	Data model implication	Problem domain
access to judgements and interpretations associated with a law	ability to reference the legislation from external documents.	citation
		linking
		namespaces
		ontology
	ability to add layer of commentary to the legislation	exegesis
inference of legislative intent	access to the notes and commentaries relating to the legislation (e.g. comments made by sponsoring members when introducing or discussing the legislation)	hypermedia
		exegesis

7. Modeling legislation

The effect of these information requirements, which vary according to the stage in the lifecycle, is to make the production of a single model for legislation within an individual jurisdiction a complex task. Layer upon this the requirements of multiple states and the task becomes even more problematic. One person's essential data element is another person's cost-sink.

In addition, the use of a single XML data model to represent a piece of legislative text over its entire lifespan will inevitably lead to design compromises. The structuring of the base-level text and its layers of meta-information can be executed in many ways depending upon which set of processing requirements are considered to be 'dominant' during model design. The structures associated with the dominant requirements will be expressed as the primary hierarchy. However, we must bear in mind that:

Few things in the universe are quintessentially hierarchical in nature. Arguably, a document does not have a "logical structure" that can be di-

rectly modeled by a hierarchical representation. Most naturally occurring physical objects and human-made artifacts (like texts) are susceptible to many kinds of analysis, suggesting multiple (simultaneous, overlapping) hierarchies, and typically involve non-hierarchical relationships.[3]

In addition to these — purely technical — issues, the idea that there should even be an electronic copy of legislation which corresponds to a standard model is relatively new. Most legislatures consider a particular *paper* copy of the legislation to be the reference version of the text. Where electronic texts do exist, they exist purely to produce the printed copy. The internal representation of the text has not been an issue, so long as the desired printed copy could be effectively produced.

8. The future for standard models?

Basic models of legislation begin with representations of the text content of legislative documents. However, even at this level, we run up against a number of issues. For example, the way that the text is organised, either on paper or on screen, has significance. Paragraphs need to be broken in the correct places. The line and page numbering system of the reference publication must be preserved, even in electronic publications where they have no direct meaning. Tables must be laid out in a way which reflects the drafter's intentions. Special styles such as underlined and stricken text have specific meaning in the context of legislation, as they are used to indicate areas of changed content. The indentation pattern of paragraphs may be important in indicating legislative intent.

However, providing that our model of the text can capture the subtleties described above, it does provide a baseline model. This model would be useful at all stages in the legislative lifecycle, as the base-text forms the core of interpretation and reuse.

Beyond this base-text, however, there may be no single standard-model but rather a series of agreed models which add or shed complexity depending upon lifecycle stage, with transformations facilitating the movement from one stage-model to another. A given model could then be optimized for the processing requirements of the stage in question. At any stage the aim would not be to produce a document which would be immediately editable by the next-stage consumers, but one which could be automatically translated into the required format, leveraging common information, and, if necessary, shedding or hiding complexity which was not required by the downstream process.

For this reason, it may be more productive to pursue 'micro-standards' rather than all-encompassing 'blockbuster' models for data exchange

---

[3] http://www.oasis-open.org/cover//hierarchies.html

between legislative stages or between legislative sections. By articulating the conceptual model in a implementation-neutral format (e.g. BNF or UML) we can also move away from the requirement to edit 'directly' against an particular implementation of the conceptual model towards a more flexible position where the key objective is produced well-structured, meaningful electronic texts which can be transformed and repurposed as necessary.

xmLegesEditor: an OpenSource Visual XML Editor for supporting Legal National Standards

Tommaso Agnoloni, Enrico Francesconi, Pierluigi Spinosa
{agnoloni,francesconi,spinosa}@ittig.cnr.it
Institute of Legal Information Theory and Techniques (ITTIG-CNR)
Italian National Research Council http://www.ittig.cnr.it

Abstract. The NormeinRete (NIR) project aims at providing improved accessibility to normative documents. To this end XML and URN standards have been established for norms representation and identification. In this paper xmLegesEditor, an Open Source visual XML editor providing a unified access to software tools for supporting the adoption of NIR standards, is presented. Thanks to its modularity and flexibility xmLegesEditor can be reused as a developing platform for supporting any XML standard and in particular other Legislative XML standards.

Keywords: Legislative Standard, XML Editor, OpenSource

1. Background

In recent years a standardization process of legislative documentation, stimulated by the migration of legislative data collections on the web, has been started both in the National and European environment. In Italy, the NormeinRete (NIR) project started in 1999, proposed by the Italian Ministry of Justice, with the aim of building a distributed cooperative system to access juridical documentation. The main goal was to improve accessibility to laws, by offering unified access to Italian and European Union legal material published on different institutional web sites through a specialised portal. The project has achieved the following results:

— a site for providing a unique access point for searching the Italian legislative corpus. The site (www.normeinrete.it) offers search and retrieval services operating on all Italian laws since 1904 and utilities for automated hyperlinking. The system is based on a federation of legislative data bases developed on different platforms and built on the basis of a co-operative technological architecture;

— an XML standard for norms representation. DTDs (Document Type Definition) for Italian legislation have been defined, able to represent metadata and all the significant information useful to automate legislative documents life-cycle management;

- a standard for norm persistent identification, based on an identifier derived from URN (Uniform Resource Name) and a resolution system able to resolve logical identifiers into physical addresses.

See (Lupo, 2005). The XML NormeinRete standard is today widespread and used by main normative document producers. Standardization allows to design cooperative systems involving different institutions achieving interoperability mainly through documents format compatibility.

In this context, a number of software tools for supporting the adoption of such standards, have been developed or are under development with the aim to cover the whole law life-cycle from drafting to Official Journal publication.

2. Introduction

xmLegesEditor is a specific integrated Legislative drafting environment developed at ITTIG/CNR for supporting the adoption of Italian Legislative National XML Standards (NIR). It is distributed with an Open Source license.

By "specific" it is meant that, besides integrating various modules for the treatment and processing of normative texts, it has been developed from scratch as a *native* XML editor oriented to Legislative Drafting and not as an adaptation of general purpose word-processors or generic XML Editor.

The peculiarity of this approach is a fundamental one in order to appreciate the features offered by xmLegesEditor.

This approach has emerged from an analysis of existing widespread general purpose editors which pointed out that none of them offers the possibility of exploiting the XML underlying document structure in a user-friendly way. In fact, typical WYSIWYG word-processors, though with the strength of being widely spread and used, are mainly oriented to texts' *style markup* than to their *structural and semantic markup*. A mapping between the latter and the software tools offered for the former has appeared as a weak and restrictive approach with respect to the development effort needed for such adaptation. On the other hand, generic XML editors are almost exclusively oriented to technical users with a strong background and awareness of XML underlying theory, which turns out to be useless in an office productivity environment in which different skills are assumed. See (Saqib, 2005) for an overview.

The effort made with the development of xmLegesEditor has been to estabilish a trade-off between a user-friendly approach to text authoring hiding the underlying XML structure, and the maximum flexibility and extensibility in the exploitation of the high potentiality of content expression offered by XML documents and grasped by Legislative XML standards. In a way an effort has been made towards the overcoming of traditional distinction between WYSIWYG and not editors, which is underlying in the XML approach where content and presentation are kept well distincted.

Moreover, a crucial point in the adoption of an XML standard and therefore with the choice of an editor handling related documents, is the issue of document validity in an XML-sense. The definition of a strict Document Type Definition (or XML Schema) is a powerful tool for the standardization of the formal structure of documents and its mandatory respect is a key tool in order to guarantee interoperability among all the software agents involved in document lifecycle.

However its enforcement and the respect of such rules during documents production is a non-trivial task for typical editors. On the other hand, failure in validation or manual management of XML tags can, particularly for complex standards as the Legislative ones, cause a complete failure of the original objectives of standard compliant document production.

xmLegesEditor proposes an original approach to this problem in which, while guaranteed to be safe and successful for XML validation (and not only well-formedness) is completely "transparent" to the user and does not require any additional effort or XML awareness than typical word processing operation. Such approach can be indicated as an *a priori validation* approach and will be more deeply described in following sections. The basic idea is that the user is transparently *constrained* by the editor to perform only valid operations on the document in such a way that, starting from a valid document, only valid documents can be produced.

Finally, the specific domain of Legal Drafting and Normative Documents Management calls for the integration of a variety of additional tools in order to setup a complete Integrated Normative Drafting Environment which are most easily integrated in a specifically developed platform.

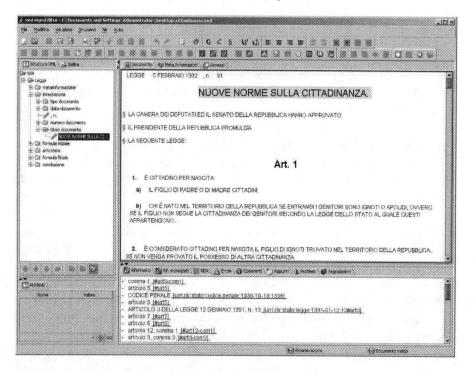

Figure 1. A screenshot of xmLegesEditor

3. xmLegesEditor

3.1. DESCRIPTION

In Fig. 1 a screenshot of xmLegesEditor is depicted. The user interface is the typical one with common functions offered by traditional word processors. However notice how the frame is divided into different panels each offering a different *view* of the document. The main one is the textual panel reporting the *full text* content of the document over which typical textual typewriting and related facilities are allowed.

Moreover, a number of different summarizing and specific panels are provided. Migrating XML approach to the editor, the idea is in fact to view and manage the same content, stored and accessed directly in XML, through different views or tabs. Each view is simply an XSLT stylesheet file applied to the content, see Fig. 2. At runtime each XML document can be associated with multiple views or tabs. Each view can deal with just one aspect of a large XML document or may simply provide another way of looking at the same content. This means that every possible view of the document obtainable by applying a stylesheet can easily become an interactive panel (not read-only) of xmLegesEditor,

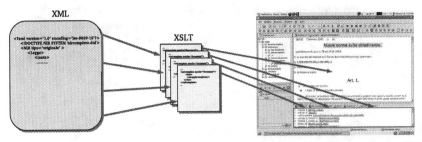

Figure 2. xmLegesEditor panels obtained by applying XSLT stylesheets to the XML document.

synchronized with all the others, and all the data inserted from each view are directly stored in the unique shared XML file.

In xmLegesEditor, besides full text view the following additional views are integrated:

Tree Panel offers a structural view of the document reproducing its tree structure. It can be browsed as a document index to quickly access document's partitions or edit partition's properties.

Attributes Panel shows the attribute contents of XML elements selected from any panel; allows editing of attributes, association of specific editors to specific data types (dates, URNs, etc.) removing/adding non mandatory/allowed attributes querying the DTD.

Reference Panel presents an index of all the normative references in the document and related URN. Clicking on the URN, web access to the resolutor and to the cited document is provided.

Notes Panel summarizing view of the notes to the document.

Annexes Panel a separated full-text view of the annexes to the main document.

General Metadata Panel summarizing view of the main document's geneal metadata.

each view can also serve as a quick access point to the corresponding content in the full text view. As all this panels are simply provided by XSLT stylesheet application to the XML document, they can be customized and parametrized in the most various stylistic and structural ways exploiting the features of XSLT standard.

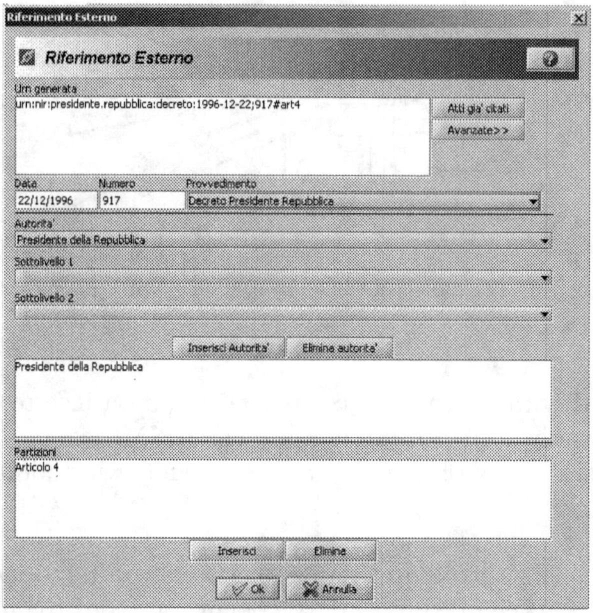

Figure 3. Guided insertion of a reference in the URN format.

3.2. XML ELEMENTS MANAGEMENT

On the top of the screen in Fig. 1 , see the specific toolbars for the access to the function for the management of NIR Elements. Buttons are grouped in toolbars by function *i.e.* red toolbar containing functions for managing normative references, green toolbar for accessing functions for managing partition insertion etc.

Each button accesses specifically developed complex function for the management of specific XML Elements and related attributes, possibly through forms guiding the user in the insertion of related informations. See for example Fig. 3 depicting the form guiding the user in the insertion of a normative reference according to the URN standard. XML Elements management is approached in an *incremental* way, from a rough mode through contextual right-click operations to evolved functions accessed by toolbars. This allowed us to cover the management of all NIR-Elements from the beginning and improve it during software development.

A fundamental feature of xmLegesEditor is the management of buttons enabling. In fact, as introduced in previous sections, in order to ensure *a priori validation* of the document, only the buttons of functions that can be applied at the current cursor position are enabled. In the same way, insertion of XML Elements from right click is managed in such a way that only the tags whose insertion preserves document validity are proposed to the user. Moreover, such information is not cabled in the program but directly accessed from the DTD files, this meaning that a change in the DTD or adoption of a different DTD directly affects such feature without additional coding. More details on the modules responsible of such feature will be given in subsequent sections. What is important at this stage is that xmLegesEditor implicitly guides the user to the production of a valid XML document according to the related DTD without additional effort than usual typewriting.

3.3. EXTERNAL MODULES INTEGRATION: XMLEGES SUITE

As pointed out in previous sections, xmLegesEditor aims to be a complete drafting environment providing facilities for handling both legacy content and drafting of new documents.

To this end, a number of independent software modules, developed for managing both formal profile (XML structure and reference recognition) and functional profile (semantic information extraction and annotation) (Biagioli et al., 2005) have been integrated into the editor in order to provide the user with a unique point of access to different tools. Notice that, external modules integration is made particularly easy by the software modules interoperability naturally offered by XML, along with the fact that xmLegesEditor natively supports standard XML format. It is therefore enough that each external module, provides an XML-NIR output for it to be connected to the editor.

For the moment, four different external modules related to the xmLeges project have been integrated:

xmLegesLinker extracts references in normative texts and describes them according to the corresponding URNs. The URN-NIR standard established a grammar to identify documents within the NIR domain. This grammar has been defined according to (Moats, 1997) andis able to generate URNs using information on: the enacting authority; the type of measure, a number of details as: date of issue, different later versions of the document; the annexes (see (Spinosa, 1997), (Biagioli et al., 2003) for details). A normative text may contain a lot of cross references to other measures that have to be described using the related URN, so that references can be transformed in effective links when documents are published on the Web. Especially in the phase of legacy content conversion, the manual construction of a URN for each reference can be a time-consuming work. For this reason xmLegesLinker, a module able to automatically detect cross-references and assigning them the related URN has been developed. The parser is generated using LEX and YACC technologies , (Lesk, 1975), (Johnson, 1975) on the basis of the vocabulary of the citations and the URN grammar expressed in EBNF.

xmLegesMarker is a structural parser able to transform a legacy normative document in plain text, HTML or doc format into XML-NIR format. Two parsing strategies have been adopted for different portions of a document. For the body of a normative document, a non-deterministic finite-state automata (NFA) was implemented. For the header and the footer a different strategy was adopted, since their partitions are not usually identified by particular typographical symbols. The identification of such elements can only be based on the sequence of words appearing within them, with a probability that can be estimated and without knowing the states which produced such sequence. The aim of this approach is to uncover these hidden states. For this reason, to parse these two sections we adopted a strategy based on Hidden Markov Models (HMMs).

xmLegesClassifier as regards the automatic detection of the semantics in a normative document, xmLegesClassifier is designed to automatically classify paragraphs into provision types according to the provisions model defined in NIR standard. Two machine learning approaches to document classification have been tested: *Naïve Bayes* and *Multiclass Support Vector Machines* (Biagioli et al., 2005)

xmLegesExtractor designed to automatically detect the arguments of a provision. Knowing the provision type detected by *xmLegesClassifier*, this module uses the provision specific grammar to extract the provision arguments using NLP techniques. Basically the purpose is to select text fragments corresponding to specific semantic roles that are relevent to the different types of provisions. It is realized as a suite of Natural Language Processing tools for the automatic analysis of Italian texts, specialized to cope with the specific stylistic convention of legal parlance (Bartolini et al., 2005).

3.4. SOFTWARE ARCHITECTURE

xmLegesEditor has been developed on the experience of prototype NirEditor (Biagioli et al., 2005). In this new version a complete reingeneering

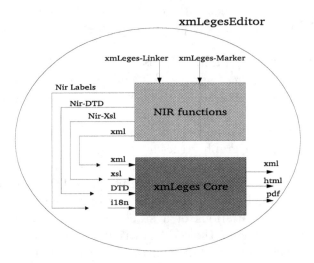

Figure 4. xmLegesEditor Architecture.

of the software has been made. The aim was to guarantee maximum extensibility, modularity and reusability of the different software modules. To this end xmLegesEditor has been structured on a component-based architecture where each component provides specific services. Moreover a strict separation between generic XML modules and specific NIR modules has been followed. This, as a by-product, gave the significant result that the developed components can be reused in order to develop other specific visual editors for supporting other XML-standards and in particular Legislative XML standards. The complete editor application is in fact obtained by simply composing the different services specified in an application composition file. Replacing NIR modules with other specific modules developed for supporting such different standards, a new editor can be obtained using the core XML editor infrastructure. In Fig. 4 such architecture is schematized. xmLegesEditor can be seen as the overlapping of two layers:

xmLegesCore At the lower level xmLegesCore provides functionality for composing a basic generic visual XML editor. Its parameters are: the DTD files of the standard to be supported, the XSLT stylesheet files for internal visualization inside the editor and for document exportation in output formats as for instance HTML or Pdf, one or more files containing textual labels and icons for the complete customization and internazionalization of the user inter-

face. All this aspects have been kept as application's parameters
rather than cabled inside the code in order to guarantee maximum
reusability. xmLegesCore provides complete functionalities for:

— **Validity Management:** This is accomplished through the access
to the *rulesManager* service. As reminded in previous sections, a
central feature in xmLegesEditor is that only valid operations are
allowed: this is obtained by contextually querying the rulesManager
which provides methods to access the DTD parsed in a Finite
State Automata graph structure in order to a priori validate in
such structure the effects of a certain operation without actually
operate over the document. Changing the DTD automatically affects rulesManager answers. This was originally needed in order
to follow the variations of a standard under evolution without
continuosly changing the code, but is of course even more useful to
provide such Validity Management strategy to different standards.
It is planned to develop a similar component providing services for
querying XML-Schema in order to extend xmLegesCore support to
standards based on such format.

— **Document Management:** A dedicated component *(Document-
Manager)* provides services for accessing a generic XML Document.
It is initially parsed into a Document Object Model format and
then made available in such format for access and modification
to any other component needing it. Functions for opening, saving, management of a multi-level undo are made available by the
DocumentManager component.

— **Document Visualization:** As reminded earlier the strategy in
document visualization consists in the visualization in the various
different panels of an HTML document obtained by applying an
XSLT stylesheet to the XML Document. However, in order to provide editing functionalities from such views, a mapping between the
original XML document elements and the visualized HTML text is
provided in order to make this process bidirectional and store the
input from the editor panels into the corresponding XML elements.
This is accomplished by two different components *XsltMapper* and
XsltPane which are at the heart of xmLegesCore visualization
functionality.

— **Internazionalization:** All the labels and the icons appearing in
the editor User Interface are actually taken from localization files
accessed through a unique key which is what is actually written in
the source code. This means that by simply changing some *locale*

file the whole UI can be translated and customized with different icons without actually changing the code. This service is provided by the *i18n* component.

each implemented in separated and standard independent components.

xmLegesNIR At the top level xmLegesNIR provides parameters to the Core level in order to specialize it to the NIR standards. Moreover, a number of NIR specific components have been developed to provide enhanced functionalities to the support of NIR-Elements. At this level external modules integration is also provided.

Notice that thanks to such architecture most of the functionalities of validation, visualization, basic elements management can then be easily shared for reuse in developing editors for other standards.

4. OpenSource Project

A fundamental feature of xmLegesEditor is that it is a free resource, distributed with an Open-Source license.

Besides a number of good motivations for being like that, especially for software in public administrations (Cospa, 2006), this is a natural choice for implementing tools supporting an *open standard* like the NIR one, shared by a number of subjects with different specific needings.

The NIR standard interests the Italian Parliament, Courts, Public Authorities, Regional Assemblies, at different levels and with different specific needings. The idea is to offer a shared highly customizable platform on which to develop specific functions and easily integrate existing or new designed tools as external modules.

Moreover xmLegesEditor is entirely written in *Java*, a platform independent language, thus leaving freedom in the choice of the platform on which to run it, included free and opensource operating systems like *GNU/Linux* which use is increasingly encouraged in Public Administrations. All the software libraries used in the development of xmLegesEditor are robust and highly reliable opensource libraries mainly from the *Apache Software Foundation*. At every level of processing, data are managed by open, *W3C* standards compliant, and commercial free, software tools. Being xmLegesEditor a *native* XML editor, this means that no conversion to or from proprietary formats is ever made, thus preventing any vendor lock-in possibility and providing the added value of complete transparency in data management which is nonnegligble especially in the context of *public data* management.

In this view the two layers architecture described in previous section should encourage contributions (Sun, 2006) from wider developer communities very active in the field of XML tools development, at least to improve *xmLegesCore* in order to obtain a robust fully functional generic Visual XML Editor shared as a common resource, which is still missing at least, but not only, among free resources. (Saqib, 2005)

xmLegesEditor is currently available for free download in its release candidate version as a binary distribution at *www.ittig.cnr.it/xmleges*, the source code repositories are currently online and a project homepage for accessing source code, documentation both for users and developers, collaborative resources like mailing lists, wiki, bug tracking system, is in preparation.

Finally, xmLegesEditor for its described features could be considered as an initial contribution for developing a shared platform over which specialize different National Legislative Editors and eventually for supporting the forthcoming European Standard of which National Standards should become specializations following the same modularity principle which inspired xmLegesEditor development.

5. Conclusions

In this paper xmLegesEditor, an Open-Source Visual XML Editor for supporting NIR standards has been proposed. xmLegesEditor can be seen as an integrated legislative drafting environment integrating a variety of software tools for supporting the adoption of Legislative standards. xmLegesEditor differs from usual general purpose word processors as well as from generic XML editors as it has been specifically designed for supporting descriptive XML documents in a user friendly way while exploting all the features offered by XML standards, with the aim of bringing non-expert users closer to XML.

Thanks to its architecture xmLegesEditor is highly customizable and extensible to support additional views and modules for improving and assisting legal drafting. Moreover the core level xmLegesCore, provides full functionalities for implementing a general purpose Visual XML Editor. As an Open-Source project the goal is to share this resource in the XML community as well as in the IT in Law community to improve it and put it at disposal of interested parties.

xmLegesEditor is currently under experimentation at Italian Senate with the aim to extend its functionalites to the support of bills, from preparatory works to amendaments management. It is also in use in Regional projects to provide mark-up of *consolidated* legislative texts (normative texts carrying all the modifications that have been introduced over time by other normative texts) to provide free access to the in-force version of laws in specific domains.

References

Bartolini, R., Lenci, A., Montemagni, S., Pirrelli, V., Soria, C. Automatic classification and analysis of provisions in italian legal texts: a case study. In *Proceedings of the Second International Workshop on Regulatory Ontologies*. 2004

Biagioli, C., Francesconi, E., Spinosa, P., Taddei, M. The nir project: Standards and tools for legislative drafting and legal document web publication. In *Proceedings of ICAIL Workshop on e-Government: Modelling Norms and Concepts as Key Issues*, 2003, pp. 69-78

Biagioli, C., Francesconi, E., Spinosa, P., Taddei, M. Legislative drafting support tool based on XML standards. In *Proceedings of DEXA 2005*, Copenhagen, Denmark, 22-26 August 2005

Biagioli, C., Francesconi, E., Passerini, A., Montemagni, S., Soria, C. Automatic semantics extraction in law documents. In *Proceedings of International Conference on Artificial Intelligence and Law*, 2005, pp. 133-139

COSPA - Consortium for Open Source in Public Administration. *http://www.cospa-project.org* retrieved on Dec. 18 2006

Johnson, S. *Yacc - yet another compiler compiler*. Technical Report CSTR 32, Bell Laboratories, Murray Hill, N.J., 1975

Lesk, M. *Lex - a lexical analyzer generator*. Technical Report CSTR 39, Bell Laboratories, Murray Hill, N.J., 1975

Lupo, C. Beyond NormeinRete. In *Proceedings of the 3rd Legislative XML Workshop*, 2005

Moats, R., K.R.S *Urn syntax*. Technical Report RFC 2141, Internet Engineering Task Force (IETF), 1997

Saqib, A. *XML: WYSIWYG to WYSIWYM A brief look at XML document authoring*. Free Software Magazine Issue 3, April 2005 *http://www.freesoftwaremagazine.com/articles/practical_applications_xml* retrieved on Dec. 18 2006

Spinosa, P. Identification of legal documents through urns (uniform resource names). In *Proceedings of the EuroWeb 2001, The Web in Public Administration*, 1997

Sun Microsystems Free and Open Source Licensing White Paper. *www.sun.com/software/opensource/whitepapers/free_open_licensing.pdf*, 2006 retrieved on Dec. 18 2006

Megale, F., Vitali F. I dtd dei documenti di norme in rete. In *Informatica e Diritto 1*, 1990, pp. 167-231

Automatic extraction of semantics in law documents

Claudia Soria*, Roberto Bartolini*, Alessandro Lenci°, Simonetta Montemagni*, Vito Pirrelli*

*Istituto di Linguistica Computazionale - CNR, Via Moruzzi 1, 56124 Pisa, Italy
°University of Pisa, Department of Linguistics, Via S. Maria 36, 56100 Pisa, Italy

Abstract. In this paper we address the problem of automatically enriching legal texts with semantic annotation, an essential pre–requisite to effective indexing and retrieval of legal documents. This is done through illustration of a computational system developed for automated semantic annotation of (Italian) law texts. This tool is an incremental system using Natural Language Processing techniques to perform two tasks: i) classify law paragraphs according to their regulatory content, and ii) extract relevant text fragments corresponding to specific semantic roles that are relevant for the different types of regulatory content. The paper sketches the overall architecture of the tool and reports results of a preliminary case study on a sample of Italian law texts.

Keywords: semantic analysis of law documents, content enrichment

1. Introduction

The huge amount of documents available in the legal domain calls for computational tools supporting efficient and intelligent search and filtering of information. Over the last several years, machine-learning oriented research in information retrieval and document classification has spawned a number of systems capable of handling structural content management, helping users to automatically or semi-automatically identify relevant structured portions of legal texts, such as paragraphs, chapters or intertextual references. However, while knowledge management systems can certainly profit from automated detection of structural properties of regulatory texts, advanced document indexing and retrieval functions are bound to require more granular and rich semantically oriented representations of text content. Suppose you are interested in finding all regulations applying to a particular type of individual, say an employer. Searching legal texts by using "employer" as a keyword is likely to return many irrelevant text excerpts, as plain keyword matching is blind to the particular semantic role played by the concept encoded by the term in context. Alternatively, one might be interested in tracking down all the penalties that a citizen or a member of a particular category of people is subjected to in connection with a particular behaviour. Simply searching for "citizen" and "penalty" would not be enough, since there are many other possible ways to express the same concepts, whose recognition requires advanced text understanding capabilities.

To successfully address all these issues, then, we expect regulatory texts to explicitly contain the sort of implicit information that human readers are naturally able to track down through reading, *e.g.* that a certain text expresses an obligation for an employer to provide a safe environment for his employees, or that another text encodes a penalty for doing or not doing something. The process of augmenting a text with labels expressing its semantic content is what we shall hereafter refer to as *semantic annotation*. In the past, indexing of textual documents with semantic tags has been a manual chore, and methods to automate this process are highly desirable. Semantic annotation of unstructured natural language texts can significantly increase the value of text collections by promoting deployment of advanced services, well beyond traditional full-text search functionalities. In this paper we intend to address the problem of automatically enriching legal texts with semantic tags through illustration of SALEM (Semantic Annotation for LEgal Management), an NLP system currently used as an advanced module of the NIR[1] legal editor (see (Biagioli et al., 2003)) to automatically tag the semantic structure of Italian law paragraphs through an integration of NLP and information extraction-inspired technology.

1.1. PREVIOUS WORK

Functionalities for retrieving relevant documents on the basis of text queries are provided by most current legal knowledge management tools, as witnessed by the well–known LexisNexis© and WestLaw© systems. Surely, systems differ as to the types of information search queries are sensitive to. In most cases only low-level text structures can be searched for. For instance, the tool described in (Bolioli et al., 2002) is used for the automatic recognition of structural elements of a law text, and allows for intra- and inter-textual browsing of documents. Fully automatic or semi-automatic systems that carry out semantic text analysis, thus providing content-based representations, are far less common. Notable exceptions are the DIAsDEM system (Graubitz et al., 2001) and the approach proposed by De Busser *et al.* (Busser et al., 2002), which is however not specialized for the legal domain. In DIAsDEM, unstructured texts are iteratively processed to yield a semantic representation of their content. Although developed for a different domain, for different purposes and with different techniques, the output of this system is

---

[1] NIR ("Norme in Rete", *Laws on the web*) is a national project sponsored by the Ministry of Justice for the free access by citizens to Italian jurisdiction.

in line with the one described in this paper: a text augmented with domain–specific tags explicitly representing portions of its content.

A technique more similar to the one presented here is adopted by Saias and Quaresma (Saias and Quaresma, 2003), who exploit NLP techniques to yield a syntactic annotation of law texts and populate a legal ontology. Their output representation allows users to retrieve a document on the basis of sophisticated queries such as, for instance, the presence of a certain action X in a document, the occurrence of individual Y as a subject of an unspecified action, or as the performer of X. SALEM identifies similar types of information in texts, but its semantic representation also contains the particular type of regulation expressed by a law paragraph, in addition to the entities and actions involved. In our view, this extra information represents an added value for effective indexing and retrieval of documents. Finally, the area of research in automatic construction and population of legal ontologies, albeit not specifically intended to address the task of semantic annotation as such, also shares many of the issues we are interested in here (see for instance the work of Lame (Lame, 2003) and Mommers (Mommers, 2001), among the others).

2. Methodology and motivations

2.1. THE LEGAL TEXT

As textual units, (Italian) laws are typically organized into hierarchically structured sections, the smallest one being the so-called *law paragraph*. Law paragraphs are usually numbered sections of an article, as in Figure 1 below[2]. As to its content, a law paragraph is associated

Article 6.
1. The Commission shall be assisted by the committee set up by Article 5 of Directive 98/34/EC.
2. The representative of the Commission shall submit to the committee a draft of the measures to be taken.
Figure 1. A typical article.

with a particular *legislative provision*, which could be seen as the illocutionary point of a law section. For instance, a paragraph expresses a

---

[2] The examples provided in the paper are taken from EC laws. Every time the purpose of the example is to illustrate semantic, language-independent phenomena, we use the English text for the sake of clarity. We remind the reader, however, that SALEM works on Italian law texts only.

permission or an obligation for some actor to perform or not to perform a certain course of action, as in Figures 2 and 3.

Directive. A Member State may provide that a legal body the head office of which is not in the Community may participate in the formation of an SCE provided that legal body is formed under the law of a Member State, has its registered office in that Member State and has a real and continuous link with a Member State's economy.

Figure 2. A Permission.

Licence applications shall be accompanied by proof of payment of the fee for the period of the licence's validity.

Figure 3. An Obligation.

Law paragraphs may also have an inter–textual content, *i.e.* they can contain some sort of amendments to existing laws. In this case they are said to be *modifications*. For instance, a paragraph may contain an insertion with respect to another law, or a replacement, or a repeal, as the Figures 4 and 5 illustrate.

The following point shall be inserted after point 2g (Council Directive 96/61/EC) in Annex XX to the Agreement: "2h. 399 D 0391: Commission Decision 1999/391/EC of 31 May 1999 concerning the questionnaire relating to Council Directive 96/61/EC concerning integrated pollution prevention and control (IPPC) (implementation of Council Directive 91/692/EEC) (OJ L 148, 15.6.1999, p. 39)."

Figure 4. An Insertion.

The text of point 2eg (Commission Decision 95/365/EC) in Annex XX to the Agreement shall be replaced by the following: "399 D 0568: Commission Decision 1999/568/EC of 27 July 1999 establishing the ecological criteria for the award of the Community eco–label to light bulbs (OJ L 216, 14.8.1999, p. 18)."

Figure 5. A Replacement.

2.2. SALEM FRAMEWORK

SALEM has a twofold task: a) to assign each law paragraph to a given *legislative provision type*; b) to automatically tag the parts of the paragraph with domain-specific semantic roles identifying the *legal entities* (i.e. actors, actions and properties) referred to in the legislative provision.

The type of semantic annotation output by SALEM is closely related to the task of Information Extraction, defined as "the extraction of information from a text in the form of text strings and processed text strings which are placed into slots labelled to indicate the kind of information that can fill them" (MUC, Message Understanding Conference). Law text analysis in SALEM is driven by an *ontology* of legislative provision types (e.g. obligation, insertion, etc.). Classes in the ontology are formally defined as *frames* with a fixed number of (possibly optional) *slots* corresponding to the semantic roles played by the legal entities specified by a given provision type. For instance, in Figure 1 above, which expresses an obligation, the relevant roles in the first sentence of paragraph 2 are the addressee of the obligation (i.e. *The representative of the Commission*), the action (i.e. what the addressee is obliged to do, in this case to *submit to the committee a draft of the measures to be taken*) and a *third_ party* (i.e. the action recipient, here *the committee*). In a similar way, a modification such as an insertion can have up to four relevant roles: (1) the reference text being modified, or *rule* (in Figure 4 above, the text *(Council Directive 96/61/EC) in Annex XX to the Agreement)*, (2) the *position* where the new text is going to be inserted (here, *after point 2g*); (3) the new text or *novella* (here, the captioned text); (4) the verbatim text to be replaced by the novella (*novellato*, not occurring in the example above). The following example illustrates the frame for an obligation:

FRAME : obligation
ADDRESSEE: the member State
ACTION: pay the advance within 30 calendar days of submission of the application for advance payment
THIRD PARTY: –

while the following is an example of the frame for a replacement.

FRAME : replacement
RULE: (Commission Decision 95/365/EC) in Annex XX to the Agreement
POSITION: –
NOVELLATO: point 2eg
NOVELLA: 399 D 0568: Commission Decision 1999/568/EC of 27 July 1999 establishing the ecological criteria for the award of the Community eco-label to light bulbs (OJ L 216, 14.8.1999, p. 18).

Automatic identification of the provision type expressed by a law paragraph is important for effective management of law texts. Law databases could be queried through fine–grained "semantic" searches according to the type of legal provision reported by a law paragraph. Furthermore, automatic identification and extraction of text portions of law that are subject to modifications could enable (semi)automatic updating of law texts, or make it possible for the history of a law to be traced throughout all its modifications; the original referenced text could be imported and modified, etc. Finally, automatic assignment of the relevant paragraph parts to semantic slots is bound to have an impact on effective legal content management and search, allowing for fine–grained semantic indexing and query of legal texts, and paving the way to real–time analysis of legal corpora in terms of logical components or actors at the level of individual provisions. In the near future, it will be possible to search an on-line legislative corpus for all types of obligations concerning a specific subject, or to highlight all possible legislative provisions a given action or actor happens to be affected by.

3. SALEM architecture

3.1. GENERAL OVERVIEW

Although legal language is considerably more constrained than ordinary language, its specific syntactic and lexical structures still pose a considerable challenge for state-of-the-art NLP tools. Nonetheless, if our goal is not a fully-fledged representation of their content, but only identification of specific information portions, legal texts are relatively predictable and hence tractable through NLP–based techniques.

SALEM is a suite of NLP tools for the analysis of Italian texts (Bartolini et al., 2002a), specialized to cope with the specific stylistic conventions of the legal parlance, with the aim to automatically classify and semantically annotate law paragraphs. A first prototype of SALEM has just been brought to completion and its performance evaluated. The NLP technology used for SALEM is relatively simple, but powerful, also thanks to the comparative predictability of law texts. SALEM takes in input single law paragraphs in raw text and outputs a semantic tagging of the text, where its classification together with the semantic roles corresponding to different frame slots are rendered as XML tags. An output example (translated into English for the reader's convenience) is given in Figure 6, where the input paragraph is classified as an *obl(igation)* and portions of the text are identified as respectively denoting the *addressee* and the *action*.

```
<obligation><obl:addressee>The Member State</obl:addressee>
shall   <obl:action>pay    the    advance   within   30   calendar
days  of  submission  of  the  application  for  advance  payment
</obl:action>.</obligation>
```
Figure 6. SALEM output example.

SALEM approach to classification and semantic annotation of legal texts follows a two stage strategy. In the first step, a general purpose parsing system, hand-tuned to handle some idiosyncracies of Italian legal texts, pre–processes each law paragraph to provide a shallow syntactic analysis. In the second step, the syntactically pre–processed text is fed into the semantic annotation component proper, making explicit the information content implicitly conveyed by the provisions.

3.2. SYNTACTIC PRE–PROCESSING

Syntactic pre–processing produces the data structures to which semantic annotation applies. At this stage, the input text is first tokenized and normalized for dates, abbreviations and multi–word expressions; the normalized text is then morphologically analyzed and lemmatized, using an Italian lexicon specialized for the analysis of legal language; finally, the text is POS-tagged and shallow parsed into non–recursive constituents called "chunks".

A sample chunked output is given in Figure 7. A chunk is a textual unit of adjacent word tokens sharing the property of being related through dependency relations (es. pre–modifier, auxiliary, determiner, etc.). Each chunk contains information about its type (e.g. a noun chunk (N_C), a verb chunk (FV_C), a prepositional chunk (P_C), an adjectival chunk (ADJ_C), etc.), its lexical head (identified by the label *potgov*) and any intervening modifier, causative or auxiliary verb, and preposition. A chunked sentence, however, does not give information about the nature and scope of inter–chunk dependencies. These dependencies, whenever relevant for semantic annotation, are identified at the ensuing processing stage (see section 3.3 below).

Although full text parsing may be suggested as an obvious candidate for adequate content processing, we contend that shallow syntactic parsing provides a useful intermediate representation for content analysis. First, at this stage information about low level textual features (e.g. punctuation) is still available and profitably usable, whereas it is typically lost at further stages of analysis. In this connection, it should be appreciated that correct analysis of modifications crucially depends on punctuation marks, and in particular on quotes and colons, which are used to identify the text of the amendment (*novella*) and the amending text (*novellato*). Secondly, chunked sentences naturally lend themselves to incrementally being used as the starting point for partial functional analysis, whereby the range of dependency relations that are instrumental for semantic annotation is detected. In particular, dependency information is heavily used for the mark–up of both modifications and obligations, which requires knowledge of the underlying syntactic structure. Finally, a third

All'articolo 6 della legge 24_ gennaio_ 1986 , n._ 17 , le parole: "entro
centottanta giorni dalla pubblicazione della presente legge nella Gazzetta
Ufficiale" sono soppresse.

1. [[CC: P_C] [PREP: A#E] [DET: LO#RD@MS] [AGR: @MS] [
   POTGOV: ARTICOLO#S@MS]] All' articolo

2. [[CC:ADJ_C] [POTGOV: 6#N]] 6

3. [[CC: di_C] [DET: LO#RD@FS] [AGR: @FS] [POTGOV:
   LEGGE#S@FS]] della legge

4. [[CC: ADJ_C] [POTGOV: 24_gennaio_1986#N]]
   24_gennaio_1986

5. : [[CC: PUNC_C] [PUNCTYPE: ,#@]] ,

6. [[CC: ADJ_C] [POTGOV: n._17#N]] n._17

7. [[CC: PUNC_C] [PUNCTYPE: ,#@]] ,

8. [[CC: N_C] [DET: LO#RD@FP] [AGR: @FP-@FP] [POTGOV:
   PAROLA#S@FP PAROLE#S@FP]] le parole

9. ...

Figure 7. A fragment of chunked text.

practical reason is that chunking yields a local level of syntactic annotation. As a result, it does not "balk" at domain–specific constructions
that violate general grammar patterns; rather, parsing is carried on
to detect the immediately following allowed structure, while ill–formed
chunks are left behind, unspecified for their category.

3.3. SEMANTIC ANNOTATION

As mentioned above, the SALEM approach is closely inspired by mainstream techniques in Information Extraction. In particular, semantic
annotation consists in the identification of all the instances of particular
provision types in text. The frame defining a provision type can then
be regarded as an *extraction template* whose slots are filled with the
textual material matching the corresponding conceptual roles.

The semantic annotation component takes in input a chunked representation of each law paragraph and identifies semantically–relevant
structures by applying domain–dependent, finite state techniques locat-

ing relevant patterns of chunks. Semantic mark–up is performed through a two–step process:

1. each paragraph is assigned to a frame (corresponding to the legislative provision expressed in the text);

2. slots of the frame identified at step (1) are turned into an extraction template and instantiated through the structural components (i.e. sentences, clauses, phrases) of the law paragraph.

The current version of the semantic annotation component is a specialized version of the ILC finite–state compiler of grammars for dependency syntactic analysis (Bartolini et al., 2002b). The SALEM version of the grammar compiler uses a specialized grammar including (i) a core group of syntactic rules for the identification of basic syntactic dependencies (e.g. subject and object), and (ii) a battery of specialized rules for the semantic annotation of the text.

All rules in the grammar are written according to the following template:

<chunk-based regular expression> WITH <battery of tests> => <actions>

The recognition of provision types and the subsequent extraction of information from the text are based on structural patterns which are combined with lexical conditions and other tests aimed at detecting low level textual features (such as punctuation) as well as specific syntactic structures (e.g. the specification of a given dependency relation). Structural patterns are expressed in terms of regular expressions over sequences of chunks, whereas all other conditions (*e.g.* lexical, syntactic, etc.) are checked through a battery of tests. The action type ranges from the identification of basic dependency relations (in the case of syntactic rules) to the semantic mark–up of the text (in the case of semantic annotation rules).

The assignment of a paragraph to a provision class is based on a combination of both syntactic and lexical criteria. As already mentioned above, a preliminary study of the linguistic features of law paragraphs revealed a strong association between classes of verbs and provision types: an obligation is typically expressed with the modal verb "dovere" (*shall/must*) or the verbal construction "essere obbligato/tenuto a" (*to be obliged to*); similarly, lexical cues for the identification of an insertion include verbs like "aggiungere" or "inserire" (*to add, to insert*). We will refer to these verbs as trigger verbs. The presence of a trigger verb in the text is only the first step towards the detection of a specific provision class which, in order to be completed, needs to be complemented with structural tests which include the role of the trigger verb as the sentence head and the types of dependency relations governed by it.

Reliable identification of dependency relations is also important for assigning structural elements to semantic roles, since the latter tend to be associated with specific syntactic functions (e.g. subject, object). To give the reader only but one example, the addressee of an obligation typically corresponds to the syntactic subject of the sentence, while the action (s)he is obliged to carry out is usually expressed as an infinitival clause, as in the example reported below:

> [[Il comitato misto] subj] addressee] è tenuto a raccomandare modifiche degli allegati secondo le modalità previste dal presente accordo
>
> [[*The Joint Committee*] subj] addressee] *shall be responsible for recommending amendments to the Annex as foreseen in this Agreement.*

Note, however, that this holds only when the verbal head of the infinitival clause is used in the active voice. By contrast, the syntactic subject can express the third–party if the action verb is used in the passive voice and is governed by specific lexical heads.

4. Case study

We report the results of a case study carried out with SALEM on the basis of a small ontology covering 8 provision types. This section presents the ontology of provisions and illustrates the system's performance against a corpus of law paragraphs previously annotated by law experts.

4.1. The frame–based legal ontology

In this case study, we have used a small ontology designed by experts in the legal domain at ITTIG–CNR.[3] The ontology distinguishes three major categories of provisions: *obligations, definitions* and *modifications*. A main distinction can be made between obligations, addressing human actors, and modifications, which are rather aimed at modifying the textual content of pre–existing laws. Obligations in turn divide into the following classes: *obligation, prohibition, permission,* and *penalty.* In their turn, modifications are further subdivided into *replacement, insertion* and *repeal.* The taxonomical structure of the SALEM ontology is illustrated in Figure 8.

As mentioned above, law paragraphs are analyzed in SALEM not only according to the particular type of legislative provision they express, but also with respect to the main legal entities involved by the

---

[3] Istituto di Teoria e Tecniche dell'Informazione Giuridica, CNR, Florence, Italy.

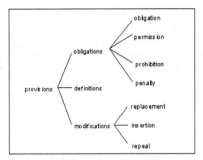

Figure 8. Taxonomical structure of the ontology of provisions

Table I. Frame-based description of the different provision types

Provision class	Slots
Obligation	Addressee, Action, Third-party
Permission	Addressee, Action, Third-party
Prohibition	Action, Third-party
Penalty	Addressee, Action, Object, Rule
Definition	Definiendum, Definiens
Repeal	Rule, Position, *Novellato*
Replacement	Rule, Position, *Novellato, Novella*
Insertion	Rule, Position, *Novella*

law. Consistently, each ontology class is formally defined as a *frame* with a fixed number of (possibly optional) *slots*. The slot types required for the description of the 8 bottom classes in the SALEM taxonomy are illustrated in Table I.

4.2. EVALUATION RESULTS

SALEM preliminary results are very promising. The system was evaluated on a sample of 473 law paragraphs, covering seven classes of the ontology of Table I. The test corpus was built by law experts at ITTIG-CNR, who also provided a hand–annotated version used as gold standard for evaluation. The aim of the evaluation was to assess the system's performance on two tasks: classification of paragraphs according to the ontology (henceforth referred to as "classification task") and mark–up of semantic roles (henceforth "information extraction task").

Table II. SALEM results for the classification task.

Class	Total	SALEM answers	OK	Precision	Recall
Obligation	19	19	18	0.95	0.95
Permission	15	18	15	0.83	1
Prohibition	15	15	14	0.93	0.93
Penalty	122	117	109	0.93	0.89
Repeal	70	69	69	1	0.99
Replacement	111	111	111	1	1
Insertion	121	119	119	1	0.98
Tot.	**473**	**468**	**455**	**0.97**	**0.96**

Table II summarizes the results achieved for the paragraph classification task with reference to the seven bottom classes of provisions,
where Precision is defined as the ratio of correctly classified provisions
over all SALEM answers, and Recall refers to the ratio of correctly
classified provisions over all provisions in the test corpus. Note that
here a classification is valued as correct if the automatically assigned
class and the manually assigned one are identical. The classification
performance is even better if it is related to the corresponding first
level ontology classes (i.e. obligations and modifications). In fact, in
some cases, mostly penalties and permissions, multiple answers are
given due to the fact that obligations bottom classes share a great
deal of lexical and morpho-syntactic properties; yet, these answers are
to be considered correct if classification is evaluated with respect to
the first level ontology classes (i.e. obligations and modifications). On
the other hand, when unambiguous linguistic patterns are used, the
system easily reaches 1 for both Precision and Recall, as with the class
of Modifications.

Table III illustrates the performance of the system in the information
extraction task. The aim of the evaluation here was to assess the system's reliability in identifying, for each provision type or frame, all the
semantic roles that are relevant for that frame and are instantiated in
the text. For each class of provisions in the test corpus we thus counted
the total number of semantic roles to be identified; this value was then
compared with the number of semantic roles correctly identified by
the system and the total number of answers given by the system. Here,
Precision is scored as the number of correct answers returned by system

Table III. SALEM results for the information extraction task.

Class	OK	Expected answers	SALEM answers	Precision	Recall
Obligation	38	38	38	1	1
Permission	20	25	24	0.83	0.8
Prohibition	21	21	27	0.78	1
Penalty	303	388	330	0.92	0.78
Repeal	104	108	106	0.98	0.96
Replacement	303	309	306	0.99	0.98
Insertion	373	376	375	0.99	0.99
Tot.	**1162**	**1265**	**1206**	**0.96**	**0.92**

over the total number of answers returned, while Recall is the ratio
of correct answers returned by system over the number of expected
answers.

5.   Conclusions and future work

In this paper we presented SALEM, an NLP–based system for classification and semantic annotation of law paragraphs. Although we follow
the mainstream trend in state-of-the-art NLP architectures towards
use of shallow parsing techniques, the novelty of our approach rests
in the incremental composition of shallow parsing with higher levels
of syntactic and semantic analysis, leading to simultaneous, effective
combination of low- and high-level text features for fine-grained content
analysis. Besides, the cascaded effect of incremental composition led to
a considerable simplification of the individual parsing modules, all of
which are implemented as finite state automata. The effectiveness and
performance of the system was tested with promising results on the
basis of a small ontology of provision types, against a test-bed of text
material hand-annotated by human experts.

We are presently working along several lines of development. On
the one hand, we intend to make the system more robust by testing
it on a larger sample of law texts. Although laws are quite stable as a
language genre, they can also be stylistically variable depending on the
personal inclinations of the author, the particular domain they apply to,
not to mention variations determined by historical changes. Collection
of a wider variety of text material is bound to have an impact on

SALEM flexibility and coverage. On the other hand, we also aim at expanding the ontology of provisions for semantic annotation to cover new provision types.

References

Bartolini, R., Lenci, A., Montemagni, S., Pirrelli, V. The lexicon-grammar balance in robust parsing of Italian. *Proc. of 3rd International Conference on Language Resources and Evaluation.* (2002).

Bartolini R., Lenci A., Montemagni S., Pirrelli V. Grammar and lexicon in the robust parsing of Italian: Towards a non-naïve interplay. *Proc. of Coling 2002 Workshop on Grammar Engineering and Evaluation.* Academia Sinica, Nankang, Taipei, Taiwan, 1st September (2002).

Biagioli, C., Francesconi, E., Spinosa, P., Taddei, M. The NIR project. Standards and tools for legislative drafting and legal document Web publication. *Proc. of the International Conference of Artificial Intelligence and Law.* Edinburgh, June 24 (2003).

Bolioli, A., Dini, L., Mercatali, P., Romano, F. For the automated mark-up of Italian legislative texts in XML. *Proc. of JURIX 2002,* London, UK, 16-17 December (2002).

De Busser, R., Angheluta, R., Moens, M.-F. Semantic Case Role Detection for Information Extraction. *Proc. of COLING 2002.* New Brunswick (2002) 1198–1202.

Graubitz, H., Winkler, K., Spiliopoulou, M. Semantic Tagging of Domain-Specific Text Documents with DIAsDEM. *Proc. of the 1st International Workshop on Databases, Documents, and Information Fusion (DBFusion 2001).* Gommern, Germany (2001) 61–72.

Saias, J., Quaresma, P. Using NLP techniques to create legal ontologies in a logic programming based web information retrieval system. *Proc. of ICAIL 2003 Workshop on Legal Ontologies and Web Based Legal Information Management.* Edinburgh, UK, June 24-28 (2003).

Lame, G. Using text analysis techniques to identify legal ontologies' components. *Proc. of ICAIL 2003 Workshop on Legal Ontologies and Web Based Legal Information Management.* Edinburgh, UK, June 24-28 (2003).

Mommers, L. A knowledge-based ontology for the legal domain. *Proc. of the Second International Workshop on Legal Ontologies.* December 13 (2001).

Law Making Environment. Perspectives.

Carlo Biagioli, Amedeo Cappelli*, Enrico Francesconi, Fabrizio Turchi
Institute of Legal Information Theory and Techniques (ITTIG-CNR)
*Institute of Information Science and Technologies (ISTI-CNR)
Italian National Research Council

Abstract. In this paper a model-driven module able to guide the legislative drafter in planning a new bill is presented. This module aims at helping the legislative drafter to build a new act from a conceptual point of view.
Using this module the classical drafting process is inverted: the structure of a bill is constructed on the basis of its semantics. The main phases of the planning process and the software architecture of this module are shown.

Keywords: Model of Provisions, Legal Drafting, Model Driven Visual Legislative Text Planning

1. Towards a Standardized-Knowledge Based Legislative Drafting

From its formulation in the beginning of '80, the subsequent prototypes (Biagioli C., 1992) and its concrete start in 2000, the general goal of the project is the implementation of a "law making environment" (LME) for planning, wording and management of legislative texts. The complete version of the law making environment software is done and consists of two modules: they are the textual "drafting environment" xmLegesEditor (the open-source version of NIREditor (Biagioli et al., 1992), a law drafting module able to produce new law texts according to the XML and URN standards established by the "NormeInRete" (NIR) project, and metaEdit (Biagioli and Turchi, 2005b), the module for the semantic mark-up of the drafted texts, according to provisions model (Section 2) and domain conceptual dictionaries.

In this paper a sketch of a second-generation LME is presented for legislative "conceptual drafting": a model driven approach for planning the new text deep structure as well as for its wording ("meta-drafting environment"). Therefore the global "law making environment" will allow two ways of drafting: textual and conceptual.

LME in general is based on a double vision of the legislative text: formal and functional (Biagioli, 1997) (or rhetorical and illocutive[1]). Articles, paragraphs, etc., are entities belonging to the formal profile,

---

[1] As those document profiles were called in (Branting et al., 1997)

while functional entities are provisions and their arguments, represented as analytical metadata in the NIR standards[2].

The formal management of texts is based on their formal entities, mainly concerned with legislative technique. Moreover metaEdit commands, based on the functional entities, allow the handling of substantial aspects of the texts and, more in general, they allow to look at them from the point of view of their content and meaning, making possible to explicit basic meanings through metadata.

The new frontier of the semantic Web will move the information searching more and more on the substantial aspects of documents, requiring the availability of advanced editing instruments, able to handle not only the body of documents, but also their semantics. The ability to deal with meaningful semantic aspects of legislative texts, is mandatory in LME, based on XML, where meanings are effectively expressed by metadata.

The law text conceptual planning system presented in this paper aims at coping with such requirements, not only providing the legislative drafter with facilities in law text semantics management through metadata, as LME already does, but also allowing the construction of a new bill directly starting from the definition of its semantics, so turning upside down the drafting process.

This paper is organized as follow: in Section 2 the two knowledge models required by LME are briefly described; in Section 3 the main features and purposes of the LME textual drafting and semantic mark-up environment are presented; in Section 4 an overview of the meta-drafting environment is described; in Sections 5, 6, 7 the process of planning a new bill from a conceptual point of view as well as the software architecture of the meta-drafting environment is shown; finally, in Section 8 some conclusions are discussed.

2. Semantic models

2.1. PROVISION MODEL

Even if the structure of legislative texts is both formal and functional, the current legistics is more concerned with formal features of legislative texts than with their semantics.

The formal structure of texts and its elements, partitions, are well described, while less attention is paid to the deep structure, viewed as a collection of "provisions", this one not deeply described and not widely involved in the organization of the text.

---

[2] NormeInRete project standards.

Paragraphs and provisions are the elements respectively of the formal (syntactic) and functional (semantic) perspective. In a paragraph every term belongs to the corresponding partition (e.g. paragraph), while every meaning belongs to the correspondent provision. For instance a cross reference is a meaningful element, but is also a part of a provision and its meaning is fully understandable only in the global provision meaning context.

Since the law structure should be one, those (syntactic and semantic) elements must correspond each other in some extent. The most simple relation is 1-to-1, but others are acceptable, if only well-known. Any known relation is necessary, to achieve the starting point: law has one structure and two faces, or, in other words, is considerable from two perspectives.

In the Italian legislation there are many cases, depending on the quality of the legislator. It is a matter of legistic quality of legislation, the degree of correspondence between the two aspects of the structure. In that vision a lack of correspondence is a lack of legislative technique quality, until a new legislating techniques will not arise. For instance in US the plain language movement suggested legislative texts based on flat common language, but, at least in Italy, the provisions approach seems to be well-grounded.

2.2. LEGAL AND DOMAIN CONCEPT MODELS: GENERAL-STATIC AND CONTINGENT-DYNAMIC MEANINGS

Legislative texts contain two kind of semantic elements: speech acts (linguistic element equivalent of the legistic element provision) and atomic concepts. The meaning of terms contained in a paragraph belongs, from a general-static point of view, to the related concept and has various relations with many others terms, as explained in the dictionaries and in terminological ontologies. On the contrary from the contingent-dynamic point of view, the meaning of every term contained in a paragraph belongs to a speech act - provision. In other words terms can be seen as atomic elements belonging to concepts and at the same time playing their role in the provision they belong to, as well explained in the speech acts theory.

Such distinction relies on Breuker and Hoekstra statement, when they speak about "epistemological promiscuity", referring to "the common practice of indiscriminately mixing epistemological knowledge and domain knowledge in ontologies" (Hoekstra and Breuker, 2004).

Therefore two kind of interacting models are needed, dynamic and static: provision theory and concepts networks (terminological ontologies)[3]. Semantic drafting supporting tools have to be based on both models, in a way that makes it possible their interaction. A provision theory has been developed (Biagioli and Grossi, 2007), while, as regards concepts, a conceptual dictionary has been made (Cappelli et al., 2006), even if every domain ontology is more or less useful and can be adopted.

3. LME - Drafting environment

The LME "drafting environment" components are xmLegesEditor and metaEdit.

xmLegesEditor (Agnoloni et al., 2007) is a specific environment for legislative drafting. It is the open-source version of NIREditor, that has been implemented within the NIR project to handle legislative documents in XML native format, within the established URN-NIR and XML-NIR standards. xmLegesEditor is conceived as a visual editor, supporting users to produce valid documents according to the NIR-DTDs. No XML validation is necessary since it allows only valid operations according to the established standard.

Specific facilities are: the insertion of partitions according to the insertion point context; the automatic numbering of the divisions; the updating of internal references in case of text movements or variations as well as the external and internal cross-references construction.

On the basis of the twofold vision of a legislative text (formal and functional (Section 2.1)) two possible text organization strategies can be followed: the *formal* and the *functional organization strategies* (Biagioli, 1997).

In the *formal organization strategy* text is considered as made up of divisions (formal profile): partitions of similar rank, to be grouped in a new partition of higher rank, are chosen explicitly by the drafter.

In the *functional organization strategy* text is considered as composed by *provisions* (functional profile): provisions to be grouped are chosen with respect to their content, affinities, etc., making queries according to the provision model; then it is decided where they should be placed, according to the preferences of the drafter and the customary procedure of presentation.

---

[3] "Ontological knowledge: Typically regulations are not given in an empty environment; instead they make use of terminology and concepts which are relevant to the organisation and/or the aspect they seek to regulate. Thus, to be able to capture the meaning of regulations, one needs to encode not only the regulations themselves, but also the underlying ontological knowledge. This knowledge usually includes the terminology used, its basic structure, and integrity constraints that need to be satisfied." (Antoniou et al., 2005).

metaEdit is a web based tool and allows the semantic mark up of the drafted text, according to the two mentioned models, epistemological (or dynamic) and ontological (or static). The user can describe the semantic contents of each partition firstly qualifying its provision type through the provision model, so capturing the basic ruling intention of the legislator. Secondly qualifying the provision contents (arguments) through the concept models available, so describing, in some extent, content and details of each provision.

Using metaEdit the user, before getting involved in the semantic mark-up process, is allowed to edit and modify the dictionary of concepts to be used in the semantic mark up, as well as to create if it is not already available from the beginning. Terms can be inserted and deleted and their relations can be introduced or modified, as well as the classes structure can be modified. It is conceived as a tool for creation and maintenance of bottom-up ontologies, starting from the relevant terms of the domain texts.

Moreover, as the ruled domains are unlimited, the system is conceived to be used with every existing dictionary, where domain relevant terms are organized into concepts and their meaning is in some way described.

4. Benefits in using semantic models

The model of provisions can be used to handle legislation with three main purposes: managing the normative system, searching for provisions and text meta-drafting.

Firstly the description of amendments (insertion, abrogation, substitution) can be used to automatically obtain the consolidated text, thus promoting the upkeep of the legal order.

Moreover it can be used to enhance the accessibility of the legal texts, giving the users advanced semantic search and retrieval facilities on legislation. To this aim a tool (metaSearch, (Biagioli and Turchi, 2005)) has been developed in the LME project able to query the functional profile of legislative texts through metadata. This module allows to query a legislative information system on the base of two modalities of reasoning: a reasoning on provisions and their relations and/or on domain concepts and their relations.

Finally the model of provisions can be effectively used to provide law-makers with tools to plan organic and well structure bills.

The use of the semantic model of provisions allows to plan new bills according to a conceptual point of view, enhancing the quality of text, structure and semantics in legislative documents. In this project the process of planning a new bill from a conceptual point of view has been called "Meta-Drafting", therefore the system implementing such legislative drafting strategy has been called "Meta-Drafting environment".

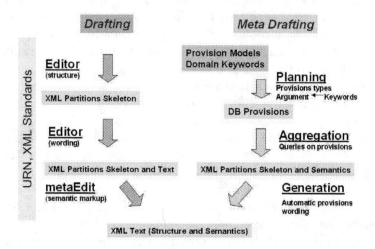

Figure 1. **Drafting and Meta-Drafting**

5. LME - Meta-Drafting environment

As discussed here and previously (Biagioli and Francesconi, 2005) the aim of this project is to provide the legislative drafter with facilities able to plan a new organic and well-structured bill. In particular the Meta-Drafting environment aims at providing users with facilities to help the organization of a new legislative text according to a semantic point of view, so that the formal profile of the text will be obtained as a result of the organization of the semantics of the text itself.

In the traditional activities of constructing a new bill, at the end of the drafting process the formal structure of the document may not be the best one to express the semantics of the text. The Meta-Drafting planning module, on the contrary, aims at turning over the traditional drafting process, providing facilities to firstly express the semantics of a legislative text, in terms of the functional profile, and only in a second phase, to organize the semantic components in a well-suited formal structure.

The semantics is expressed, as mentioned, in terms of type of provisions and arguments, usually added to the documents as metadata, chosen by documentalist or by specialized software. In our framework they play a different role: firstly they are chosen by the legislative drafter himself and, secondly, they are chosen during the text drafting, helping the drafting process itself. Therefore, firstly they are authentic metadata, as chosen by the legislative drafter, and moreover they are used not only in the searching process, but also in the drafting phase. The first point, authenticity of metadata, is a very crucial issue in Legislative XML community, as recently pointed out (Lachmayer and Hoffmann, 2005).

6. The process of planning a new bill

According to a semantic point of view, planning a new bill may be seen as an activity that consists basically in describing how the domain of interest of the human activities (a scenario) will be regulated by the new act. The formalization of this can rely on a model of the scenario to be regulated and on a model of the possible ways the act will be able to regulate the scenario. The scenario will consist of terms and concepts of the real world that can be drawn from or organized into term hierarchies (thesauri) and concept taxonomies (ontologies).

Similarly, a possible model of the legal order can rely, to some extent, on the concept of provision. According to this point of view "a legislative text may be seen as a vehicle that contains and transports provisions and the legal order as a set of provisions rather than of laws"(Biagioli, 1997).

For the activities of planning a new bill, facilities can be provided which are able to help the legislator to establish relations between instances of the provision model and the entities of the scenario to be regulated. The collection of the established relations and the instances of these models will represent the semantics, namely the functional profile, of the bill under construction.

After having defined the functional profile of the new bill, facilities will be provided helping the organization of the semantic components (provisions) into formal partitions of the constructing act, according to several criteria (expressed by query selections) derived from legislative technique rules. At the end of this process, the formal partitions of the act will contain semantically correlated components (provisions), and the semantically qualified formal structure skeleton of the new act can be obtained.

Partition wording can rely upon the user, or proposals of partitions wording can be generated on the basis of the semantics of the provision associated to each partition.

In Section 6.1, 6.2, 6.3 and 6.4 the main phases of construction of a new bill by using the Meta-Drafting environment module are described in more details.

6.1. Defining the scenario to be regulated

Traditionally the body of legislative acts begins with the introduction of definitional provisions concerning the most important concepts that are: the description of the involved actors (norm addressees), the main activities, the regulated actions, and in general the entities belonging to the domain regulated by the law.

The terms (subjects, actions, etc.) introduced by the drafter will update the description of the scenario to be regulated and defined (this can be done using a specific module within the Meta-Drafting environment, for example the functionalities of metaEdit dealing with terms and concepts management), giving place to voices, composed by the name of the entity and the correspondent definition.

Moreover, the drafter can be given the possibility to correlate terms under construction by means of the basic relations ("is a", "is part of", etc.), creating therefore a taxonomic tree structure, in the metaEdit application. Graphical instruments can be added to such application. The outcome will be a set of graphs representing the key-terms of domain to be regulated by the bill under construction.

6.2. Constructing provision instances (Planning)

The next step will consist in the construction of provision instances by correlating (regulative correlation) terms of the adopted conceptual dictionary to the provision arguments. Basically, such terms become contents of provision arguments; so instances of provisions are constructed. To obtain a provision instance from the corresponding model the drafter may choose among the arguments those which are relevant for the provision under construction; such arguments will be filled by the drafter with terms. In constructing a provision instance, the drafter is therefore guided by the provision model and by the tree-structure associated to the terms of the domain to be regulated.

For example the following fragment of the Italian privacy law:

"*A controller intending to process personal data falling within the scope of application of this act shall have to notify the 'Garante'...*"

can be described, according to the NIR metadata scheme, as a provision instance of type *Obligation* and arguments *Addressee*, *Action* and *Counter-party* as follows:

Obligation

Addressee: "Controller";

Action: "Notification";

Counter-party: "Garante".

6.3. GROUPING PROVISIONS INTO FORMAL PARTITIONS (AGGREGATION)

This phase will consist in the organization of provision instances into formal partitions by means of aggregations. The drafter will be allowed to group, directly or by means of meta-commands (basically queries on metadata), semantically correlated provision instances. Criteria of aggregation can be both thematic, depending on contents of the arguments, and regulative, deriving from the types of provisions and their typical structure.

Following legislative-technique criteria on the organization of the texts, the selected provisions will be collected in higher hierarchy level partitions of the formal structure. For instance, according to a common and simple criterion followed at least by the Italian legislative drafter and in the European directives drafting, the provisions of type *Definition* will be grouped in a single partition, on the beginning of the text. Another typical criterion is the aggregation of the type of provisions *Obligation, Procedure, Derogation*, related to a specific *action*.

When the obtained aggregations are considered satisfactory by the drafter, a stable functional structure of the legislative text is obtained and the automatic conversion of the functional structure into the final formal structure will be possible.

6.4. GENERATING PROVISION AND HEADLINE WORDING (GENERATION)

A further phase, here reported as a future research issue, will be able to help the drafter in the formulation of the body of the single provision and the headlines of formal partitions.

It will allow to construct sentences for provision instances wording, using tools based on computational linguistic techniques for language generation. Several styles of provision wording might be possible, including at least the active and passive form of a sentence.

Similarly, a semi-automatic headline wording could complete the process of constructing the body of the bill. In the Italian legislative technique titles of the partitions express both thematic and regulative aspects of the provisions. The automatic headline function will help the drafter in formulating a sort of virtual title of each provision, starting from its term-arguments.

Since in the Italian legislative technique a provision usually corresponds to a formal paragraph, such provision virtual title represents *de facto* the title of the corresponding formal paragraph.

The titles of the higher level container partitions will be a synthesis, as common denominator, of the titles of the contained partitions.

A possible implementation of the provision wording generation module can be based on an EBNF grammar which expresses the "productions" for each type of provision.

Ex:

$< ProvisionType > \rightarrow < Definition > \mid < Competence > \mid < Obligation > \mid$
$< Permission > \mid < Procedure > \mid < Penalty >$

$< Definition > \rightarrow < Definition\ syntactical\ structure >$

$< Competence > \rightarrow < Competence\ syntactical\ structure >$

. . .

$< Obligation > \rightarrow < Obligation\ syntactical\ structure >$

Each specific syntactical structure is related to the structure of the arguments of each provision type.

7.   The Meta-Drafting environment software architecture

The Meta-Drafting environment system is conceived as a visual editor of provisions and it is composed by three main components:

1. a Model of *Provisions* and *Arguments*;

2. a Model, represented as *concepts* and *terms*, of the scenario to be regulated;

3. a Visual Provision Manager.

7.1.   MODEL OF PROVISIONS AND ARGUMENTS

As discussed in Section 6, planning a new bill from a conceptual point of view can be based mainly on the model of Provisions and Arguments able to describe the semantics of the acts.

To the aim of providing a standard description of such a model, we suggest OWL as a language able to represent the model properties. An example of a taxonomic description of a provision model portion and its OWL implementation is reported in Fig. 2.

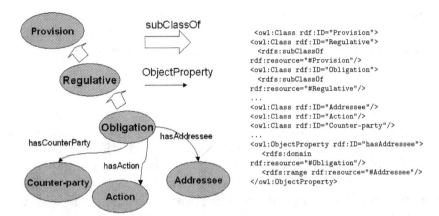

Figure 2. **Taxonomy of a provision model portion (*Obligation* model hierarchy path) and its OWL representation.**

OWL will provide a well-established implementation of the provision model which guarantees interoperability among the applications and a well-grounded framework for reasoning on provisions instantiation within a single act or within a legislative corpus.

7.2. MODEL OF THE SCENARIO TO BE REGULATED

As discussed in Section 6, the description of the main entities of the scenario to be regulated can be based on domain ontologies and thesauri.

In this context the use of an ontology is of primary importance. Laws in fact usually contain provisions which deal with entities (arguments) but they do not provide any general information on them: for example the Italian privacy law regulates the behaviour of the entity "Data controller" who is the owner of a set of personal data, but such law does not give any additional information on this role in the real domain-life. The use of an ontology allows to obtain such additional general information on the entities the new act will deal with. Moreover, the use of an ontology, and particularly of the associated lexicon, allows to obtain a normalized form of the terms with which entities are expressed, so that they can be indexed and used in the law document metadata querying process.

Legislative acts are made of terms both from the ruled domain and from the legal domain. The last ones are more or less common to every legislative act.

The system will rely on ontologies and lexicons: the knowledge they describe is both thematic (related to the scenario to be regulated) and legal (pure juridical concepts).

Similarly, the user may, if allowed, insert new terms or concepts of the particular domain he is going to regulate by using the functionalities of metaEdit dealing with terms and concepts management[4].

7.3. VISUAL PROVISION MANAGER

The Visual Provision Manager is a visual panel where provisions types and their arguments can be handle as visual objects (Fig. 3).

User will be able to plan a new act from a conceptual point of view by inserting provision instances as building blocks of the act under construction. The arguments of the provision instances will be given values obtained from the ontologies or thesauri of the domain of interest. At the end of this process the functional profile of the new act is defined in terms of its regulative (provision types) and thematic (provision argument values) profiles. This way the new act is constructed starting from the description of its semantic components, basically instances of the provision model.

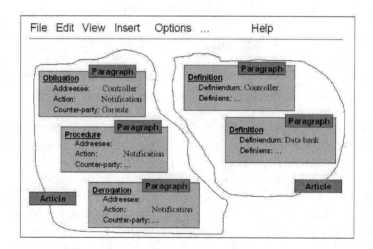

Figure 3. **Visual Provision Manager and the result of the provision grouping process.**

---

[4] An example of use of metaEdit for conceptual dictionary bottom up construction from domain lexicon in (Cappelli et al., 2006)

Only in a second phase the user will be able to construct the best structural organization (formal profile) of the text, with the benefit to see the building blocks of the bill under construction from the point of view of their meaning. The basic assumption allowing the organization of the structure of a legislative document while organizing its semantics, is that a "paragraph", the basic component of the formal profile, usually contains a provision, basic component of the functional profile, assumption which is widely observed by the legislator (this is represented (see Fig. 4) by the "concrete" (Niemann et al., 1990) relation between a type of provision and the corresponding paragraph; the "concrete" relation connects different representations of an object in different levels of abstraction).

At this stage the objects, representing provision instances, introduced within the visual panel, can be grouped into semantically correlated clusters. On the basis of the previous assumption, while organizing provisions into semantically correlated clusters, we obtain the organization of the same objects, viewed as paragraphs of the formal profile, into clusters representing higher level formal partitions, basically "articles" (Fig. 3). This process can be recursively repeated, so to obtain clusters representing higher level formal partitions, organized in a tree representing the document formal profile (Fig. 4).

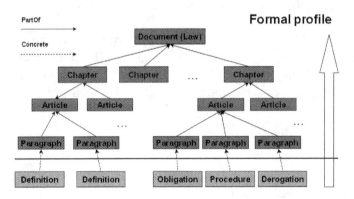

Figure 4. **Building document tree.**

The user will have the possibility to use an interface where grouping criteria can be expressed by queries on the provision model structure and on the content of its current instances (provision argument contents). Predefined criteria derived from legislative technique rules can be foreseen.

At the end of this process the document tree, where leaves are semantically annotated in terms of provisions and their arguments, is obtained. At this point the XML skeleton of the new bill can be generated according to a specific standard (in Italy, for example, the NIR standard), composed by semantically annotated formal partitions. Then the user will be allowed to complete the document structure, by wording each paragraph, being guided by the semantic annotation (Fig. 5).

```
...
<capo id="cap1">
<disposizioni>
<analitiche>
<dsp:definizione xlink:href="#art1-com1">
 <dsp:definiendum>Controller
<dsp:definiendum>
</dsp:definizione>
...
   <articolo id="art1">...</articolo>
</capo>
<disposizioni>
<analitiche>
<dsp:obbligo>
  <dsp:destinatario
xlink:href="#art7-com1">
  Controller
  </dsp:destinatario>
  <dsp:azione>
  Notification
  </dsp:azione>
  </dsp:obbligo>
<capo id="cap2">
  <articolo id="art7">...</articolo>
</capo>
```

Law n.

           Chapter 1

Art. 1

       Definition(Controller, ...)

1. [to be filled]

       Definition(Data bank,...)

2. [to be filled]

  ...

           Chapter 2

Art. 7

       Obligation(Controller,
         Notification, Garante)

1. [to be filled]

       Procedure(.., Notification, ...)

2. [to be filled]

       Derogation(.., Notification, ..)

3. [to be filled]

Figure 5. **XML-NIR skeleton of a new bill and its WYSIWYG view.**

As discussed in Section 6.4, a further development could be the semiautomatic provision wording phase by using NLP techniques on the basis of each provision model instance and the automatic summarisation of the meanings of provision groups to generate their titles.

8. Conclusions

In this work a system able to guide the legislative drafter in planning a new bill has been presented.

The new system, called "Meta-Drafting Environment" (MDE), is conceived to help the legislative drafter to build a new act from a conceptual point of view. Using the Meta-Drafting Environment system the classical drafting process is inverted: the structure of a bill (formal profile) is constructed on the basis of its semantics (functional profile), so to obtain a well-structured legislative text, where the chosen formal profile fits well the functional one.

The system can contribute to improve the legislative process, in particular the phase of legislative drafting, enhancing the quality of legislative texts.

In particular the "planning" and "aggregation" functionalities will improve external quality (semantics and structure) of legislative texts, while the functionality of "generation" will improve their internal quality in terms of coherency, consistency, improvement of the quality of provision wording, by using a key-language limiting the ambiguity of legislative texts. This will improve the accessibility of legislation for legal experts, decision-makers as well as citizens, thus promoting a democratic participation in the legislative process.

References

C. Biagioli. *Law Making Environment.* In Proceedings of the International Symposium "Legal Knowledge and Legal Reasoning Systems", pp. 83-103, Tokyo, 24-25 October 1992.

C. Biagioli, E. Francesconi, P. Spinosa, M. Taddei. *A legal drafting environment based on formal and semantic XML standards.* In Proceedings of International Conference on Artificial Intelligence and Law, pp. 244-245, Bologna, 2005.

C. Biagioli. *Towards a legal rules functional micro-ontology.* In Proceedings of Workshop LEGONT, 1997.

L.K. Branting, J.C. Lester, C.B. Callaway. *Automated Drafting of Self-Explaining Documents.* In Proceedings of the VI International Conference on Artificial Intelligence and Law, Melbourne, Australia, ACM Press, pp. 72-81.

C. Biagioli, D. Grossi. *Towards a Formal Foundation of Meta Drafting.* (To appear).

C. Biagioli, F. Turchi. *Model and Ontology based Conceptual Searching in Legislative XML Collections.* In Proceedings of the LOAIT Workshop, Bologna, 2005.

C. Biagioli, F. Turchi. *MetaSearch: Searching for Provisions and their Relevant Conceptual Contents in Legislative XML Database* Presentation at the IV Legislative XML Workshop, Klagenfurt, 2005.

T. Agnoloni, E. Francesconi, P. Spinosa. *xmLegesEditor: an open-source Visual XML Editor for supporting Legal National Standards* In Proceedings of the V Legislative XML Workshop.

A. Cappelli, V. Bartalesi Lenzi, R. Sprugnoli, C. Biagioli. *Modelization of Domain Concepts Extracted from the Italian Privacy Legislation.* In Proceedings of the Workshop IWCS-7, Tilburg, 2006.

C. Biagioli, E. Francesconi. *A Semantics-based Visual Framework for Planning a New Bill.* In Proceedings of the Jurix Conference: Legal Knowledge and Information Systems, 2005.

J. Breuker and R. Hoekstra. *Epistemology and ontology in core ontologies: FOLaw and LRICore, two core ontologies for law.* In Proceedings of EKAW Workshop on Core ontologies. CEUR, 2004.

H. Niemann, G.F. Sagerer, S. Schröder and F. Kummert. *ERNEST: A Semantic Network System for Pattern Understanding.* In Transactions on Pattern Analysis and Machine Intelligence, vol. 12, n. 9, pp. 883-905, 1990.

F. Lachmayer and H. Hoffmann. *From Legal Categories Towards Legal Ontologies.* In Proceedings of the LOAIT Workshop, Bologna, 2005.

Grigoris Antoniou, David Billington, Guido Governatori and Michael J. Maher. *On the modeling and analysis of regulations.* In Proceedings of the Australian Conference Information Systems, pages 20-29, 1999.

Author Index